Labour Relations in the Global Fast-Food Industry

The fast-food industry is one of few industries that can be described as truly global, not only in terms of the vast number of restaurants located in most countries around the world but also in terms of employment in an industry in which many millions of people are employed worldwide.

This edited volume is the first of its kind providing an analysis of labour relations in this important industry. It focuses on fast-food multinational corporations and their large national competitors in nine countries: the US, Canada, the UK, Germany, the Netherlands, Russia, Singapore, Australia and New Zealand.

The authors use a common framework focusing less on work organization but more on the outcomes of employment practices for employees and their rights to trade union organization and interest representation. This kind of analysis also allows the authors to examine the extent to which multinational enterprises impose or adapt their employment practices to differing national industrial relations systems.

The findings reveal that multinational corporations have been very effective in undermining national systems of employee interest representation, particularly in the workplace. While trade unions have had some successes in organizing workers and gaining improvements in working conditions, these have been mostly in the countries of mainland Europe where more stringent labour laws are in force. However, even in those countries such successes have been limited. Overall, the global fast-food industry is typified by trade union exclusion, high labour turnover, low skilled work, low pay and paternalistic management regimes and work organization that allows little scope for developing workers' participation in decision-making, let alone advocating widely accepted concepts of social justice and workers' rights.

Dr Tony Royle is Reader in International and Comparative Industrial Relations at the Nottingham Business School, Nottingham Trent University. He has published widely in the field of industrial relations in multinational corporations and is the author of *Working for McDonald's in Europe: The Unequal Struggle?*

Professor Brian Towers is currently Associate Fellow at the Industrial Relations Research Unit at the University of Warwick. He has held a number of teaching and research appointments at British and American universities. He is Consulting and Founding Editor of the *Industrial Relations Journal* and has arbitrated for ACAS since 1975. He has published widely on trade unions and industrial relations public policy including *The Representation Gap: Change and Reform in British and American Industrial Relations.*

This fascinating account of the control of labour in the multi-national fast-food corporations is also a remarkable comparative study of the protections provided for unorganized workers. Through a carefully orchestrated study of the employment experience of fast-food workers in nine countries, the reader is provided with a vivid, if discouraging, 'natural experiment' in how far different regulatory systems protect the weak.

Professor William A. Brown
Master of Darwin College
Montague Burton Professor of Industrial Relations
University of Cambridge

Anyone interested in knowing what's brewing in human resource management and labour relations under those Golden Arches and behind the drive-up windows of fast-food outlets should definitely read this book. Very well written and rich in detail, the authors lay out the global employment and labour relations strategies of fast-food multinationals across a wide array of countries. Ever clever and generally underhanded, the corporate strategies being played out have suppressed employee interest in union representation, persistently frustrated union efforts to organize these low-wage workforces and allowed employers to slip through the loopholes of regulations intended to protect worker rights to interest representation. In spite of its focus on fast-food, this book offers the reader a full-course international feast and one I highly recommend.

Professor William Cooke
Director, Douglas A. Fraser Center for Workplace Issues
Wayne State University
USA

This excellent and well researched book on the global fast-food industry confirms the ability of multinational corporations to subvert employment rights under different national cultures and employment laws. It is a valuable contribution to the growing literature on the regulation of multinational companies and will be of particular interest to policy makers, academics and employers. I strongly recommend it to anyone interested in these important issues.

Robert Taylor
Employment Editor
Financial Times

Labour Relations in the Global Fast-Food Industry

Edited by Tony Royle and Brian Towers

London and New York

First published 2002 by Routledge
11 New Fetter Lane, London EC4P 4EE

Simultaneously published in the USA and Canada
by Routledge
29 West 35th Street, New York, NY 10001

Routledge is an imprint of the Taylor & Francis Group

Typeset in Times by BC Typesetting, Bristol
Printed and bound in Great Britain by The Cromwell Press Ltd, Wiltshire

British Library Cataloguing in Publication Data
A catalogue record for this book is available from the British Library

Library of Congress Cataloging in Publication Data
Royle, Tony, 1957–
    Labour relations in the global fast-food industry/Tony Royle and
    Brian Towers.
        p.   cm.
    Includes bibliographical references and index.
        1. Industrial relations–Case studies. 2. Fast food restaurants–
    Employees–Case studies. 3. Fast food restaurants–Employees–
    Labor unions–Case studies.   4. Chain restaurants–Employees–
    Case studies. 5. Chain restaurants–Employees–Labor unions–
    Case studies. I. Towers, Brian. II. Title.

    HD6976.H8 R69 2002
    331′.04164795–dc21   2001058181

ISBN 0–415–22166–8 (hbk)
ISBN 0–415–22167–6 (pbk)

Contents

Illustrations

Figures

Tables

Contributors

Cameron Allan holds a PhD and teaches in the School of Industrial Relations at Griffith University in Australia. His research interests include non-standard employment, labour market flexibility, management strategy, and employment relations in the service industry.

Greg J. Bamber is Professor and Director, Graduate School of Management, Griffith University, Queensland, Australia. He was formerly at Durham University (UK) and an arbitrator with the Advisory, Conciliation and Arbitration Service (UK); his (joint) publications include: *Employment Relations in the Asia Pacific*; *International and Comparative Employment Relations*; and *Organizational Change Strategies*. His publications have been translated into several languages.

Sonja Bekker is a PhD student at the Nijmegen School of Management, University of Nijmegen, the Netherlands. Her research concerns the development of work organization in the Dutch chemical industry.

Jos Benders is at the Nijmegen School of Management, University of Nijmegen, the Netherlands, and Honorary Research Fellow at the Business School of Manchester Metropolitan University, UK. His research interests include medieval coinage from the Low Countries and organization concepts.

Glenda Fryer is a senior Lecturer in the School of Hotel and Restaurant Studies at the Auckland University of Technology, New Zealand. She was previously a union official with the Northern Hotel, Hospital and Restaurant Union for ten years. She now lectures and researches in employment relations in the hospitality industry, human resource management and organizational behaviour.

Peter Haynes lectures in the Department of Management and Employment Relations at the University of Auckland in New Zealand. He has worked as a trade union advocate and is completing a PhD in industrial relations. His research focuses on union strategy, union–management cooperation and employment relations in the service sector.

Robin Leidner is Associate Professor of Sociology at the University of Pennsylvania in the US. She is the author of *Fast Food, Fast Talk: Service Work and the Routinization of Everyday Life*. She has also written numerous articles on emotional work, feminist organizations, and parenting.

Daniel J. McCarthy, DBA (Harvard University) is Professor of Strategic Management, Northeastern University, Boston US. He has held the McDonald and Walsh Professorships, he is also a Fellow at the Davis Center for Russian Studies, Harvard University and is a member of the editorial board of *The Academy of Management Executive*. His publications include: *Business Policy and Strategy*, *Business and Management in Russia*, and the *Russian Capitalist Experiment*. He is a corporate director and does consultancy work in the US and Europe.

Birthe Mol is an entrepreneur and runs her own shop *Wijn & Spijs* in Haarlem, the Netherlands. For her MBA from the Nijmegen Business School, she wrote a thesis on McDonald's in the Netherlands.

Alexius A. Pereira teaches at the Department of Sociology, National University of Singapore. He received his PhD from the London School of Economics and Political Science. His research focus is in economic sociology and he has published papers on industrialization in China and on employment in Singapore.

Sheila M. Puffer PhD (University of California) is Professor of International Business and Human Resources Management, Northeastern University US. She also graduated from the Plekhanov Institute of the National Economy in Moscow and is a Fellow at the Davis Center for Russian Studies, Harvard University. She is the editor of *The Academy of Management Executive*. Her publications include *Behind the Factory Walls: Decision Making in Soviet and US Enterprises*, *The Russian Management Revolution*, and *The Russian Capitalist Experiment*.

Ester Reiter is Associate Professor of Social Science and Women's Studies at York University in Toronto, Ontario Canada. She is the author of *Making Fast Food: From the Frying Pan into the Fryer*. She is currently researching the culture of the Secular Jewish Left in Canada in the pre-World War II period.

Tony Royle PhD is Reader in International and Comparative Industrial Relations at Nottingham Trent University in the UK and is the author of *Working for McDonald's in Europe: The Unequal Struggle?*. He has published widely in the field of industrial relations in multinational corporations. He is currently engaged in further research in the food service sector in both Eastern and Western Europe.

Stanislav V. Shekshnia is President and CEO of Millicom Russia and is based in Moscow.

Nils Timo holds a PhD and teaches in the School of Marketing and Management at Griffith University, Australia. He is a former industrial advocate for the AWU with 20 years' experience as a labour relations advocate in numerous labour tribunals. He has been intimately involved in labour relations in the fast-food industry in Australia. His research interests cover managerial and trade union strategies, employee relations and labour utilization in services

Professor Brian Towers is currently Associate Fellow at the Industrial Relations Research Unit at the University of Warwick. He has held a number of teaching and research appointments at British and American universities. He is Consulting and Founding Editor of the *Industrial Relations Journal* and has arbitrated for ACAS since 1975. He has published widely on trade unions and industrial relations public policy, including the comparative study, *The Representation Gap: Change and Reform in British and American Industrial Relations.*

Acronyms

ABS	Australian Bureau of Statistics
ACAS	Advisory Conciliation and Arbitration Service
ACLU	American Civil Liberties Union
ACTU	Australian Council of Trade Unions
AFC	America's Favorite Chicken
AFL	American Federation of Labor
AIRC	Australian Industrial Relations Commission
ALHMWU	Australian Liquor, Hospitality and Miscellaneous Workers' Union
ALP	Australian Labor Party
AWA	Australian Workplace Agreement
AWU	Australian Workers' Union of Employees
BdS	German Fast-Food Employers Association (Germany)
BLS	Bureau of Labor Statistics (US)
BNA	Bureau of National Affairs (US)
CAW	Canadian Auto Workers Union
CBS	Centraal Bureau voor de Statistiek
CFAWU	Canadian Food and Allied Workers Union
CGB	Federation of Christian Trade Unions (Germany)
CLA	Collective labour agreements
CNV	Christelijk Nationaal Vakverbond
CURRE	Canadian Union of Restaurant and Related Employees
DAG	German Union of Salaried Employees
DBB	German Civil Service Federation
DEHOGA	German Hotel and Guesthouses Employers' Federation
DGB	German Trade Union Federation
DHV	German Association of Commercial and Industrial Employees
EEA	European Economic Area
EEOC	Equal Employment Opportunities Commission (US)
ETUC	European Trade Union Confederation
EU	European Union
EWC	European Works Council Directive

FNV	Federatie Nederlandse Vakbeweging
GBR	Company-level works council (Germany)
GDP	Gross Domestic Product
GMB	General Municipal and Boilermakers Union
GmbH	Limited liability company (Germany)
HACCP	Hazard Analysis and Critical Control Point
HERE	Hotel Employees Restaurant Employees Union
HR	Human Resource
HRM	Human Resource Management
ILO	International Labor Organization
IR	Industrial relations
IUF	International Union of Food, Agricultural, Hotel, Restaurant, Catering, Tobacco and Allied Workers' Associations
KBR	Group-level works council (Germany)
KFC	Kentucky Fried Chicken
MNC	Multinational corporation
NAFTA	North American Free Trade Agreement
NDP	New Democratic Party
NGG	Food, Restaurant, Hotel and Guesthouse Union (Germany)
NLRB	National Labor Relations Board (US)
NTUC	National Trade Union Congress
OECD	Organization for Economic Cooperation and Development
OCL	Operation check list (see also SOC)
PAL	Personal action letter
QSC	Quality, service and cleanliness
QSR	Quick service restaurant
RAP	Real approach to problems
SDA	Shop, Distributive and Allied Employees' Union (Australia)
SEIU	Service Employees International Union
SOC	Station observation checklists (see also OCL)
SWF	Service Workers Federation of Aotearoa (New Zealand)
TGWU	Transport and General Workers Union
TQM	Total quality management
UFCW	United Food and Commercial Workers
USDAW	Union of Shop, Distributive and Allied Workers
USDL	United States Department of Labor
Ver.Di	German Service Workers Union
VNO–NCW	Verbond van Nederlandse Ondernemingen – Nederlands Christelijk Werkgeversverbond
WERS	Workplace Employment Relations Survey
WRA	Workplace Relations Act (Australia)
WUL	Workers Unity League

1 Introduction

Tony Royle and Brian Towers

Mrs Thatcher once said 'you can't buck the market'. Yet it seems that the fast-food industry has been able to do just that. McDonald's, the best known brand in the world and often cited as the driving force behind the success of the industry, appears, so far, to be able to operate free of the capitalist trade cycle. Regardless of downturns or weaknesses in national economies McDonald's continues to expand at a breathtaking rate. Every day on average four new McDonald's restaurants are being opened somewhere around the globe. It plans to have 50,000 restaurants by 2010 (double the number it had in 2000) and already employs over two million people in 118 countries. Although there is some evidence of diversification much of its future growth is likely to depend on overseas expansion. While there are 46 McDonald's restaurants for every million residents in the US, there are only three outlets per million people on average elsewhere. Per capita annual sales in the US are $54, whilst elsewhere in the world they average only $4. However this growth is not only restricted to McDonald's: other burger and chicken companies as well as pizza companies and sandwich shops are also expanding rapidly. For example, seven of the largest fast-food operators in the European Union already employ well over half a million workers and multinational corporations (MNCs) such as KFC, Burger King, and Pizza Hut each, in 1999, generated sales of around $550 million outside the US. In part this reflects broader changes in society. As the chapters on both Russia and Canada reveal, in the industrialized countries eating is no longer primarily concerned with survival or even social interaction, but with convenience. Of course the rapid expansion of fast-food is also reflected in the dramatic growth of the service sector over the last 30 years, which now accounts for around 70 per cent of employment in the UK, Canada and the US. MNCs are driving much of this growth including retailers such as Wal-Mart, the largest private employer in the US, and McDonald's, the largest in Brazil (Klein, 2001; Schlosser, 2001).

However, the growth and success of the service sector and particularly fast-food has arguably come at high cost in terms of workers' rights, pay levels and conditions of work.[1] The key to the success of fast-food revolves around limited menus and highly standardized product offerings, which permit the use of low skilled and easily replaceable labour. Fast-food companies are in the vanguard of companies demanding ever more 'flexibility' of working conditions and have frequently been involved in lobbying governments to introduce lower rates of pay for young workers (Royle, 2000; Vidal, 1997).[2] There also seems to be little doubt that the fast-food chains have played an important role in developing the growth of part-time, insecure, and low paid employment. At the same time employment in these companies almost invariably means there will be no easy access, even in most continental European countries, to independent representation through a trade union (Royle, 2000). Indeed, as the following chapters indicate, many fast-food companies are vigorous in denying employees their rights to independent representation. Furthermore, the competitive nature of the fast-food market means that fast-food brands exert considerable pressure on their suppliers, which in turn has a negative impact on workers' rights, pay and conditions in those companies. Schlosser (2001), for example, reports that in the American meat packing industry 'union busting' is commonplace.[3] The consequences are that each year one in three of the US's 43,000 meat packing workers goes to a doctor with a work related injury or illness; they are paid a third less in real terms than they were 40 years ago; they have to be on the job six months before they get health insurance and for one year before they get holiday pay; and many workers leave before the first and most before the second year of employment.[4] Although these supplier companies are not the focus of this book, they serve to highlight many of the basic assumptions about the nature of the employment relationship and which the fast-food industry generally operates: low pay, poor working conditions, if possible, no trade unions and the ability of fast-food companies to influence the employment practices of dependent suppliers. This influence does not necessarily mean direct control but there is an imperative for suppliers to drive down their costs, not least their labour costs, to compete for business in a highly competitive industry.

What is 'fast-food'?

Although the fast-food industry is an important, still expanding and frequently controversial sector, fast-food as a product is not easy to define and is becoming increasingly difficult to do so. In some respects the broader but less common term 'quick-service' might be more appropriate than 'fast-food' to cover the types of operations under consideration in this book. For example, fast-food can include service with or without plates and be consumed inside or outside the business and pizza companies are sometimes considered to be quick service but not 'fast-food' per se. For the purposes of this study we consider 'fast-food' in fairly broad terms meaning food consumed rapidly either in or outside units. But this broad definition, despite its convenience for this study is not without its difficulties. These must be kept in mind throughout the text.

First, fast-food 'restaurants', 'stores' or 'outlets' come in a wide variety of forms and varying product offerings ranging from hamburgers, pizzas, fish, baked potatoes and French bakery products to ethnic foods such as Indian curries and Chinese meals, Turkish or Greek kebabs, coffee shops and soup outlets. However, though sandwich shops, burgers, pizzas and other products are dominated by large companies, ethnic foods tend to be the domain of the small independent owner. The focus here is on the larger national and multinational fast-food chain operations and not the very large number of independent owner-operators.

Second, the distinction between what is and is not fast-food is becoming increasingly blurred. Driven by the growth in chain operations more and more restaurants now offer standardized menus and limited product offerings for quick consumption and in an increasing number and variety of locations. Large companies originally focused on brewing and leisure have entered the market in recent years and increased the competition in the industry. This has also led to aggressive pricing policies amongst the large brands and an increase in menu diversification and new product developments in order to increase sales and market share. As the high street has become increasingly saturated, the leading fast-food chains have stepped up their store expansion programmes into new kinds of locations and 'markets'. These include hospitals, military bases, prisons, and schools and a wider variety of locations other than on the high street, such as kiosks, carts, 'drive thrus', sites in motorway service stations, retail and leisure parks, shopping centres, petrol forecourts and trains and other travel terminals. McDonald's has even opened its own motorway service station in the UK!

Third, although large national players still play a significant role in this sector, multinational fast-food chains have now become household names, and in terms of sales and units tend to dominate national markets. Indeed, the industry is becoming more internationalized with brands like Burger King being bought by the British multinational Diageo; and McDonald's has recently bought a stake in Prêt à Manger. However, some of the largest brands in this sector are still American-owned, such as McDonald's, KFC, Pizza Hut, and Wimpy.

Finally, in international terms (as we shall see in the following chapters) the industry is required to operate within differing employment relations and statutory contexts in different countries. These contexts are also changing over time. New Zealand is a good example. This country has experienced considerable changes in labour legislation covering both left and right of the political spectrum. The UK has also seen much change in its labour laws between 1979 and 1999, with possibly more changes yet to come from the recently re-elected Blair administration, and partly influenced by membership of the European Union.[5] It has therefore been necessary for the authors in each case to attempt to track relevant changes in the broader context of the employment relationship and the impact upon the fast-food sector.

The role of the franchise in fast-food

One final and important organizational feature of fast-food is the franchise. Indeed it has become one of the most important means of achieving volume growth in a largely saturated marketplace and it is increasingly associated with multinational expansion (Felstead, 1993). The franchise systems operated by most of the large companies in the fast-food sector are based on the 'format' franchise. This is a type of franchise which is now more common than any other franchise system (Felstead, 1993). Under this arrangement the franchisor (for example McDonald's or Burger King) not only supplies the product, but also lays down precisely the rules and procedures that have to be followed by the franchisee within a set of detailed pre-determined procedures or 'format'. The franchisee is in effect purchasing a carefully prepared 'blueprint', which minimizes the risks involved in setting up a conventional small business. According to Felstead (1993) the format franchise has enjoyed unprecedented growth since the mid-1980s, not only in the UK and the US but also in Europe. One reason for this may be that little experience is required. Second, this kind of franchise is well suited to those who have an interest in running their own business, but do not know what sort of business it should be; the franchisor makes the decision for them.

Chan and Justis (1990) suggest that maintaining uniformity, whilst franchising across different societal cultures, is particularly complex and difficult. A question which arises therefore is: if franchisees are independent operators, how can multinationals maintain the internal consistency and uniformity of their operations across differing societal frameworks? The answer, we suggest, is that although franchises are usually considered to be separate legal entities, and so far treated as such in national and some limited supranational law (for example the European Works Council Directive), they are, for all practical purposes, de facto 'subsidiaries' of the brand owners. At McDonald's, for example, this is achieved by a variety of methods and processes. First, there are elaborate selection processes with various interviews and a process of socialization in which the prospective franchisee must work many unpaid hours in the restaurants before a franchise is granted; second, the franchisee is required to make a considerable financial commitment including a non-refundable deposit of well over £10,000; third, there are very tight and finely detailed sets of rules and procedures; fourth, there is an ongoing and thorough monitoring of performance and standards; and, finally, franchisees face very tough sanctions for non-compliance with set standards, losing the opportunity to run additional restaurants and culminating in the loss of the franchise altogether.

McDonald's can be said to have pioneered and refined many of these processes and procedures and it appears that most aspects of the McDonald's franchise system have been emulated by its main competitors. Furthermore, we argue that a franchise provides multinationals with distinct advantages over other forms of expansion. First, it provides them with much needed capital and involves franchisees in a share of the costs and risks associated with international expansion. Second, it allows multinationals to gain the valuable local knowledge of on-site entrepreneurs. Finally, franchise operations are likely to be more efficient in driving down labour costs, because franchisees take much more care of every aspect of profit margins, being motivated by profits unlike wage earning managers. This is particularly important in an industry where labour costs account for 30 per cent or more of the total costs of the business. Similarly when franchisees break the law, or from time to time risk damaging the corporate brand in the name of enhanced profitability, the brand owner can distance itself from the actions of franchisees but, at the same time, continue to take a cut of their improved profitability; a classic 'win–win' outcome. As the analysis in Chapter 5 also suggests franchises can also be used to interfere with collective bargaining and statutory mechanisms of employee representation at both national and European levels. This is an increasing issue of direct concern for trade unions and their members as well as other employees and, more widely, those involved with implementing and protecting employee rights in the modern economy and democratic rights in the wider society.

Research methods and issues

Many comparative studies tend to focus on the pragmatic issues of 'managing' across borders or about the implementation of different production systems; few focus on the implications for employee representation and employment conditions, and the few that have been carried out tend to focus on manufacturing industry rather than services. In particular, there has been a paucity of serious industrial relations research in the hospitality and fast-food industries. This is particularly surprising when one considers the scale of some of the main operators in terms of turnover, and the industry's size and growing importance in terms of employment and employment growth.

The research methods used in the various chapters in this book vary to some extent from one chapter to another. However, most chapters are based on a combination of qualitative interview material, survey and documentary evidence and with authors encouraged to keep to a basic framework suggested by the editors. Some chapters are written by authors who have already undertaken substantial earlier research on the fast-food industry. For example, those who have already published extensively on the sector have contributed the chapters written on the US, Canada, the UK, and

Germany. Other chapters have been written by individuals or teams of authors who have more recently become interested in the industry and have been specifically brought together to contribute to this book.

Managements are often unwilling to take part in a study of this kind, which focuses on labour relations and employees' rights and terms and conditions of work. This is especially the case with fast-food. As we shall see in the following chapters, many employers in this industry prefer to operate without trade unions, a stance compounded by strong pressure to keep labour costs to a minimum. We offer no apology, therefore, that some chapters have, to a lesser or greater degree, not systematically accessed management representatives in the companies concerned. However, we have encouraged authors to use whatever sources were available, and practicable, in order to gain insights into the reality of management views and employer practices in the different countries.

The book in outline

In writing their chapters we asked authors to consider a number of issues. First, each chapter should provide a political and economic context, which would include some analysis of the system of industrial relations and the broader economic and political trends in the country concerned. Second, there should be an industry analysis giving some attention to market competition, the main market leaders and some details of the development of the industry. We also asked authors to include one or more companies as case studies. This may often include the McDonald's Corporation because it is usually the market leader in most countries. But we have also encouraged authors to examine the activities of other MNCs and significant national competitors where this is possible and appropriate.

The book is largely silent about the nature of fast-food products and we do not address work procedures and methods in any great detail because we feel that these have already been covered adequately elsewhere (see for example Love, 1995; Ritzer, 1996; Watson, 1997). The book sets out to examine the following themes. Where MNCs are involved in the sector, to what extent are they able to impose common employment practices on diverse national systems of labour regulation? What implications do such MNC operations have for the future development of labour market regulation and trade union organization? What impact have MNC operations had on the activities of national competitors? What problems does the industry pose for trade unions and how have trade unions responded? What are the realities of employment practices in the country concerned? How are employees' interests supposed to be represented in theory and how, and to what extent are they represented in practice? Whilst not providing extensive detail of production processes and work organization, what relevance do such matters have for unionization, employee representation and employment conditions? How is labour paid and pay determined – through collective bargaining or unilaterally by the employer? What are the pay structures, and to what extent is performance related pay relevant? Who is employed and what are the main characteristics of the workforce?

In their conclusions we asked authors to draw out the extent to which the state, its agencies, the law, collective bargaining, and cultural influences on employer attitudes impact on MNC employment policies in practice. We hope that the book will raise an awareness of broad issues affecting not just fast-food, but most other sectors, that is, the exigencies of the market within the globalization process driving multinational activity in a way which is arguably undermining national labour relations systems and workers' democratic rights.

We present the chapters moving from West to East beginning with the original home of modern fast-food, the US, followed by Canada. Later chapters cover the UK, Germany, the Netherlands, Russia, Singapore, Australia and New Zealand. In the final chapter the editors draw out some of the key findings; come to some conclusions concerning the future of employment relations in this sector; and consider the extent to which the findings for this industry offer a contribution to wider empirical and theoretical debates on comparative industrial relations.

Notes

1 In addition to concerns about the massive and increasing advertising spend targeted at young children, Schlosser (2001) also argues that fast-food companies are making profits at the expense of people's health, through the increasing sales of their sugar, salt and fat-rich product offerings.
2 See also Chapter 10.
3 Historically this industry has been synonymous with employees' struggles for representation against determined union busting by employers vividly portrayed by the writings of Upton Sinclair. These struggles now seem to be more or less lost and non-unionism has become widespread.
4 The fact that there are so many work related injuries is hardly surprising when one considers the relentless and unforgiving nature of the abattoir slaughter process: America's biggest slaughter house butchers five thousand cattle a day (Schlosser, 2001).
5 For example the directives on equal opportunities and working time and, more recently, the EU directive on information and consultation rights in workplaces which will be implemented in stages from 2004.

2 Fast-food work in the United States

Robin Leidner

Introduction

The fast-food industry that now extends throughout the world has its roots in the United States. Fast-food restaurants are often regarded as emblematic of a new global culture, but the industry has indisputably been shaped by its American origins. The informality of the restaurants, their uniformity of service to everyone, their focus on speed, their promised smiles are all distinctively American. They grew out of a cultural ethos that values friendliness more than propriety, practicality more than traditions of gracious living, and democratic egalitarianism over status-based distinctions (Bellah *et al.*, 1985; Lipset, 1991; de Tocqueville, 1969). As the industry expanded internationally, these features of fast-food restaurants struck citizens of many countries as novel when they first encountered them, as did the types of food available. The introduction of new eating habits and behavioural norms by powerful American companies raised concerns about cultural imperialism which have been widely aired, although careful studies of how fast-food restaurants become part of local cultures around the world suggest a more complicated two-way dynamic.[1]

Employment practices in the fast-food industry similarly emerged in a distinctively American social landscape. The balance of power between owners and management, on one side, and employees on the other is weighted much more heavily in employers' favour in the United States than in most other industrialized nations. As the major fast-food companies have gone abroad in search of new markets, they have sought to implement American patterns of employee relations and working conditions in new contexts (Royle, 2000, 2001).

The story of a brief 1998 strike vividly illustrates some of those patterns and provides a revealing view of the industry in its native habitat. In April 1998, about twenty young workers in the town of Macedonia, Ohio, picketed their employer for five days. They did not shut down the business, yet this small and short-lived strike generated national news coverage. What made the story newsworthy was its novelty: the strikers were high school and college students, their target was a McDonald's franchise, and, once a local Teamsters official offered support, a union campaign seemed possible. McDonald's has more than 12,400 restaurants in the United States (Sacks, 2000: 1); not one is unionized.

News organizations played up the David vs. Goliath angle in covering this strike, emphasizing the youth and lack of resources of the rebellious employees who dared to stand up against McDonald's. In fact, McDonald's Corporation was not the target of this labour action: the strikers' complaints were with the managerial practices of a locally owned franchise. But McDonald's – the large and powerful corporation and the hugely valuable brand name – suddenly seemed potentially vulnerable, if not to widespread unionization, then certainly to damaging publicity. And since McDonald's, the industry leader, has set the pattern for many aspects of employment relations in fast-food, other major chains could be similarly vulnerable. *The Tonight Show*, a late-night network television programme that is a national institution, featured a 'running skit in which the strikers were intimidated and beaten by fast-food mascots like Ronald McDonald, Col. Sanders and Wendy' (Colton, 1998). As Bryan Drapp, the 19-year-old who began the walk-out put it: 'All of a sudden we were representing fast-food workers across the country' (Drapp, 1998).

The walk-out was sparked by a manager's harsh treatment of a 66-year-old worker. The manager allegedly grabbed her arm and yelled at her. When she ran out of the restaurant in tears, the manager told Drapp to take over her lobby-cleaning duties. He refused, was reprimanded, and walked out. Unable to get management to talk with him afterwards, Drapp and a co-worker, Jamal Nickens, decided to picket. Twenty workers joined the walk-out and signed union cards indicating their support for affiliation with the powerful Teamsters union. The modesty of their demands was notable, including such workplace basics as fully equipped first aid kits and posted schedules, in addition to improvements in pay, working conditions, and relations with management (Colton, 1998).

Americans following this story in the national media learned that the strikers were victorious. *Business Week* reported that 'McDonald's caved' (Bernstein, 1998: 6), and it agreed to send supervisors to a training course in 'people skills', to pay retroactive wage increases corresponding to increases in the federal minimum wage, and to give full-time workers a week's paid vacation after one year on the job (Colton, 1998: F1). However, the story was not over when the national media coverage ended. About a month later, the franchise owner distributed a new employee handbook specifying that employment was 'at will', meaning that McDonald's managers can fire workers for any reason. The two strike leaders, who said that the handbook barred workers from talking to a union or to journalists, refused to sign it. They also charged management with not following through on promises to correct wage disparities and with retaliating against former strikers. They therefore took the next step in pursuing unionization, presenting signed union cards to the National Labor Relations Board. The store's owner claimed that 'the vast majority' of his workers did not support this action because 'we already do the types of things unions would advocate, such as open communication, training, rap sessions,' and providing opportunities for advancement (Robb, 1998a). Management ordered Drapp and Nickens not to discuss unionizing at work and they were fired after appearing at work with 'Go Union' painted on their faces. The National Labor Relations Board sought back pay and reinstatement for them because they 'found probable merit in the charge that the workers were discharged because of their union activities' (Robb, 1998b: 1B). The scheduled hearing on the matter was cancelled when the parties agreed to a confidential settlement (Robb, 1999). Drapp and Nickens did not resume work at McDonald's.

Although the authoritarian management and inflammatory treatment of workers that sparked the strike was in sharp contrast to McDonald's espoused corporate policy,[2] the strikers' grievances were ones that many fast-food workers across the country would echo. Understaffed shifts, unpredictable schedules, skimping on equipment repairs and supplies, and wage inequities, as well as tyrannical supervision, are not unusual. In fact, in October 1998 a 17-year-old McDonald's worker led a six-day strike against a company-owned store in Virginia on quite similar grounds (Salmon, 1998) and in the wake of the Ohio strike the Teamsters received requests for union cards from workers at twelve other fast-food restaurants in the area, including a Taco Bell outlet (*Nation's Restaurant News*, 1998). None the less, McDonald's Corporation's dismissal of the strikes as isolated incidents was borne out, no broader movement to unionize McDonald's or the rest of the US fast-food industry has yet materialized.

To understand the kinds of working conditions typical in the fast-food industry, including the absence of unionization, we must examine both what is distinctive about the industry and how it fits into the overall pattern of labour relations in the United States. The next section outlines the general features of the fast-food industry and describes its rapid growth. To put industry employment practices into context, an overview of US employment law follows, arguing that the balance of power in the American workplace favours employers far more than in many other countries. The section on fast-food work in the United States demonstrates that the industry relies on low-paid, part-time workers whose tasks have been rigidly standardized. This employment system generates extraordinary rates of labour turnover, presenting a formidable obstacle to unionization, especially in combination with industry decentralization and determined employer opposition. Extreme routinization, which affects customers and managers as well as workers, supports the industry's low-wage, low-commitment employment strategy. In recent years, tight labour markets have made it harder for fast-food employers to find and retain qualified workers, yet, as described in the concluding sections, there is little evidence of a marked increase in fast-food workers' compensation or power. Data for this account are drawn from government and industry sources, mass media, and scholarly literature. The analysis builds on my previous ethnographic work at McDonald's, reported in Leidner (1993). That research, conducted in 1986, included: attending management training classes at McDonald's corporate head-quarters; training at a Chicago-area franchise and work experience behind the counter; interviews with the franchise owner, managers, and twenty-three workers who served customers; and informal conversations and observation at the franchise.

The US fast-food industry

The most common type of restaurant in the United States is a franchised operation of a nationwide fast-food chain (BLS, 2000b: 126). McDonald's, the largest food service company in the world, greatly outdistances its nearest competitors in the US both in sales and number of outlets. The next largest chains, based on sales in the United States, are Burger King, Taco Bell, Wendy's, Pizza Hut, and KFC (formerly Kentucky Fried Chicken). Ranked by number of outlets in the US, McDonald's is followed by Subway, Pizza Hut, Burger King, Taco Bell, and KFC. Taco Bell, Pizza Hut, and KFC are all owned by Tricon Global Corporation. While their combined total number of outlets in the US exceeds McDonald's, their combined sales do not (Sacks, 2000: 5).[3] According to one estimate, there are approximately 2.5 million fast-food workers in the United States, making them the country's largest group of low-paid workers (Schlosser, 1998). To understand employment relations in the fast-food industry, however, it is important to remember that most workers at McDonald's and other chains in the US are not employed directly by the fast-food giants but rather by franchisees. On average, franchisees operate 70 per cent of the outlets of US restaurant chains (full-service as well as fast-food chains), though the proportion of company-owned stores varies widely across chains (Sacks, 2000: 13). The corporations exercise extensive control over how the franchised outlets operate, yet franchisees can face some of the same difficulties as entrepreneurs operating small businesses, including intense local competition. Industry employment conditions reflect both the policies of some of the largest and most profitable corporations in the world and the decisions of individual franchisees operating in highly competitive environments.

Fast-food businesses or, as the US industry press likes to call them, quick-service restaurants (QSRs) share several features that distinguish them from other kinds of food service establishments: limited menus, limited service, and standardization. Customers choose their meals from a short list of offerings, with most chains specializing in hamburgers, chicken, or pizza. Typically, customers place their orders at a counter or window, rather than being waited on at a table.[4] The food is served quickly, either packaged to take elsewhere or placed on trays that customers carry to tables them-selves. In many cases no plates or eating utensils of any kind are provided, but where these are in use they are disposable. Eat-in customers are expected to throw out their own trash when they finish eating and to clear away the only non-disposable items they've used, the trays. The industry caters to people who want inexpensive meals in a hurry. Indeed, the trend has been toward ever-greater emphasis on convenience: easily accessible outlets, orders delivered quickly, foods that can be eaten on the run. While ethno-graphic accounts of American-based fast-food chains in some other countries report that customers particularly enjoy the atmosphere of the restaurants and often choose to linger (Fantasia, 1995; Wu, 1997; Yan, 1997), the pattern in the United States is for customers to take their food elsewhere. In 1974, Wendy's introduced 'drive-thru' service, which allows customers to order and receive their food without ever leaving their cars, or even turning off the engines. Drive-through business has grown in importance over time, now accounting for more than half of sales at McDonald's and Burger King's US outlets. Overall, 64 per cent of fast-food sales in the US derives from 'off-premise traffic', whether drive-through, carry-out, or delivery (Jekanowski, 1999).

By 1998, more than one out of every three 'eating and drinking places' in the country was a fast-food outlet, compared with fewer than one in five in 1970 (BLS 2000b: 126). The spectacular growth of the industry was fuelled by a variety of trends: the postwar rise of an automobile-based culture; the prodigious increase in women's paid employment, which raised household incomes while greatly decreasing time available for meal preparation; the increase in single-parent families; and the success of the franchise system that allowed companies to expand rapidly with relatively small capital out-lays. In 1999, Americans spent $109.9 billion dollars at fast-food restaurants, a 2.3 per cent increase (inflation-adjusted) over the previous year, according to the National Restaurant Association (Sacks, 2000: 3). Fast-food outlets more than doubled their sales between 1987 and 1997, making them the largest and fastest-rising share of sales in the food service industry in the United States (Price, 1998). However, Standard & Poor's, a leading analyst of American business, anticipates slow growth in the US restaurant industry overall in the future, predicting greater competition for market share and ongoing reshuffling of assets in what is now a mature industry (Sacks, 2000: 7). The Bureau of Labor Statistics predicts that growth in the fast-food industry will slow as the ageing of the baby boom generation increases the proportion of the US population over 45 years old (BLS, 2000b: 129).

To generate continued growth in US sales in what some market observers describe as an 'overstored environment' (*U.S. Industry & Trade Outlook* 1999: 42–7) and despite opposition from trade unions, fast-food chains have sought new types of markets, including schools (Beaver, 1999) and hospitals (*Nation's Restaurant News*, 1997c), and they have also opened satellite outlets in discount stores, service stations, and other venues (Jekanowski, 1999; Price, 1996). By the mid-1990s, though, the growth of US fast-food outlets came to outpace growth in demand, leading the major chains to concentrate more on increasing sales per store than on opening new outlets (Edgecliffe-Johnson, 1999). The crowded US fast-food market has intensified the incentives for the major chains to seek growth opportunities abroad. In 1998, the number of international units of restaurant chains (including full-service as well as fast-food chains) increased 7.8 per cent, compared with only 1.7 per cent growth of units in the United States (Sacks, 2000: 10). Foreign operations are now crucial to the economic success of many of the major chains. Almost half of McDonald's 1999 worldwide sales – $18.8 billion – came from the more than 13,500 outlets it operates in 117 countries outside the United States (Sacks, 2000: 10; Zuber, 1999c). Moreover, the company's future growth depends on overseas expansion: there are forty-six McDonald's restaurants for every million residents of the US, but only three outlets per million people in the other countries where it does business. While per capita sales in the US are an astonishing $54 annually, per capita sales elsewhere in the world average only $4 per year. Other major chains have also become powerful multinational operations: KFC, Burger King, and Pizza Hut each have foreign sales of at least $550 million per year (Sacks, 2000: 10). As they have expanded globally, the fast-food companies have sought to transplant not only foods, styles of eating, and forms of sociability developed for the American market, but also patterns of work organization and employment relations that reflect conditions in the United States.

Labour relations in the United States

American employers have much greater freedom to establish the conditions of employment than do their counterparts in other industrialized countries, thanks to extremely low rates of unionization and a legal framework that reflects the national valorization of 'free enterprise'. While employers customarily describe the economy as greatly over-regulated, managers in the United States, compared with those in other countries, may make decisions and establish policies with minimal intervention by federal and state governments. Most notably, the legal principle governing employment relations in most circumstances is 'employment-at-will', which means that workers have no right to ongoing employment and that employers have no legal obligation of fairness (ACLU, 2000; Gould, 1993; Rasnic, 1995; Rothstein *et al.*, 1994). 'In the classic judicial statement, an employer may dismiss an employee "for good cause, for no cause, or even for cause morally wrong"' (Summers, 1995: 1067).

As of 2000, only one state, Montana, had legislation preventing dismissals without a 'just cause' (Summers, 2000). Elsewhere, employers can fire workers 'at will', with several specific exceptions. Some reasons for firing workers are illegal because they violate public policy (e.g., dismissal for engaging in legally protected behaviour, including pro-union activities or reporting safety violations). Others are prohibited by anti-discrimination statutes, such as Title VII of the Civil Rights Act or the Americans with Disabilities Act. Anti-discrimination statutes, which are unusually strong and well-enforced in the United States (Summers, 2000), make it illegal to fire a worker for reasons based on race, sex, religion, national origin, age, or disability. Finally, employers may forfeit the power to dismiss workers at will by agreeing to other employment terms, for example, by signing a union contract or by issuing an employee handbook that specifies a 'just cause' for discharge standard. When the management of the Macedonia, Ohio, McDonald's issued a handbook stating that employment was 'at will', it was making explicit that in settling the strike it had not ceded its prerogative to fire workers at any time for any reason.

In contrast to employment law in the countries of the European Union, American law endows workers with few positive rights; rather, it imposes minimal restrictions on employers by establishing what they cannot do (Rasnic, 1995: 497). The absence of legislation mandating many kinds of prerogatives to workers greatly enhances American employers' freedom of action. While the right to form unions is guaranteed by law, no laws require that employees be granted a voice in their conditions of employment. Statutory works councils in their European forms do not exist in the US. In most states employers may fire workers without prior notice and without providing severance pay. Paid vacations, paid holidays, and paid maternity or paternity leave are provided at the discretion of American employers, not legally mandated (Rasnic, 1995).

Furthermore, most Americans must rely on their employers for social protections that elsewhere are provided by the state. Most notably, US citizens are not guaranteed access to medical care unless they are elderly (through the Medicare program) or utterly indigent (through Medicaid). Rather, health insurance – like life insurance and disability insurance – is an employee 'fringe benefit' in the United States and people who do not receive free or subsidized insurance through their jobs or those of family members may well be unable to afford to buy it. While many employers provide such benefits, many do not. Even employers who do provide fringe benefits to full-time employees are not obliged to do so for their part-time workers; consequently, part-time workers are far less likely to receive them (Tilly, 1996). The only kinds of non-wage compensation that federal law requires of employers are contributions toward Social Security (retirement) benefits and unemployment insurance.

Federal and state laws do provide some restrictions on the conditions of employment by establishing a minimum wage, limiting children's hours and types of work, and setting safety standards, as well as by regulating the establishment and conduct of collective bargaining between employers and unions.

Unions have historically played a crucial role in extending fringe benefits to their members and in providing them with a collective voice, but unionization rates in the United States are at their lowest level in half a century (Kelly, 2000), far lower than in most other industrialized nations (ILO, 1997). As of 1999, 13.9 per cent of all American wage and salary workers were unionized, and only 9.4 per cent of the private-sector workforce. In service industries, unionization rates are even lower than in private-sector employment as a whole; 5.5 per cent compared with 9.4 per cent (BLS, 2000a). The fast-food industry, with its complete absence of unions, is an extreme but not unparalleled case.

The great imbalance in the power of employers and workers in the United States results from a complex interplay of structural and cultural forces affecting national and state governments, corporations, businesspeople, and the American workforce. One factor is the comparatively weak role of the federal government, a limitation established in accordance with, and sustained by, strong cultural predispositions toward suspicion of centralized government authority and insistence on individual rights (Shafer, 1991). The United States' federal system of government grants states significant autonomy in many matters relevant to economics and employment. In addition, American law and culture accord corporations great latitude to pursue their own interests, generally accepting the laissez-faire economic view that the workings of the market will discipline employers to the extent necessary, promote economic innovation and growth, and generate prosperity. As there are few limitations on the power of corporations to influence government (let alone to influence public discourse) the lobbying and public relations efforts of American employers have been remarkably effective in sustaining a legal and cultural environment supportive of a relatively unregulated market. Powerful and well-financed associations of employers continue to work zealously to influence federal legislation of concern to them, such as the level of the minimum hourly wage. Competition among states and municipalities to attract corporate investment pressures state and local governments to promote 'business-friendly' policies. The behaviour of individual Americans as workers and citizens is affected not only by explicit corporate efforts to promote free-market policies, but also by strong cultural valorization of self-reliance, based on the belief that success is and should be determined by individual effort.

Employment and working conditions in fast-food

The American fast-food industry was built on the promise of low prices. Profitability therefore depends in large part on keeping labour and other operating costs down. Low wages, minimal benefits, tight staffing, and efforts to intensify labour are the predictable results of strong competitive pressure in a legal and cultural setting that grants employers remarkable discretion and does not guarantee workers a voice in influencing employment conditions. While workers do not necessarily accept such treatment without resistance, resentment about wages and working conditions has not led to unionization, as the story of the Macedonia, Ohio, McDonald's exemplifies.

A number of features of the fast-food industry make it especially difficult to organize. The major fast-food companies do not directly employ most workers; rather, they are employed by franchisees, many of which own only a few restaurants or just one.[5] This decentralization greatly increases the difficulty and expense of organizing unions. The nature of the jobs and the characteristics of the workers, two closely related factors which will be discussed in detail below, present further obstacles to unionization. Employee turnover is extraordinarily high, with estimates typically ranging from 200 per cent to 300 per cent annually for crew workers (*Chain Store Age Executive with Shopping Center Age*, 1999; Kreuger, 1991; Bond, 1998; Lardner, 1999). The challenge of organizing an ever-shifting labour force is formidable. As an official of the Hotel Employees and Restaurant Employees union put it, 'By the time you've talked to them about the union, they've quit or been fired' (Romano, 1993). A related difficulty is that the industry predominantly employs young people: a 1994 study reported that nearly 70 per cent of fast-food workers were 20 years old or younger (Van Giezen, 1994). Many young workers have no knowledge or experience of unions, have low expectations of wages and benefits, and in any event view their jobs as temporary. Moreover, unions have typically emphasized issues such as seniority rights and retirement benefits that are of little interest to young people planning to move on to work in other fields (Tannock, 2001).[6] Other categories of workers widely recruited for fast-food work, including the elderly and women with school-age children, share some circumstances with youth workers. They often need or prefer part-time work, their opportunities for paid work are constrained, and some, though by no means all, have access to income and benefits from alternate sources, such as family members' jobs, pensions, or government programmes. The large majority of fast-food employees work part-time, 72 per cent in one study (Prewitt, 1999b). The prevalence of part-time work further complicates union organizing efforts, both by increasing the difficulty of reaching all employees and by minimizing the likelihood that workers will see the potential benefits of unionization as worth their time and energy.[7] Finally, all efforts to organize fast-food workers have met with prompt, determined, and well-funded opposition from the major fast-food companies, which are openly anti-union and which steadfastly resist unionization in either company-owned or franchisee-owned outlets.[8]

The key factor making it possible to run an industry with a workforce dominated by young, inexperienced part-time employees who do not stay on the job for long is the extreme routinization of the work. When work is routinized, each worker repeatedly performs a limited number of tasks according to instructions provided by management, which minimizes – in fast-food, virtually eliminates – the need or opportunity for workers to exercise discretion. This sort of standardization has a variety of benefits for employers. It increases managerial control over the operation and cuts wage costs by eliminating the need to hire skilled workers. The simplified jobs can be learned quickly, making employers less dependent on experienced workers. Routinization is especially advantageous to fast-food companies because of its capacity to promote uniformity of outcomes. Massive advertising campaigns promise fast-food customers a particular standard of food and service and a predictable kind of experience. To ensure that thousands of outlets across the country and around the world, most of them not directly owned by the fast-food companies, will deliver on those promises, the companies promulgate precise instructions specifying every detail of food preparation and customer service. A variety of mechanisms reinforce these standards, many of which contribute to the routinization of crew workers' jobs.

Contracts between franchisees and companies require that owners meet company specifications by following a wide range of company procedures and by using products and equipment from company-approved distributors. The companies assure franchisees that their systems for producing and serving food are the most efficient ones possible for meeting the expectations of customers and for generating profits. Corporate-produced training programmes for managers and for crew members inculcate company standards and practices. The level of detail in specifying work routines is remarkable: at McDonald's, for instance, workers are instructed in the precise arm motion to use when salting a batch of fries. Moreover, since the jobs of many fast-food workers involve serving the public, their appearance, words, and facial expressions are also subject to managerial oversight and control. Customers are promised an enjoyable experience as well as a particular quality of food, and fast-food companies try to ensure that such experiences will be reliably produced by standardizing the interactions between customers and workers even as they encourage workers to inject a touch of 'personal' service through eye contact, smiles, and friendly delivery of scripted lines (Leidner, 1993).

Technology plays an important part in standardizing the work of fast-food crews and, not coincidentally, minimizing the amount of skill and discretion required of workers. Over the years, the fast-food companies have designed grills and fry vats that use lights and buzzers to tell workers when to proceed with the next step in their routines; have provided numerous food products in forms that need only be heated, rehydrated, or assembled rather than prepared from scratch; have computerized cash registers so that counter workers do not have to memorize the prices of different items, know how to calculate tax or make change, or remember to 'suggestive sell' (encourage customers to buy more items). Computerized systems have also standardized much managerial work, such as scheduling work shifts, handling payroll, ordering supplies, determining how much food to have ready to serve throughout the day, and monitoring sales, inventory and waste. Computerized cash registers also play a role in monitoring work, for example by keeping track of counter workers' relative success in promoting sales.

The degree of supervision of crew workers varies (Tannock, 2001) but the fast-food companies typically encourage close monitoring of workers to ensure that company standards are met and that workers are busy every moment of their shifts. It is not unusual for multiple layers of supervisory personnel, ranging from hourly workers to owners, to be present behind the counter at any given time. Furthermore, crew members who serve the public are often acutely aware that their work is monitored by customers. Dread of the nasty looks and comments that can be provoked by longer-than-average waits for service or by errors in meal assembly keeps many workers on their toes, and the wish to avoid complaints to managers helps persuade harassed workers to hold their tongues when provoked.

Fast-food companies have also routinized the behaviour of their customers. The smooth functioning of the outlets depends on customers' familiarity with and willingness to perform their parts of the routine (Leidner, 1993). They are expected to be prepared to give their orders promptly and properly and also to do a share of the work. Labour costs are kept low in part through what has been termed 'work transfer': shifting work that might be done by paid employees to other people (Glazer, 1993). As in self-service generally, fast-food customers perform tasks that are handled by employees at other kinds of restaurants, such as bringing food to tables, serving beverages, gathering condiments, napkins, and utensils, clearing tables, and discarding trash. That the knowledge and effort required of customers cannot be taken for granted is demonstrated whenever a fast-food outlet opens in an area of the world in which these behavioural rules are novel.

The extreme standardization of work is key to numerous features of the fast-food industry. It justifies low wages and benefits. Young, inexperienced people, who are competent to perform the simplified jobs, are especially likely to be able to accept – or have no choice but to settle for – these low rewards. The youth of the workforce and the low wages and benefits contribute to high labour turnover. Young workers generally do not see fast-food work as a long-term career, so quitting is a more common response to dissatisfaction with wages, working conditions, or management, than is a collective effort to improve the work ('exit' rather than 'voice'). However, routinization makes high turnover less problematic by widening the pool of potential replacements and speeding training. High turnover also makes unionization extraordinarily difficult, hence the vicious circle: the higher the turnover rate, the more fast-food companies are motivated to increase routinization and automation.

Fast-food outlets usually offer some opportunity for advancement into jobs that allow workers to exercise limited discretion. Young crew workers typically can be promoted a step or two to such positions as 'crew trainer' and 'crew chief', usually with a small wage increase. The lowest level of store management, 'swing manager', is also an hourly-paid position in most fast-food chains, but since it generally requires full-time work, young people still in school usually cannot qualify. Fast-food companies can justly claim that, compared with other industries, they provide unusual opportunities for workers who begin at entry-level jobs to move into salaried management positions (Newman, 1999). However, the large majority of fast-food workers have no intention of staying in the industry in the long term and are not interested in moving into management (Tannock, 2001). For them, working conditions and compensation levels are probably more important than opportunities for promotion.

While fast-food work is generally treated as unskilled, it is not easy to perform well, requiring grace under pressure along with physical dexterity, endurance, a capacity to keep many things in mind at once, and particularly for those serving the public, substantial 'emotional labour'.[9] It can be hard and exhausting work, especially during busy periods, because managers are highly motivated to limit labour costs by minimizing the number of workers per shift and by eliminating idle time. The public perception of fast-food jobs as the quintessential unskilled work increases the stressfulness of that work by making it more likely that customers will treat crew members with minimal respect and by generating a stigma that weighs especially heavily on workers who are no longer in their teens (Leidner, 1993; Newman, 1999). Also contributing to both the stress and the stigma of the jobs of those who serve the public are scripts and interaction rules that undermine the dignity of job-holders and make it hard to defend themselves against insult. Workers are sometimes required to behave as though they do not understand basic rules of interaction, for example by suggesting an additional product even to a customer who has just said, 'That's it', or to deliver lines that make them feel ridiculous, such as: 'Would you like to Dino-Size that for only thirty-nine cents more?'[10] If customers respond with exasperation or derision, workers are supposed to apologize or swallow their resentment rather than to defend themselves or respond angrily. The stigma attached to fast-food work is intensified by the widespread knowledge of its low levels of pay and benefits.

The fast-food corporations set wage and benefit levels for workers in company-owned outlets, but they cannot dictate the compensation of franchisees' employees. Wages, and to a lesser extent fringe benefits, therefore do vary with local labour market conditions and with franchisees' ideas about how best to balance compensation costs and profitability. But clearly the employment strategy promoted by the corporations is to use the lowest-cost labour available, to keep turnover within acceptable limits by providing workers with 'recognition' and a 'fun' working environment rather than increased compensation, and to minimize the number of workers on any given shift.

Compensation in the industry is consistently among the lowest available in the United States, excepting only occupations exempt from the Fair Labor Standards Act and work in the underground economy. Lots of fast-food workers do have fun on the job and appreciate what may be the only employment opportunity open to them (Leidner, 1993; Newman, 1999; Tannock, 2001). Yet the fact remains that compensation is well below the level required for workers to be self-supporting, let alone to support dependants. The National Restaurant Association, an employers' association, is heavily involved in lobbying against increases in the federal minimum wage, local 'living wage' ordinances, and any kind of mandated benefits (National Restaurant Association, 2000a, 2000b).

As of 1998 (the most recent year for which data are available), the median hourly wages for workers in the detailed occupational titles most likely to include fast-food workers were $6.00 an hour for 'Cooks, Fast Food' and $6.04 an hour for 'Combined Food Preparation and Service Workers', compared with a minimum wage of $5.15 (BLS, 1998). Part-time workers, the large majority of industry employees, typically receive no fringe benefits at all beyond discounted meals. When industry executives and trainers speak of employee benefits, they refer to crew meetings, work-evaluation sessions, and incentive systems offering prizes for good work. Rather than providing significant material advantages, these policies are intended to promote team spirit, energize workers, and create the impression that management is attentive to workers' concerns.

Not all observers agree that this low-compensation strategy minimizes labour costs. In a study of 255 hamburger chain outlets (mostly in Indiana), researchers at Purdue University found that restaurants that provided their workers with scheduled wage increases, bonuses, or benefits such as insurance or paid vacations had significantly lower rates of employee turnover than those that did not.[11] The costs associated with turnover, including hiring and training new workers, can be greater than these expenses (Prewitt, 1999a; Purdue University, 1999).[12] James C. Doherty, former publisher of *Nation's Restaurant News*, urged the assembled chain-restaurant operators and executives at the 1997 Multi-Unit Food-Service Operators Conference to develop employment policies that would encourage careers in the food-service industry, lessening their dependance on a low-wage labour force with high turnover rates. They could not expect workers to make careers in the industry he pointed out, when they are paid the minimum wage and receive no health benefits (Schlosser, 1998: 3). But Doherty's speech received only 'polite applause'.

Compensation for workers in the food-service industry increased somewhat in the last years of the century, however, because labour markets have been unusually tight by US standards. By mid-1997, unemployment rates had fallen below 5 per cent for the first time in almost a quarter century and they continued dropping through 2000. In the first five months of that year, the national unemployment rate fluctuated between 3.9 per cent and 4.1 per cent, the lowest levels since 1970 (BLS, 2000c). Partly as a result of the tight labour market, restaurant industry labour costs rose about 4.4 per cent in 1999, compared with 3.7 per cent overall for US workers (Sacks, 2000: 3). Finding and retaining workers was especially difficult in the fast-food industry because of a combination of demographic trends and economic ones. Between 1988 and 1998, the number of 16–24-year-olds in the US civilian labour force dropped 2.8 per cent, shrinking the industry's primary labour pool (BLS, 1999b).[13] With many American families experiencing good economic times, more young people could choose not to seek paid work. In 1998, the percentage of young people aged 14 to 24 who want to work declined to 72.8 per cent, a 25-year low (Nathan, 1999). Moreover, the tight labour market meant that many of the teenagers, college students, and low-skilled adults who might otherwise have accepted fast-food jobs were able to find work in other, better-paying industries (Ginsberg, 1999; Maharaj, 1998; Smart *et al.*, 1999). Since the fast-food industry was adding outlets at a rapid rate (Jekanowski, 1999), franchisees and managers in many parts of the country reported unprecedented difficulty in staffing their restaurants.

Reflecting these trends, numerous newspaper accounts described desperate employers offering workers unprecedented levels of pay and new fringe benefits: Burger King's vice president for human resources said that in some areas of the country, counter clerks got $200 'retention bonuses' if they stayed on the job six months (Uchitelle, 1998), while company-owned McDonald's restaurants in Atlanta offered new employees a $50 bonus for showing up on the first day (Bond, 1998); in Southern Maryland, average wages at KFC were said to be more than $7 an hour and full-time employees were 'eligible for' vacation time, health insurance, and dental coverage (Ginsberg, 1999); in Michigan, where unemployment rates were below the national average, some fast-food chains offered $7.50 as an entry-level starting wage, and a McDonald's franchisee offered workers stipends toward college textbooks, optional health insurance, and $50 bonuses for bringing in a new employee (Lienert, 1998). However, despite these reports of fast-food employers offering unusually generous wages and benefits, available evidence suggests that significant increases in compensation were not typical and primarily reflected local labour market conditions. Overall wage levels in the industry remain low and most fast-food workers receive minimal non-wage benefits, if any. In 1998, when the labour market was already quite tight, the median hourly wage for crew workers was around $6.00 (BLS, 1998).

In terms of labour costs the National Restaurant Association reported that wages and salaries made up 26.4 per cent of fast-food restaurants' expenses in 1998, while employee benefits accounted for 2.5 per cent of expenses (Sacks, 2000: 14). Workers' compensation is a relatively high percentage of the fast-food operator's expenses (second only to food costs, at 31.1 per cent), but employee benefits are only 8.65 per cent of total compensation, an extraordinarily low figure. By comparison, in 1999 employee benefits were 27.5 per cent of total compensation for the average US civilian worker and 26.2 per cent for the average US worker in a service occupation. Indeed, for service workers, legally required benefits, such as Social Security and unemployment insurance, accounted for 9.5 per cent of total compensation. If we limit the comparison to part-time workers, fast-food workers' benefit levels are still strikingly low: as of March 1999, benefits made up 18.7 per cent of total compensation for all US part-time workers in private industry, and 16.6 per cent of total compensation for part-time workers in service occupations (BLS, 1999a). While unusually high wages could produce a low ratio of benefits to total compensation, that explanation clearly does not apply to the fast-food industry.

Apart from the low level of earnings, unpredictability of earnings is a problem for many fast-food workers who are not guaranteed a specified number of hours of work per week. Some favoured employees can count on working their preferred shifts regularly, but many workers struggle with highly variable work hours, both in number and in timing. Of course such unpredictability not only affects workers' capacity to plan their budgets, it also makes it difficult for them to plan their daily lives, since they have neither regular working hours nor, often, much advance notice about their scheduled hours. For example, in some McDonald's franchises the work schedule, posted one week in advance, explicitly demands flexibility from workers. For each employee, a solid line on the schedule indicates the hours that person can count on working and a zigzag line marks an additional hour or so. Whether or not the worker is asked – or allowed – to work during that additional time depends on whether or not the store is busy. In addition, workers might be pressured to leave early if business is slow or discouraged from leaving even after the 'extra' scheduled time if the restaurant is busy (Leidner, 1993: 63). Under this system, the workers rather than the employer bear the costs of uncertain demand, and workers' arrangements for transportation, child care, social activities, or other responsibilities can be upset without compensation.

Fast-food workers commonly report that scheduling is unfair or unpredictable. They complain that they are given insufficient notice of their scheduled hours; that they are assigned too few hours to earn as much as they need; that they are assigned more hours or later hours than they can handle on top of their schoolwork; that they are scheduled for hours they explicitly said they could not work and then held responsible for finding a replacement; that managers play favourites in assigning desirable shifts; and that posted schedules are not adhered to if there is more or less business than anticipated. The computerized systems provided by the fast-food companies keep track of the volume of sales throughout the course of the day and week and determine how many workers should be on hand at any given time based on the predicted demand. Managers, acutely aware of the balance of labour costs and sales volume, try to match the number of workers to consumer demand, broken down into small segments of an hour, as precisely as possible, rather than assigning workers to standard shifts. Managers are judged by whether or not they exceed their labour budgets, so they are under pressure to avoid paying workers for 'extra' time (Leidner, 1993; Tannock, 2001). Fast-food employers also commonly minimize labour costs by distributing hours among workers in ways that do not trigger extra expenses under state or federal law. For example, the scheduling programme can keep shifts below the number of hours that would entitle workers to a longer paid break and can make sure that workers are not assigned so many hours in a week that they are entitled to overtime pay.

The scheduling of workers' hours is a means of exercising control over labour, as well as an important element of managerial strategies for keeping employment costs down. Limiting the number of workers per shift effectively intensifies the labour of fast-food crew members, for many workers who might resist direct injunctions to work more quickly none the less intensify their effort because they do not want to let down fellow employees by not doing their share or because of the pressure exerted by lines of impatient customers. Moreover, managers can use scheduling explicitly as part of the discipline system to motivate or punish workers. In some fast-food outlets, workers are told that they have to earn extra hours or desirable shifts through hard work and a 'good attitude'. Conversely, managers can show their displeasure with a worker by cutting hours, sometimes drastically enough to prompt the worker to quit (Leidner, 1993). By making dismissal unnecessary, this technique can eliminate some unpleasant scenes, and it also allows management to get rid of unwanted employees without affecting the rate of the employers' contributions to unemployment insurance.

All of the scheduling practices described above are legal in the United States, where non-union workers have no guarantees of steady hours, advance notice of schedule changes, continued employment if they are unwilling to work when directed, compensation for irregular hours, or minimum shift length.[14] One illegal practice that is widespread in the fast-food industry is 'off-the-clock work', which Tannock found to be endemic even in unionized Canadian outlets (Tannock, 2001; Geoghegan, 1999). That is, many fast-food workers perform labour, often in small segments of time, for which they are not paid. For example, they may work through their break time; may 'help out' co-workers before or after their own shifts; may be required to do preparatory work (such as counting the money in a cash register drawer or stocking supplies) before a shift starts or to do clean-up work after a shift ends. In some cases, workers may be unaware that they are not being paid for this time, but workers sometimes 'choose' to do extra work, either out of loyalty to employers or co-workers or because tight labour scheduling does not allow them to complete all of the necessary work during their shifts. Such 'volunteer' work is nevertheless illegal, but even workers who are aware of that may find it difficult to resist pressures to work off the clock. In 1997, a jury in Washington State found Taco Bell Corporation guilty of intentionally cheating hourly workers out of wages. In this class-action suit representing 12,000 workers, the plaintiffs' lawyers persuaded the jury that the company's 'obsession' with profits had 'fostered an atmosphere in which managers felt they must, at almost any cost, maintain recommended labour costs-to-sales ratios' (Liddle, 1997: 1). To do so, managers under-reported employee hours, 'permitted' employees to work after clocking out or asked them to wait to clock in until the restaurants got busy, failed to provide state-mandated paid breaks, and circumvented overtime-pay rules (Liddle, 1997). Taco Bell and Wendy's have also faced class-action suits in California charging them with misclassifying workers as assistant managers and managers in order to avoid paying overtime wages (Norman, 1999).[15] Krystal, a regional hamburger chain, filed for bankruptcy in 1995 in the face of litigation charging it with wage violations of the Fair Labor Standards Act, which it settled for $13 million in 1997 (*Nation's Restaurant News*, 1997a).[16]

Future developments in employment practices

In Standard & Poor's assessment: 'the lack of qualified workers will remain the [restaurant] industry's No. 1 problem' in the short term (Sacks, 2000: 4). Some observers comment on 'a shift of power to workers' in fast-food (Rodriguez, 2000) because:

> near-record employment and a long period of economic prosperity have created headaches for employers and businesses – and golden opportunities for once-downtrodden workers.
>
> (Lienert, 1998: 1)

Used to hiring interchangeable workers only for the times they are necessary, some fast-food employers are now struggling with a lack of employee loyalty as entry-level workers jump from job to job to get the highest possible starting wage (Bond, 1998). Managers and consumers report declining standards of service as fast-food outlets, desperate for staff, put newly hired employees to work without proper training and tolerate lower levels of courtesy and competence because of the difficulty of replacing even bad workers (Rodriguez, 2000).

At the turn of the century fast-food employers were pursuing a variety of strategies to overcome staffing difficulties. While some were offering higher wages and fringe benefits, so far national data reveal only modest increases in wages and little evidence that fringe benefits are broadly available. In many parts of the country, fast-food employers addressed the worker shortage by expanding their recruitment efforts. The implementation of 'welfare reform' has meant that many poor single mothers who previously could rely on state support are now required to find jobs. Employers earn tax credits for hiring such workers and the fast-food industry has welcomed this new pool of labour (Papiernik, 1999). In 1999, Burger King committed itself to recruiting 10,000 welfare recipients, having achieved a 45 per cent retention rate with the 10,000 such employees already working for the company (*Nation's Restaurant News*, 1999). A Maryland Burger King franchisee established partnerships with 'local high schools, handicapped organizations and welfare-to-work programmes to attract employees' (Ginsberg, 1999: M3). The question of whether 'burger-flipping jobs' can lead to self-sufficiency for women supporting children has frequently been raised in national debates about welfare reform, and fast-food employers have had to work to convince welfare recipients that jobs in the industry do not deserve their 'no future' stigma (Ellis and Ellingwood, 1998; Shapiro and Murray, 1997).[17] To persuade high school students that jobs in the hospitality industry, including fast-food, do indeed provide a future, the National Restaurant Association and the American Hotel & Motel Association formed the Hospitality Business Alliance, which develops special curricula, arranges internships, and has industry executives address high school students across the country (Bond, 1998; Pauly, 1998). Since it is difficult for workers to reach many suburban fast-food outlets on public transportation, employers in some areas have begun providing private transportation to expand their recruitment range (Lienert, 1998). To attract workers to Florida, recruiters for McDonald's joined colleagues from Disney World on trips to Puerto Rico; Disney offered $1500 bonuses and one-way airfare to workers willing to spend one year as $6.25-an-hour fast-food workers or maids (Blank, 1999).

Given the difficulty of attracting new employees, many fast-food employers have looked for ways to lower employee turnover rates. Tactics range from weeding out poor prospects with background checks (Bond, 1998) to expediting promotion opportunities (Ginsberg, 1999), paying bonuses to workers who stay on the job (Uchitelle, 1998), and offering fringe benefits (Leming, 1998). McDonald's encourages its managers to use low-cost strategies to keep workers happy, distributing a book called *300 Ways to Have Fun at Work* that offers suggestions such as holding ice cream parties, handing out candy, and offering on-the-spot recognition to workers who do things right (Rodriguez, 2000). To help fast-food restaurants cope with high turnover and other staffing problems, agencies that provide trained fast-food workers for temporary employment have opened in several cities (Meyers, 1998).

Labor shortages also encourage fast-food employers to alter their work systems in ways that minimize the demand for labour through reorganization or technological change. Subway Sandwiches supplies franchisees with pre-sliced and pre-portioned sandwich ingredients from centralized food preparation plants; McDonald's has experimented with robotic french fry makers, automated touch-screen ordering machines, and automatic electronic payment systems for cashless drive-through service (Liddle,

2000; Murphy, 1996; Zuber, 1999b). McDonald's also expects its new 'Made for You' food preparation system to reduce employee turnover and 'provide some labour savings' (Hamstra, 1998a; Sacks, 2000: 8).[18]

These special efforts to recruit employees, retain employees, and reduce the demand for employees in the face of the tight labour market do not seem to have altered the nature of employment relations in the fast-food industry to a significant degree. They have, however, improved compensation and perhaps enhanced workers' power in areas where staffing is particularly difficult. While changes in equipment and production processes may well last beyond the labour shortage, it is not clear that higher wages, bonuses, and fringe benefits will. Standard & Poor's, describing the US restaurant industry as a 'low-growth area', predicts increased competition for market share and greater emphasis on lowering costs and increasing service. It warns (Sacks, 2000: 7): 'Competition to boost sales, lower costs, and improve over-all profitability can create a cut-throat environment.' Such an environment is unlikely to generate improved working conditions or compensation.

Summary and conclusions

The typical worker in an American fast-food restaurant is a young woman in a highly routinized, closely supervised, non-union job. She works part-time, with no guarantee of a minimum number of hours per week or of specific hours. She earns a bit above the minimum wage and gets no fringe benefits. She will move on to another job before long.

The youth of the workforce, the prevalence of part-time work, the low compensation, and the high turnover are closely intertwined elements of the employment system in fast-food. The jobs are designed so that they can be learned quickly and carried out competently by people with little work experience. None the less, they are high-pressure jobs that require hard work under frequently stressful conditions.

In the absence of unions and other forms of employee representation, the wages and working conditions of American fast-food workers are set by employers constrained only by the competitive environment and by minimal legal regulation. The large fast-food companies set employment policies for company-owned stores and guide franchisees to adopt similar practices in dealing with their employees. No overall standards prescribe even such minimal benefits as uniform laundering or sick pay, or dictate that workers with greater job tenure receive preferred work hours or higher pay. Federal legislation does however, regulate which jobs and how many hours minors can work. It also establishes which employees are entitled to overtime pay for work beyond forty hours per week, although this is rarely an issue in fast-food. Federal and state minimum wage laws set a floor on wages; beyond that, wages and benefits depend on the abundance of the labour supply and therefore vary by area. The supply of labour for the fast-food industry depends on the overall state of the economy and on the number of available workers with little experience or marketable skills. When the economy is strong, some teenagers (and others who can be supported by family members' wages) stay out of the job market altogether, while those who do seek employment may find more attractive opportunities than fast-food work. Demographic trends determining the size of the teenage population influence the number of available workers who have little experience or marketable skills, but so do government decisions about income support for the poor. 'Welfare reform' legislation enacted during the 1990s set time limits on government income support and established work requirements for poor mothers, increasing the pool of potential fast-food workers.

Threats of unionization can have some effect on labour practices, but as we have seen, the American fast-food industry has faced few serious challenges from organized labour. High labour turnover in the industry, the prevalence of part-time work and the youth of the workforce, in addition to unsupportive labour laws, have been major influences in discouraging any large-scale organizing efforts.

The fast-food companies are not immune to bad publicity, but the degree of public outrage that, for example, McDonald's business practices have generated in Europe is not echoed in the United States (Jardine, 1999; Royle, 2000). By and large, to judge by public discourse, Americans simply do not regard the fast-food industry as offering the kinds of jobs that could or should provide a worker with economic autonomy or career prospects. Rather, fast-food jobs are seen as appropriate first labour-force experiences for teenagers, while older workers who cannot get better jobs elsewhere tend to receive little sympathy. The American values of individualism and meritocracy suggest that workers should improve their lot by moving out of fast-food jobs rather than by improving the compensation and working conditions in these jobs. To the extent that the quality of fast-food jobs receives public discussion, concern is limited to whether or not the work is a valuable learning experience providing new entrants to the labour force with habits, values, and skills that allow them to move on to better jobs (Newman, 1999; Shapiro and Murray, 1997; Tannock, 2001).

Many aspects of the organization of the fast-food industry – from uniformity of design, to extreme routinization of labour, to provision of standardized experiences as well as standardized products – have been replicated or adapted in other industries, significantly reshaping the American physical and social landscape. As the fast-food companies continue to expand internationally, they confront cultures, legal frameworks, and social policies quite different from the ones that spawned them. People in many host countries may associate these companies' products and practices with American values they view positively, such as modernity, efficiency, informality, and fun. However, the companies' assumptions about the proper relations between employers and workers may be much less welcome imports.

Notes

1 See especially the fascinating discussions of how McDonald's has been received in various East Asian countries in Watson (1997).
2 At Hamburger University, McDonald's management training centre, the company attempts to give managers the skills to avoid antagonistic relations and promote a harmonious and cooperative workplace (Leidner, 1993).
3 Looking only at the domestic fast-food hamburger market, which was worth $42.3 billion in 1998, McDonald's held a 42.8 per cent market share; its closest competitor, Burger King, held 20.2 per cent (Sacks, 2000: 8); and Wendy's held 11.5 per cent (Edgecliffe-Johnson, 1999).
4 Industry statistics include a few companies with a somewhat different service system. Pizza Hut provides table service, for example, and Domino's Pizza is primarily a delivery business.
5 For an extended discussion on the McDonald's franchise system and its impact on worker representation see Royle (2000).
6 In 1999, 6.0 per cent of American workers aged 16 to 24 years belonged to unions, compared with 15.5 per cent of those 25 years and over (BLS, 2000a).
7 In 1999, 6.9 per cent of part-time employees in the United States were union members, compared with 15.3 per cent of full-time employees (BLS, 2000a).
8 Love (1995) provides details of McDonald's efforts to keep its restaurants 'union-free'; also see the 'McSpotlight' website at http://www.mcspotlight.org/campaigns/tactics/unionall.html.
9 On emotional labour, see Hochschild (1983); Steinberg and Figart (1999).
10 That script was imposed during a McDonald's promotion of a dinosaur-themed movie (Luhrs, 2000).
11 The Starbucks Coffee chain, which offers medical and dental coverage, stock options, and pension contributions to part-time employees who work at least 20 hours per week, claims to have an employee turnover rate under 60 per cent (Leming, 1998).
12 AFC, the parent company of several fast-food chains, 'estimates it wastes $800 in ill-spent time and training for each hourly employee who quits after a few months on the job' (Bond, 1998: 1R).
13 That trend is turning around: the Bureau of Labor Statistics predicts a 15.1 per cent increase in the number of workers in this age group between 1998 and 2008 (BLS, 1999b).
14 The federal Fair Labor Standards Act does impose some restrictions on the work schedules of minors, as well as on the types of task they can perform.
15 Salaried managers are exempt from the provision of the Fair Labor Standards Act requiring employers to pay overtime wages (150 per cent of the usual wage) for hours worked beyond 40 hours per week, and from some state wage and hour laws. The plaintiffs' attorney claimed that the 'managers' in question, who put in between 50 and 70 hours per week, spent most of their time 'mopping floors, making tacos and doing the exact same job as crew members', and thus should not have been considered exempt employees (Norman, 1999). Such misclassification also adds yet another barrier to unionization (see Gould, 1994).
16 Legal proceedings document other abuses of power by fast-food employers: in 1999 the U.S. Equal Employment Opportunity Commission filed sexual harassment charges against Domino's Pizza Inc. and Carrols Corp. (one of Burger King's largest franchises) (Zuber, 1999a); an Illinois jury awarded $900,000 in damages in 1997 to four young women who, when employed as cashiers in 1992, were allegedly strip-searched by two Hardee's restaurant managers looking for a missing $50 (*Nation's Restaurant News*, 1997b); in 1996 the U.S. Equal Employment Opportunity Commission filed for a restraining order to prevent

the Midland Food Services Inc., owner of 75 Pizza Hut franchises, from requiring workers to sign a waiver saying they would not file employment discrimination charges with the EEOC (*Cleveland Plain Dealer*, 1996).

17 One Burger King franchisee in Grand Rapids, Michigan, has teamed up with a manufacturing firm in a programme intended to address the hiring problems of both companies and to get unskilled workers out of dead-end jobs. Welfare recipients participating in this 'work-to-work' programme spend six months working for Burger King for $6–7 per hour while they take night classes in remedial reading and technical skills. They then start working night shifts in one of Cascade Engineering's plastics factories. They start there at $7 per hour but can move up to $12.50 per hour, or $26,000 per year (Naughton, 1998).

18 By replacing its batch cooking system with this made-to-order system, McDonald's further hopes to produce fresher, hotter food, cut waste, increase speed of service, and broaden its range of offerings. By the end of 1999, all of McDonald's US outlets had the equipment and software the new system requires. The Jack-in-the-Box chain simultaneously introduced similar changes (Hamstra, 1998b). The president of Consortium Members, Inc., an organization of McDonald's franchisees, argued that the 'Made for You' system actually increased labour costs slightly (Zuber, 1999c).

3 Fast-food in Canada
Working conditions, labour law and unionization

Ester Reiter

Eating together has been central to how we maintain emotional connections with each other. However, gathering around a table at home to share a meal is a custom becoming increasingly rare for many Canadians. With the proliferation of non-standard employment and the entrance into the labour market of all members of the family, it is becoming a rare occasion when all members of the household can sit down together to share a meal. The site of meal consumption is changing as well. Thus mom is no longer in the kitchen; she, along with her teenage children, are to be found at the local fast-food outlet as customers, and often as workers. As more and more jobs become part-time and contingent like fast-food, people do not have regular schedules. In an increasingly commodified world, even minimum wage employment is necessary to help the family make ends meet. One consequence is that a larger and larger percentage of the family food budget in Canada is spent on food consumed in restaurants away from home, a trend that continues to grow. According to the Canadian Restaurant and Foodservice Association, by 1997, 39.8 cents of every food dollar was spent on food away from home (Cook, 1999: 30). McDonald's alone reports that more than three million Canadians visit their restaurants daily, or 10 per cent of Canada's population (McDonald's, 1999).

This chapter explores the fast-food industry in Canada with an emphasis on the working conditions of the people employed in this industry. It will examine the growth and history of the industry, as one of the first areas for expansion of the United States based fast-food giants outside the US. The chapter examines the working conditions and management practices found in the industry. It also provides a brief overview of the Canadian labour relations regime in order to help the reader understand the broader context in which fast-food companies operate. This analysis will indicate that workers' representation rights are at risk in the Canadian fast-food sector despite the union-friendly industrial relations system in some provinces. Finally it examines some of the future prospects for workers' representation in this sector.

The research for this chapter is based on a wide range of sources. The research began with a period of participant observation undertaken by the author in a Burger King outlet in Ontario in the 1980s (this also formed the basis for the author's book *Making Fast-Food* first published in 1991 (2nd edn 1996). The period of observation was undertaken for a total of twelve months, five months full-time and seven months part-time, supplemented by a literature review which included industry journals, Statistics Canada material, archival materials, as well as a number of qualitative interviews. This work formed the basis for this chapter which includes a review of labour legislation in several provinces, interviews with workers and union officials, representing three Canadian unions involved in food service and one young trade union organizer. The Canadian Auto Worker (CAW) staff in British Columbia generously photocopied their entire file on the McDonald's organizing drive in Squamish. An additional literature review was also undertaken using a wide variety of sources including information on various recent organizing drives and official Canadian statistics.

The development of the fast-food industry in Canada: an historical overview

As immigrants to Canada arriving in the late nineteenth century transformed the Canadian wilderness into a settler society, so restaurants sprang up. The restaurant business in Canada was traditionally the kind of enterprise where a disproportionate number of proprietors were immigrants with little capital. Chinese, Macedonian or Jewish immigrant groups, who faced discriminatory treatment in getting factory jobs, often set up their own small businesses. Employees were either immigrants like themselves, or young Canadian women coming to the city from rural backgrounds.[1] Although the industry remained one avenue for small entrepreneurs, some larger Canadian chains such as Murray's, Fran's and Diana Sweets developed in the 1920s as the urban areas in Canada grew.

Despite the diversity of new immigrants working in this industry speaking different languages, the very low wages and long working hours contributed to an organized response. Even in the difficult conditions of the depression of the 1930s, there are accounts of successful unionizing efforts in restaurants. Unions associated with the left wing Workers Unity League organized hundreds of restaurants across the country by industry rather than by craft (Reiter, 1996: 33). In a number of cases these organizing efforts were sabotaged by union rivalries. For example the craft based American Federation of Labor undermined the work of the Workers Unity League by arrangements with the employer that did not respect the striking union. The *Financial Post* reported that:

> This adolescent organization [the Restaurant Employees Union, part of the Workers Unity League] has in its brief career, instigated no less than nine strikes in the city of Toronto. Not one of these strikes has been started or aided by the AFL unit, the Hotel and Restaurant Employees

Union. The aim of the W.U.L. is to link every restaurant in every city across Canada in their union. Sims (W.U.L. general secretary) complained to the *Financial Post* that where these strikes were in progress, the AFL union allowed their men to work for the restaurant.

(*Financial Post*, 1934: 5)

Canada's economy boomed during the World War II years, and despite the rationing, restaurants also prospered. These were good years as restaurant owners had a ready clientele, serving food to people who were working odd hours with spouses overseas. Just after World War II, Canadian restaurant owners feared the end of the prosperity they had experienced during the war years now that eating at home was once again an option for families. They looked to how and where they could create a market for their food to keep themselves in business. Luring the average family into buying ready-made food held the promise of a new market that looked

like magic. . . . It's a magic that enables any restaurant to be as big as a city, to gather profits as big as the operator's imagination and to do these without major capital outlay.

(*Canadian Hotel and Restaurant*, 1955: 23)

This, however, was no small challenge as it meant stiff competition with mom. After all, 'she puts love into her cooking' (ibid.: 23). This new marketing technique of using advertising to target the family at home was successful in expanding the restaurant business, franchising provided a way for large corporations to harness the capital and energies of small entrepreneurs. For an investment fee, a percentage of gross sales, and another percentage that went to advertising, large companies sold their logo, and dictated how the business should be run. In return, success was guaranteed. Colonel Sanders Kentucky Fried Chicken system made a number of early franchisees in Canada into millionaires (Reiter, 1996). Giant food processing multinationals such as Pillsbury and Unilever then entered the restaurant business directly by buying out a number of these chains. These provided the financial base for aggressive advertising strategies, which in turn developed a broader market for fast-food. The ingredients were in place for the implementation of different kind of labour process, one that replaced the 'erratic elegance of the craftsman' with the munificent predictability of the machine minder (Reiter, 1996: 48).

By the 1960s and 1970s, the fast-food restaurants of a handful of fast-food chains transformed the regional landscapes of Canada. US chains such as A&W and Kentucky Fried Chicken arrived first. If a Canadian owned company, such as Gentleman Jim's Steaks, wanted to make a go of it, it was necessary to conceal its Canadian origins by obtaining a Detroit address from which to promote its product. By 1970, 66 per cent of the fast-food business in Canada was in the hands of fourteen companies. Mergers and acquisitions mushroomed as fast-food companies were taken over by even larger food processing giants.

As the fast-food industry developed in the l960s, the new restaurants became franchisees within large corporate structures. Although the family-run business could compete in terms of food quality, the tremendous marketing advantages of the large corporations made staying in business very difficult. One company, McDonald's, controlled as much as 50 per cent of the hamburger market in Canada by the mid-l980s.

The trend of increasing concentration, as well as foreign ownership, continues to this day. In the five year period from 1992 to 1997, restaurant chains in Canada increased their sales by 65 per cent and the number of establishments increased by 76 per cent, while independently owned and operated restaurants increased by only 8 per cent during the same period (Canadian Restaurant and Foodservice Association, 1999a, 1999b). The Canadian Foodservices and Hospitality Association does not appear to see this level of concentration as a problem. Indeed, when Burger King used their resources to expand in Canada in the early 1980s, the Association presented them with a 'Hospitality Leader' award. Most of the fast-food businesses, with the exception of Cara Foods, remain in the hands of companies based in the United States. McDonald's leads the pack, controlling 18.7 per cent of the Canadian fast-food industry (*Market Share Reporter*, 1998). It is said that schoolchildren in Canada are more familiar with the cartoon character Ronald McDonald than they are with Canada's first premier, Sir John A. McDonald! Sales in the foodservice industry were approximately $36 billion in 1999 and the industry association is optimistic about growth in the immediate future, although they observe that food-service growth now occurs primarily through acquisitions and strategic mergers (Cook, 1999).

In the 1980s, Kentucky Fried Chicken, Pizza Hut, and Taco Bell became part of PepsiCo and from 1997 were operated by Tricon Global Restaurants. In Canada, Scott's Food Service, a division of Scott's Hospitality, operate some Kentucky Fried Chicken, Tim Horton's and Wendy's franchises but a merger is currently underway between Scott's and Tricon. This is illustrated in Table 3.1.

The North American market has become saturated with fast-food outlets, and in Canada as in the United States, companies continue to seek out hitherto untapped areas in institutional venues such as hospitals, prisons, zoos and schools to enlarge their market. As we can see from the other chapters in this book an even more promising growth area is selling fast-food outside North America. Indeed as we can see in Chapter 7 on Russia it was George Cohon, Canadian president of McDonald's since 1968, who engineered the expansion of McDonald's Canada into what was previously the Soviet Union. Burger King was taken over by Diageo in 1997, a food and drink conglomerate which includes Pillsbury, Haagen Daz and

Table 3.1 The leading fast-food companies in Canada

Company	Number of units	Revenue ($ Canadian millions)
McDonald's	1,065	2,400
TDL group Tim Horton's subsidiary of Wendy's International	1,817	1,603
Cara Operations Harvey's Swiss Chalet Kelsey's and others	1,681	1,526
Tricon Global restaurants KFC Pizza Hut Taco Bell	1,520	1,215
Subway Franchise Systems	1,371	454
Burger King	316	408
Wendy's Restaurants (Canada)	298	390

Source: Food Service and Hospitality (2000: 36).

Guinness. More than 50 per cent of McDonald's operations are now outside the US.

Working conditions in the Canadian fast-food industry

All members of the family, from young children to ageing grandparents, are the targets of a variety of marketing strategies geared toward increasing consumption. By the 1980s, most women and young people in Canada had paid jobs, more than seven out of every ten of all women in Canada between the ages of 15 and 45 were in the labour force by the end of the decade. Canadian women have one of the highest rates of labour market participation in the world, they ranked seventh among the 29 OECD countries in 1995 (Yalnizyan, 1998).

As we move into the twenty-first century, we find that this mass entry into the labour market is taking place under particular conditions. Canada has the second highest incidence of low paid employment of all OECD countries at 23.7 per cent, second only to the United States with 25 per cent. Low paid employment for Canadian women was even worse at 34.3 per cent, second only to Japan at 37.2 per cent. For young Canadian workers under the age of 25, 57.1 per cent were said to be in low pay, again this was only second to the United States with 63 per cent (OECD, July 1996: 2). Many of these low paid jobs are part-time non-standard work arrangements. In 1996, virtually all job growth for Canadian women was in part-time work. Accommodation, food and beverage services have the highest proportion of part time workers at around 41 per cent of all industries. Despite the evidence that more people than ever are working, and the economy is growing, this has not been reflected in rising family incomes. Indeed, in 10 of the last 20 years, there has been a reduction in average family income (Yalnizyan, 1999).

Analysts have noted the huge gap in wages between younger and older workers in the 1990s. Average hourly wage rates for young people (15–24) were Canadian $9.11 in 1998. Workers over 25 earned $17.12 an hour on average. Indications are that young male workers in particular can expect much lower earnings in the future (Marquardt, 1998: 92). Wages for young people tend to be lower than those of older workers in all sectors, but wages in accommodation and food service is lower than other industries for all types of workers. In 1998 the average hourly wage for occupations in hospitality was $9.06, while the average hourly rate for those between the ages of 15 to 24 was $7.47 (*Statistics Canada*, 1998). The findings from a York University (Canada) Study also suggests that half of the young working population is employed in wholesale or retail trade, and food services and accommodation (Laxer, 1999: 37).

In the fast-food sector the larger companies have found it to their benefit to use minimum wage, part-time employees, who they 'hire and fire' depending on the demand for their labour at any particular hour on any particular day. Turnover in the industry is high, and replacement costs minimal because this kind of low skilled work means that new workers can be easily trained to take the place of those who have left. Fast-food companies depend on and encourage a patriarchal system that involves a very lopsided distribution of wages and responsibilities. Women work for minimum wage at fast-food outlets because it is one of the few jobs that allows them to meet their responsibilities outside the workplace. Low wages tend to reinforce the notion that these women and teenagers will consider themselves not to be *bona fide* workers. Survival is not thought to be possible without the wages of the 'head' of the family, the main breadwinner. Additionally there is some contradiction between work organization and marketing strategy. This kind of work is intensive and stressful, yet at the same time the marketing of the product is based on telling women that they deserve to 'give themselves a break today'. A visit to a restaurant as a consumer is a good experience and will give them a rest from cooking at home. The sale of fast-food as a fun, healthy dose of Americana masks the actual conditions of work for people who work there.

The fast-food industry led the way in work organization and the use of technology in the service sector, developing and enhancing 'Taylorist' and

'Fordist' principles established years earlier in manufacturing. Theodore Levitt, a business analyst, admiringly reported in the *Harvard Business Review* that a fast-food outlet could be seen as:

> a machine that produces, with the help of totally unskilled machine tenders, a highly polished product. Through painstaking attention to total design and facilities planning, everything is built integrally into the machine itself, into the technology of the system. The only choice available to the attendant is to operate it exactly as the designers intended.
>
> (Levitt, 1972: 50)

Large fast-food companies were also quick to introduce the latest techniques in the management of their workforces. 'RAP' sessions (real approach to problems) were introduced where selected crew members were invited to express their grievances. An emphasis on 'teamwork' between workers and managers to together better serve the customer were also part of this approach. Burger King training manuals emphasized the need to train managers in 'people skills' that emphasize that low morale is the manager's fault. A store manager's responsibility is to indicate appropriate 'appreciation of work' to manage discontent. In this context the issue of decent wages and working conditions are 'not the first concern of their workers', and should be played down.

In fast-food, as in other service occupations, there is a tremendous emphasis on having the 'right attitude'. Indeed, an improper attitude was *the* most common reason for being fired. Challenging any of the directives of the managers, no matter how contradictory or confusing, was not acceptable, taken together with 'insufficient smiling', this kind of behaviour indicates that the worker might be as one restaurant manager put it: 'a bad apple, that could ruin the whole barrel'. Thus, a good positive attitude is essential, which will reflect 'feelings for the job, the company, their fellow workers and their superiors'. Smiling is part of how one displays a 'good attitude' particularly if the employee is working at the cash register where customer contact is closest. A handout for Burger King counter employees in Mississauga, Ontario contained the following instructions:

> Smile with a greeting and make a positive first impression. Show them you are 'glad to see them'. Include eye contact with the cheerful greeting. When the customer feels and sees a good attitude, they sense concern for them and their needs. This then presents one reason for their liking for Burger King and ultimately they return. An excellent employee attitude will be pleasant, cheerful, smiling and courteous at all times with customers, fellow workers and supervisors . . . they should show obvious pride in their work and employment.

In a service industry, the emphasis is on the common interests of the company and the workforce in producing what they call 'customer satisfaction' which in turn is related to satisfied and loyal employees. Employee satisfaction is described as resulting primarily from the ability of employees to adequately serve their customers, thus producing a profit for the company. The idea is to teach the workforce to do things 'not well, but right'. As one McDonald's' worker described it: 'When you go to work for McDonald's, you leave your brains at home.'

Labour law and unionization

Given these conditions, one would expect that there would be considerable interest in trade union representation. However, the large chains in the fast-food industry with a few exceptions have been remarkably successful in remaining free of unions. In 1998, when Statistics Canada reported a total of 811,500 workers in hospitality, only 9 per cent of workers were unionized, although the average for all Canadian workers was 33 per cent, 75 per cent of the crew consist of young people between the ages of 15 and 19. Women make up 60 per cent of the total workforce in the industry. The average unionization rate for young people aged 15 to 24 is low at only 13 per cent, but in fast-food it is even lower at 3.2 per cent. However the evidence indicates that workforce characteristics are not the reason for low unionization rates, but rather the limited work opportunities available to these workers (White, 1993). In the next section we examine the role played by labour law in Canadian industrial relations.

Labour law and the Canadian fast-food industry

In Canada, a federal state with ten provincial governments and two territories in the North, labour law, with a few exceptions, is a provincial matter. During the postwar period, the federal government established a rather extensive 'social wage' that included aid to the provinces for the provision of health care, education, unemployment insurance, and welfare, all of which are under provincial jurisdiction. In recent years, the power of the federal state over the provinces has become more and more limited, as federal fiscal policy has limited cash payments to the provinces, thus essentially giving up its ability to direct social policy.

The federal government has jurisdiction over only about 10 per cent of the labour force, primarily those workers employed directly by the federal government itself or in banking. As a consequence the majority of workers come under the jurisdiction of the provinces which have varying and diverging laws, policies and practices regarding the minimum wage, employment standards and collective bargaining. Although unions in Canada have a history dating back to the early nineteenth century, Canada's collective bargaining regime, often called the 'postwar compromise', dates from 1944.[2]

The Canadian labour relations system is largely based on the US National Labor Relations legislation, in particular the US Wagner Act. This approach to labour relations was marked by freedom of association, certification of trade unions approved by a majority of workers in a workplace, and free collective bargaining. As such the rights of workers to organize in trade unions were defined and unfair labour practices by employers and/or workers made explicit. For example procedures for settling disputes during the terms of a collective agreement forbid work stoppages, strikes and lock-outs within fourteen days after a conciliation board report. An arbitration compromise decision in 1946 put in place the Rand Formula. This specified that although all workers in a unionized shop do not have to join the union, an automatic union dues check-off for all employees in a unionized work-place can be negotiated, whether or not workers join the union (Craig, 1986). The result was a collective bargaining system that served the purpose of keeping workers on the job and away from picket lines in between con-tracts. It is also enterprise based, enabling unionized workers in a particular workplace to extract what they can from their employer. Designed to main-tain labour peace, the legislation benefited one particular group of workers, those (predominantly male) workers in mass production, manufacturing industry and in vertically integrated firms such as auto or steel (MacDonald, 1997). It was not designed to protect vulnerable workers with the kind of employment found in sectors like fast-food.

The building block of this system is the 'bargaining unit' that defines the group of employees eligible to join together and form a union which will then be the exclusive bargaining agent for that group of workers. In each provincial jurisdiction, a Labour Relations Board determines the unit appro-priate for the purposes of collective bargaining. A Labour Relations Board is an administrative agency established by statute in each jurisdiction in Canada. Thus the size and composition of the bargaining unit is not based on a particular union's ability to organize a group of workers, rather it is determined by the Board on the basis of a rather vague standard called 'community of interest' (Adams, 1993). The preference of the Labour Rela-tions Boards in almost all cases is for single enterprise bargaining units and consequently negotiations overwhelmingly take place at the workplace level. Union benefits therefore become wedded to the individual employer. Thus for certain groups of workers, legislation and labour board policies contri-bute to a two-tiered labour market, where certain groups have had great difficulty in organizing (Adams, 1993). Union recognition is integral to the regime of collective bargaining in Canada, as it is this clause that determines the bargaining unit. It is also the presence of the union that limits managements' ability to impose conditions, negotiate with employees or take individual punitive action against employees.

The fast-food industry, where there are a few large corporations but many small units has been extremely difficult to organize. One important con-sideration is the nature of legal institutions that can play a vital role in the ability of unions to organize and service these small workplaces. In small units, where individuals are highly visible, and where young people with little experience or knowledge of unions predominate, the level of fear and intimidation can be considerable. This coupled with an aggressive anti-union strategy and high turnover rates, has made it difficult for workers to organize and stay in a union.

The provincial variation in the number of unionized restaurants is significant. British Columbia is the only province where Kentucky Fried Chicken outlets are organized; one person, a Canadian entrepreneur who also owned a chain of family restaurants called White Spot, formerly owned these outlets. An employees' association representing all the employees in both these restaurants bargained under one master collective agreement. When they were sold to General Foods in 1971, the employees were able to retain their certification and transformed their association into the Canadian Food and Allied Workers Union (CFAWU), a much more activist Canadian union. Any new outlet could, if it wished, opt into the master collective agreement through voluntary recognition. In the late 1980s, attempts were made by some of the White Spot franchisees to break away from the master collective agreement, but the British Columbia Labour Relations Board ruled that the franchised restaurants and the non-franchised restaurants are deemed to have common employers. In the early 1990s, the CFAWU became part of the Canadian Auto Workers Union. The definition of what is a 'bargaining unit' and who is the employer is key to the successful unionization of fast-food workers. In this case the history of a common owner of both the KFC and White Spot's outlets in that province provided the legal basis for one master collective agreement.

Certain features of the British Columbia labour code, established by a New Democratic government to facilitate organizing, also helped in a successful unionization of the coffee chain, Starbucks (another US import). When a majority of the workers sign union cards, certification is automatic. Thus, the possibility for the employer to influence the outcome, always possible with an open vote, is minimized. Most important is the ability to bargain a master contract ensuring workers of common working conditions in a sector. Although no province, with the limited exception of Quebec, has sector-level bargaining, British Columbia has a tradition of master agreements in KFC and Starbucks. That means that once employees decide to form a union in their workplace, they can be rolled into the collective agreement that already exists for that company, and do not have to face this difficult task on their own.

Quebec is the only province in Canada that has a form of broader based bargaining in its legislation. The Quebec Collective Agreement Decrees Act was put in place at the height of the great depression in 1934, before the right to bargain collectively at a federal level was recognized. The government of Quebec has the power to proclaim, by decree or order-in-council, to extend a collective agreement to all employees and employers doing the same work, even those who are not unionized. Although this has been used as originally defined in four sub-sectors of Quebec's garment industry, there has been no attempt to apply similar decrees to other sectors such as fast-food. Indeed, the opposite appears to be the case with increasing pressure from employers to amend the law to eliminate the decree system (MacDonald, 1997).

One chain of fast-food restaurants, Swiss Chalet,[3] is unionized in Ontario. However, the background to this case highlights some of the problems associated with union certification when collective bargaining arrangements become subject to inter-union rivalry and internal union power struggles. Over a two-year period from 1978 to 1980 and without any apparent employer opposition, thirty-six Swiss Chalet restaurants in Southern Ontario, Quebec, Nova Scotia and Alberta were unionized by CURRE (the Canadian Union of Restaurant and Related Employees) (Sanginese, 1999). In 1981, a master agreement was negotiated in Ontario between the company and CURRE, thereby protecting CURRE against raiding by other unions. In the fall of 1983, CURRE's legitimacy was challenged by the United Food and Commercial Workers (UFCW), which had started an organizing campaign of Swiss Chalet restaurants, and filed applications for the certification of twenty-nine locations in Ontario by the end of 1984. In the evidence presented to the labour board it emerged that there been some collusion between the company and CURRE. For example some employees who had been encouraging workers to join CURRE turned out to be on Cara's payroll. Furthermore CURRE operated without a constitution, financial statement or indeed even a bargaining committee to negotiate collective agreements.

CURRE responded by quickly arranging a merger with the Hotel Employees and Restaurant Employees (HERE) International Union, a move that was challenged by the UFCW. Although the Labour Board supported the UFCW allegations, the UFCW backed off and made a deal. It accepted voluntary recognition at nine locations (it had four in addition to these) and agreed to drop all outstanding litigations and not organize any further in Swiss Chalet. Apparently without consulting its members the UFCW agreed to drop attempts to represent the more profitable Swiss Chalet locations and to accept the CURRE/HERE provisions for its own members. An employee who worked in the Industrial Relations Department of FoodCorp, a Cara subsidiary at the time, contends that the explanation for this lies in internal UFCW disputes reflecting very different visions of unionism. The more militant UFCW director who had initiated events at Swiss Chalet was defeated in a power struggle with other senior UFCW officials. It can be argued that worker's interests were sacrificed because some union officials deemed fast-food workers to be of little significance and looked the other way when the CURRE began to 'organize'.

Since the early 1990s, the labour laws in Ontario have changed twice: the first time in order to facilitate union organizing, and the second to make it more difficult than it had been in the 1980s. When the New Democratic Party (NDP) government in Ontario took power from 1990–1995, they put in place a new labour bill that contained compulsory first contract provisions and prohibited the use of strikebreakers. At the time, critics were disappointed; they hoped for legislation that would encourage unionization of home workers, domestic workers and other difficult to organize sectors. Under the right wing conservative government of Mike Harris, who took power in 1995, Ontario became 'open for business'. One of their first pieces of legislation, Bill 7, changed the provisions that the NDP had put in place. No matter how large a majority of cards requesting a union were signed in a workplace, a certification vote became mandatory. However, the law still gave the Labour Board the authority to certify a union despite the outcome of the vote where it determined that the Act was contravened. Threats of store closure and other forms of intimidation were considered violations of the Labour Relations Act. The Labour Board had the power to grant automatic certification if it deemed that employees' true wishes about union representation were not reflected in the vote. Wal-Mart, the large retailing chain had a store in Windsor, Ontario that was certified in 1997 under these provisions (Gale, 1997: 3–4). Very quickly, the government reacted with its so-called Wal-Mart Bill which in 1998 became the *Economic Development and Workplace Democracy Act*. The remedial action of the board is now limited to ordering a new representation vote (Kleiner, 1998). As the following analysis indicates this new Act has considerable implications for organizing in fast-food.

Some recent illustrative case studies

Employees are expected to make themselves available for work for a maximum number of hours with no guarantees about when they will be called. Each week, the outlet manager posts the list of which workers are assigned to what shifts for the coming week. In the past, when workers have become disillusioned with the one-way nature of these obligations they simply quit; labour turnover in this industry is estimated at 300 per cent per year. Even if employees have some knowledge of provincial employment standards, they have limited options. A worker who objects when asked to leave before a three hour shift is over – because the restaurant is quiet, or requests a break when legally entitled to one, or refuses to stay longer when asked – is at risk. Given the scheduling system, an employee can in effect be fired by simply not being put on the work schedule. Consequently there have been a number of attempts to organize in this industry in recent years. In the large companies, McDonald's in particular, workers have found that they were facing an opposition funded by the resources of the entire corporation. The details vary but, in each case, McDonald's was able to fend off a successful unionizing drive. In one case, in St Hubert, Quebec, the outlet was suddenly deemed to be 'unprofitable' and was closed. In two others, one in Ontario and the other in Squamish, British Columbia, legal loopholes were found to prevent certification in one case and, in the other, to decertify before a collective agreement could be concluded.

What follows is the detailed events surrounding one such organization attempt. A 17-year-old teenager named Sarah Inglis challenged McDonald's union-free record in North America by signing up a majority of the workers in her restaurant (north of Toronto) in the autumn of 1993. She had been working at McDonald's since she was fourteen and this was her first job. After a change in the management at her restaurant working conditions became much worse than normal. She states that she was annoyed by management's allegedly rude and sexist behaviour: 'management making people feel disgusting about themselves, getting yelled at, even fired'. After an exhausting and busy Saturday when the rush of customers had finally quieted down, the young worker was publicly dressed down for not smiling enough and not running as she puts it: '[at] five hundred miles an hour'. An employee from the day shift with a six-year history at the store was fired for speaking to the store manager about the treatment of workers. In addition the shift schedules for workers were reduced so that people could no longer count on the hours each week they had typically received under the old manager and they pleaded to have their old hours back. Even in a relatively affluent community like Orangeville, Ontario, workers relied on their wages for rent money, mortgage payments and savings for university tuition.[4]

The teenager stated that just because McDonald's was the first job for many of them, there was no reason for McDonald's to 'treat us like dogs', so she decided to organize her workplace. By this time in early 1993 the provisions of the new labour bill in Ontario had come into effect, theoretically at least making certification easier.[5] The teenager contacted a number of unions but they refused to help because of her age. Finally she contacted the SEIU (Service Employees International Union) without mentioning her age. By the fall of 1993, she and her friends had signed up 67 of the 102 workers in her restaurant. Acquiring signatures was apparently straightforward; most people approached agreed to sign cards, exchanging horror stories of their work at McDonald's.

With that kind of majority, certification should have been automatic, but management heard about the organization drive and appealed to the Labour Board before certification was awarded. McDonald's charged that there had been irregularities in that some of the young people did not know what they were doing when they signed the cards, and now wanted to change their minds. Three sets of lawyers representing the franchise owner, McDonald's and the intervening employees, appeared before the board. Thirty-five days of hearings and five months later, the issues grew ever more confused. One of the main rank and file organizers for the union changed his story as the hearings progressed. Workers, paid standard Labour Board compensation for missing a day's work, found their testimony was worth more money than they earned in a week. Some workers perhaps tempted by the compensation and free trips to Toronto at the employer's expense were soon giving evidence on behalf of McDonald's. The biggest concern for the union was the allegations that some employees were promised their cards back if they changed their minds. Finally the Board ordered a new vote.

By this time the McDonald's anti-union machine was in full swing. Conditions in the workplace improved, 'just vote no' badges were distributed at work, 'no union' tee-shirts were given out, and free Winter Olympics hats for all. Interviewees report that at the local high school and at the McDonald's outlet, concerns were raised about the withdrawal of employment related perks such as 'McGold' cards. These cards allow all workers to get a 50 per cent discount on food purchases at McDonald's. McDonald's also hosted a party for the workers on the weekend before the vote, and the night before the vote invited all workers to a paid meeting to 'explain' about the 'dangers' of unionizing the restaurant. The young organizer and her friend attended the meeting and tried to challenge the managers as best they could. Life was becoming difficult for those teenagers who supported the union organization drive; they were increasingly being subjected to abuse and intimidation, not only at work, but also at school and elsewhere in their small community.

Not surprisingly, given the extent of the intimidation, and the general lack of education about workers' rights, combined with the SEIU's apparent failure to help rally support in the community, the certification vote was lost, 77 to 19. For a while the crew enjoyed improved working conditions but, soon after, conditions returned to the way they had been when the union drive began. Although the unionization attempt had failed, the teenager stated that:

> We have opened the eyes of teenaged workers about what their rights in the workplace are . . . we wanted a union because we wanted job security, dignity and respect, but at least we have let the world know that McDonald's is not just food, folks and fun.

Since this unsuccessful attempt in Orangeville, there have been two instances of partially successful organizing campaigns. The first, in St Hubert, Quebec, successfully organized in February 1997, when over 80 per cent of the workers signed union cards. According to the president of the local Teamsters Union (973), McDonald's used all the legal resources at their disposal and they delayed certification by requests for a review hearing, a ploy successfully used in the Orangeville case. However, after the last hearing was scheduled, it appeared that no further delay was possible and the Quebec Labour Commission would probably not dismiss the employees' certification request. McDonald's response was to close the outlet, stating that it was 'unprofitable'. The Teamsters trade union responded by sponsoring a campaign to unionize all the McDonald's outlets in the Montreal area. Sixteen months and $100,000 later, only one unit had been organized and the certification vote was lost. Workers who initially had signed union cards left for other jobs, and 90 per cent of the workers in one Montreal outlet voted against unionization.

Squamish[6] in British Columbia had the only unionized McDonald's outlet in North America for almost a year. Again two of the organizers, Tessa Lowinger and Jennifer Wiebe, were teenagers both 17 years old. Lowinger stated in a talk to the CAW council that: 'public humiliation, unsafe working conditions and total lack of respect and dignity' were the reasons people were unhappy at McDonald's and became interested in unionization. Lowinger's father was a CAW member and put them in touch with a CAW youth organizer, Ryan Krell. In July 1998, CAW Local 3000 applied to represent the workers; three and one half days after they had contacted Krell, they applied for certification. McDonald's immediately responded by hiring twenty-eight new employees and rapidly improving working conditions. One of the teenagers reported that the workplace was dramatically transformed: 'anything we asked for was fixed or added to our restaurant'. Despite these improvements, the 'Mcflurry' of legal activity trying to obstruct the process and, as Jennifer Wiebe put it: 'management becoming incredibly nice', the organization drive went ahead and the restaurant acquired union certification on 19 August. However, nine months later, the workers were still without a collective agreement. In December 1998, the workers voted to go on strike in an attempt to bring McDonald's to the table. The legality of the strike was challenged by McDonald's, but was upheld by the Labour Relations Board. Under British Columbian labour law, this is significant, as it lays the groundwork for the imposition of a first collective agreement. The franchise owner promptly appealed the ruling, delaying the Board's mediator from ordering binding arbitration. Although the mediator's suggestions for a pay rise were modest, workers voted unanimously in favour of a collective agreement in March. Nevertheless, McDonald's eventually prevailed. Its delaying tactics finally paid off owing to a loophole in the province's otherwise fairly labour-friendly labour law. This allows for a decertification vote if a collective agreement is not established within ten months of certification. Intimidated by a whispering campaign of threats of closure, and with a large influx of new employees since the restaurant was unionized, the vote was lost. In view of the fact that the employees were just three weeks away from the imposition of a collective agreement the decertification vote was extremely disappointing. As the union organizer put it: 'We did everything humanly possible.' One positive outcome of the 'threat' of unionization is that, for the time being at least, working conditions appear to have improved in the restaurant.

Future prospects for unionization

Union officials and labour lawyers stress the importance of union friendly labour laws in addition to rank and file and community organizing if the problems in fast-food are to be overcome. Both the CAW and the Teamsters union argue that the only way to do this would be to change the law to allow for master agreements involving not only multi-unit, but also multi-employer bargaining. This would then eliminate the expensive and difficult process of negotiating collective agreements for individual restaurants. A legal amendment of this kind was proposed to the provincial government in British Columbia in 1992, known as the 'Baigent–Ready' proposal. It built on the collective bargaining arrangements established at KFC in British Columbia. It proposed that workers in each enterprise should independently decide whether or not to unionize, where there was a clear majority the employer would be automatically covered by a master agreement in that sector. At the point where a majority of the workers voted to unionize, then there would be one master agreement for that sector. This proposal would allow for not only multi-unit, but multi-employer bargaining that could involve more than one union. (MacDonald, 1997).[7] However, the proposal was dropped by the provincial government.

Paul Clifford, an international union organizer from the Hotel and Restaurant Employees Union (HERE), suggests that it is possible to organize fast-food workers in larger institutional venues in places such as racetracks or stadiums. The idea is to have a multi-location approach and target the larger franchises.[8] Clifford also argues that in addition to jurisdictional strategies, traditional organizing methods need to be supplemented with gathering community and political support. Existing unionized members can then be called upon to assist in other efforts in their sector, to raise the standards for all restaurant workers, a strategy HERE is implementing in the hotel sector. In this regard there have been examples of unified action when labour allies itself with other social movements in Canada. In March 2000, the International Women's March against poverty and violence against women was launched, sponsored in Canada by the Quebec labour movement, the Canadian Labour Congress and the National Action Committee on the Status of Women, to draw attention to labour and social rights (Canadian Women's March Committee, 2000).

One final issue is the fact that many fast-food workers are very young. At a conference sponsored by the Centre for Research on Work and Society at York University, more than 250 young activists gathered to talk about what it means to be a young worker in precarious employment. As one participant, Njeri Damali Campbell, noted, it is important that young people, and people from ethnic minorities, see themselves represented not just in posters, but also in union leadership positions. Unions, she added have to understand that people identify in many ways:

workers are a conglomerate of other identities they are not a homogeneous group with one set of interests . . . the workplace is changing
and so is the face of Canada.

(Our Times, 1999: 27)

The point for unions to take on board is that they cannot just be identified
with a white, male, middle-class, middle-aged group if they are to be taken
seriously by young workers in the new economy.

Conclusion

In Canada, it has often been noted that the most exploited workers – immigrants and young people, in part-time, contingent work – have been the ones
for whom it has been most difficult to guarantee representation rights. The
reasons for this are varied. High labour turnover, and the predominantly
part-time, low-skilled nature of the work make it difficult in practical
terms to organize these workers in an enterprise based collective bargaining
system. Nevertheless, as we have seen, and despite these obstacles, workers
have at times banded together to establish their rights to independent representation. This analysis shows that even the reasonably sympathetic labour
legislation in certain provinces in Canada falls short in this respect. Faced
with the willingness of employers to adopt a combination of legal, quasi-
legal and sometimes illegal practices, workers' representation rights have
been and continue to be undermined.

However, as we have seen, despite this power imbalance, there are still
regular eruptions when workers have been willing to take on these corporations. In these cases it is not traditional union sentiments that have spurred
the moves to unionize, but unacceptable and arbitrary management practices. In the current neo-conservative climate the problems of successfully
organizing workplaces and then negotiating and keeping collective agreements in place are considerable. The combination of a well-resourced
employer opposition, enterprise based labour law that privileges large workplaces and a predominantly young workforce with high turnover mean that
organizing fast-food workers in Canada is an uphill struggle. However
corporations are vulnerable because of the pressure to continually protect
and expand their markets, and spend billions promoting 'consumer choice'
for their product. Consumers might include labour concerns, environmental
concerns and targeting little children in advertising campaigns as considera-
tions in where they choose to eat out. One important way forward, among
others, is to develop an alliance of workers and consumers in demanding
ethical conduct from employers. However, forging this alliance is likely to
prove a continuing challenge.

Notes

1 For a more comprehensive development of this argument see Reiter (1996).

2 It was first enacted as a wartime measure, known as Privy Council Order 1003, and then made permanent by legislation after World War II was over.

3 Swiss Chalet restaurants are part of 'FoodCorp', a subsidiary of Cara.

4 Interview with Sarah Inglis, Orangeville, Ontario, April 1994.

5 This was a bill passed by the New Democratic Party which included 'no scab' provisions, the right to first contract arbitration, statutory protection against discipline or discharge without just cause during the period after certification before a first contract is in place, and access to private property open to the public (e.g. shopping malls) for organizing and picketing. Since the 1940s, a card based system for certification has been in place, allowing for automatic certification with 55 per cent of the employees signing union cards. After the defeat of the NDP government in 1995, all these provisions were repealed in a new labour bill, Bill 7. Regressive measures include replacing the card-based system with a US style electoral certification process arguably providing an employer with more opportunity to intimidate employees.

6 Squamish is a union town where the local rail and pulp workers belong to the Canadian Auto Workers, the largest union in Canada. British Columbia is also the only province where the employees of two other fast-food chains are unionized (also with the CAW). Wage rates in these union outlets are above the norm for the industry and workers have managed to negotiate a benefits package.

7 Note this is not sectoral certification, although it could lead to an entire sector being certified.

8 Interviews with Roger Crowther, National Union Representative, CAW (March 2000); Rejean Lavigne, president Teamsters local 973 (March 2000), and Paul Clifford, President, Local 75, HERE (March 2000).

4 The 51st US state?

Labour relations in the UK fast-food industry

Tony Royle

Politicians of most political persuasions have at different times emphasized the importance of the UK's 'special relationship' with the US, something that was arguably at its peak during World War II and under the Conservative Thatcher governments of the 1980s and early 1990s. Under the Thatcher administrations, government policy appeared to be drawing strongly on the US economic model and trying to move away from Europe; indeed the 'special relationship' has often been cited as one reason why Britain should not be part of Europe at all. Yet, perhaps somewhat paradoxically, American policy since the 1940s has tended to be in the other direction, that is to encourage Britain to become more, not less, involved in Europe (Palmer, 1988).

In addition, during the 1980s the UK was rapidly de-industrializing and the service sector was growing rapidly. US style, out of town shopping malls were springing up all over the UK, and the American-style 'chaining' of previously independent businesses such as car exhaust fitters, opticians and fast-food was becoming an established feature of British life. In addition the promotion of the American Human Resource Management (HRM) concept, the 'individualization' of the employment relationship, the attack on trade unions and various measures aimed at deregulating the UK labour market led some commentators to revive earlier postwar observations, that the UK had become little more than the 51st state of the US. In recent years there has also been some evidence that policy makers in European countries have sought to shift Europe towards more 'flexible' economic structures, influenced by the sustained growth of the US economy. In particular this has tended to manifest itself in increasing pressure on existing systems of corporate governance especially in Germany. In other words European companies are being urged to become more 'Anglo-Saxon' and likewise European countries are being urged to do away with 'burdensome' regulation (Morgan, 1999). Despite New Labour's apparently more positive European stance, Pilger (1999) suggests that little has changed since the previous Conservative administrations; he suggests that New Labour's foreign policy is the most 'Atlanticist' of all British governments since World War II. It is interesting to note in this respect that the new 1999 Employment Act owes much in its design and origins to the US industrial relations system (with some Canadian modifications) exerting only a light, regulatory hand on the UK labour market (Towers, 1999a).

The shift towards the service sector and the promotion of HRM often associated with American non-union or union avoidance management styles has undoubtedly created problems for British unions. Many of the new service companies have no history of union organization and this is particularly so in the case of the fast-food industry where most chains operating in the UK tend to be strongly anti-union. As we shall see in the following pages, UK trade unions have had little or no success in recruiting members, achieving recognition or establishing collective agreements in the UK fast-food industry. This chapter examines why this is so and asks whether the 1999 Employment Act will be likely to have any significant impact on this situation in the near future. The chapter begins by providing an analysis of the UK industrial relations system and then an analysis of the fast-food market and the main companies operating within it. We then provide a review of labour relations in the fast-food sector. The bulk of the chapter draws on data on the McDonald's Corporation; first, because as the market leader it is seen as a highly successful system that others try to emulate; second, it can therefore provide us with unique insights into the way such systems operate in practice and arguably the attitudes of employees and managers in the fast-food sector as a whole.

This chapter is based on the findings of an ongoing study, which builds on over six years of empirical research on the McDonald's Corporation and continuing research which focuses on McDonald's main competitors in the European fast-food industry. This includes multinationals such as PepsiCo/ Tricon (KFC, Pizza Hut, Taco Bell), Whitbread (Churrasco, Maredo), Burger King, Autogrill, and a number of large national players such as Nordsee and Quickburger and in several countries: Germany, the UK, France, Spain, Italy, Denmark, Ukraine and the Czech Republic. In addition to appropriate documentary analysis most of the data for this chapter are based on close to 100 qualitative interviews, which have been conducted with management, employees, international trade union federations, national trade union officials and employer associations over a period of seven years. We begin by providing a brief analysis of the UK industrial relations system.

Industrial relations in the UK

Until the 1980s, the regulation of UK union activities had been minimal and they enjoyed reasonable statutory immunity from the strictures of common law, a system aptly described as 'collective laissez fire'. Rules governing bargaining had been largely established by custom and only loosely defined, with the absence of regulation leaving UK workers without formally guaranteed rights, although many workers remained effectively protected by union membership and union influence (McCarthy, 1992). The UK has seen major changes in its system of industrial relations since that time, and these changes have seen some shift away from traditional patterns of collective bargaining towards a new emphasis on the role of the individual. Terry (1994), amongst others, suggests that the traditionally voluntarist approach to industrial relations combined with the changes in union legislation introduced in the 1980s have left UK trade unions in a vulnerable position. The key influence, however, has been the steep decline in trade union membership and the weakening of collective bargaining. The coverage of collective bargaining in the UK has fallen considerably since the 1970s. In the early 1970s collective agreements covered 80 per cent of all male employees and over 70 per cent of female employees. By the mid-1990s only about 45 per cent of the UK workforce as a whole was covered by collective agreements. Nevertheless, collective bargaining is still the predominant form of pay setting for some groups of employees and trade union membership remains at relatively high levels in the public sector at about 60 per cent (Lecher and Naumann, 1994; Brown *et al.*, 1995; Ackers *et al.*, 1996; Edwards *et al.*, 1998).

The 'Fairness of Work' White Paper made much of the need to provide a basic platform of statutory rights for workers. However, a number of concerns were raised about the adequacy of the proposals even in its early stages. The 1999 Employment Relations Act which finally emerged was strongly influenced by pressure from the employers' organisations, notably the CBI, and consequently the TUC's influence was much less than it would have wished, especially in respect of the statutory recognition procedure. The outcome is that the UK labour market, even after the 1999 legislation, remains far less regulated than most other European countries (Milne, 1998). It could be argued therefore that the UK regulatory system does not significantly challenge MNCs over their preferred forms of employee relations practices. This situation represents a positive advantage for US companies with anti-union or union avoidance policies interested in moving into the UK market, even where unions are recognized. The recent absorption of the ASDA supermarket chain by the giant US Wal-Mart Corporation may be a case in point. Although ASDA has a 'social partnership' agreement with the GMB union there is some anecdotal evidence to suggest that this 'union-friendly' approach was never strongly supported by ASDA management so that the agreement is much more a case of form rather than substance. Wal-Mart's record in the US is one of strong anti-unionism. Should Wal-Mart decide to do so, current conditions may allow it to limit the coverage of the present agreement or even to seek the de-recognition of the union at ASDA, leaving its employees in a vulnerable position.

There are essentially three strands to New Labour's legislative framework for the employment relationship: new individual and collective rights and policies to make it easier for employees to achieve a satisfactory balance between work and family life. The last strand includes the implementation of EU (European Union) directives on working time, the employment of young workers, parental leave and maternity leave. However, the government's policies in this regard go little further than that already required by the EU directives. The 'new' individual rights that the Act provides would perhaps be better described as ameliorations of the onerous restrictions put in place under previous governments. For example, the reduction of the qualifying period for unfair dismissal claims to one year, though welcome to unions and employees, is still higher than the six months that applied under the last Labour government of the late 1970s. The national minimum wage, although it has been increased, has been set at a low level, which clearly reduced the number of employer protests and therefore, whilst it may be radical in principle, it is not so radical in practice. The final strand of the new framework – collective rights – does not introduce a legal right to strike (as exists in most continental European countries). In addition employers will still have substantial rights after eight weeks of a lawful dispute and although employees will no longer be vulnerable to employer inducements to opt-out of collective agreements, they will still be able to do so voluntarily (Towers, 1999a). What is new is the new statutory recognition procedure. This important feature of the new legislation draws upon the recognition procedures of North America and as Towers, quoting from Tony Blair's Foreword to the White Paper 'Fairness at Work', points out:

> intends to maintain the absence of strikes without ballots, mass picketing, closed shops, and secondary action [in] the most lightly regulated labour market of any leading economy in the world.
>
> (Towers, 1998b: 83)

However, although the final legislative outcome was strongly influenced by employer pressure, the legislation does halt and to some extent reverse the apparently inexorable tide of ant-union legislation introduced by successive Conservative governments from 1980 to 1993.

Developments in the UK fast-food market

The UK is the largest European market for fast-food, probably because the market is more developed than in other European countries. The concept is widely and firmly established, with the UK population showing a growing preference for convenience foods (*Euromonitor*, 1998). Before the advent of the fast-food brands, fast-food in the UK revolved around fish and chips and sandwiches. The first burger bar of any significance was the Wimpy chain that appeared in the mid-1950s. KFC was the next after Wimpy, opening its first outlet in 1965 in Preston. McDonald's did not arrive until nearly ten years later, opening its first outlet in Woolwich in 1974. Much has changed since that time; the market for fast-food has expanded rapidly and now includes a wide diversity of products ranging from hamburgers, pizzas, baked potatoes and French bakery products to the more recent coffee shops and soup outlets. Ethnic foods have grown in popularity at the end of the twentieth century and there is a much greater acceptance of 'foreign' foods. Indeed Indian style curries and Chinese takeaways have become part of the staple diet of many people in the UK.

However, while sandwich shops, burgers, pizzas and other products are dominated by large companies, ethnic foods are still the domain of the small independent operator. Increasing competition has also led to aggressive pricing policies amongst the large brands and an increase in menu diversification and new product developments in order to increase sales and market share. As the high street has become increasingly saturated the leading fast-food chains have stepped up their store expansion programmes and introduced new formats such as 'drive thrus', kiosks, carts sites in motorway service stations, retail and leisure parks, shopping centres, petrol forecourts and other travel terminals. McDonald's has now gone beyond this by opening its own motorway service station called McDonald's Services which it opened on the M5 in Devon in 1999. The continued expansion of the market has prompted the entry of leisure and catering companies and large breweries. For example, Compass Leisure Group has developed its Select Service Partner Ltd division linking up with leading fast-food brands including Burger King, Harry Ramsden's and O'Briens. Similarly the Granada Group has also expanded its roadside catering operations linking up with Burger King and Harry Ramsden's. The leading fast-food brand owners and their brands are detailed in Table 4.1. As we indicate in the introduction to this book there are different ways in which fast-food can be defined. In Table 4.2 we differentiate fast-food chains by the main product offerings, for example, Burgers, Pizzas, Chicken and Others.

The fast-food sector is growing steadily; in the period 1995 to 1999 the number of units grew by over 14 per cent from 22,959 units to 26,189 units. Although there are more independently operated fast-food units than chained units (87 per cent are operated independently) average value sales per unit are significantly higher in chained outlets – over £600,000 per unit as opposed to just over £170,000 in 1999 – probably a reflection of the chains' greater experience and financial backing.

Euromonitor who do not include Pizza operations in their UK fast-food statistics suggest that chained burger outlets such as McDonald's and Burger King are by far more important than the rest of the fast-food chains – chained bakery outlets (sandwiches), ice cream, fish and chicken outlets – in terms of units, transactions and value sales. In 1999 they accounted for 64 per cent of chained units, 80 per cent of chained transactions and 80 per cent of chained value sales. This is almost entirely due to the efforts of the two most heavily branded operators, McDonald's and Burger King. Both have made heavy use of advertising, give-aways and other promotional tools. According to *Euromonitor* (2000) there appears to be no limit to the demand for burger outlets in the UK with new units being rolled out a strong rate. McDonald's dominates the chained fast-food sector both in terms of company and brand terms, taking a share, by value, of 52 per cent

Table 4.1 Leading fast-food brand owners and their brands, 2000

Brand owner	Brand
McDonald's Restaurants Ltd	McDonald's, Aroma, Prêt à Manger
Tricon Global Restaurants Inc.	KFC, Pizza Hut, Taco Bell
Diageo PLC	Burger King
Allied Domecq PLC	Dunkin Donuts, Baskin Robins
Domino's Pizza Ltd	Domino's Pizza
Pizza Express	Pizza Express, San Marzan, Café Pasta
Perfect Pizza Ltd	Perfect Pizza
Whitbread PLC	Pizza Hut, Bella Pasta, Costa Café
City Centre Restaurants PLC	Deep Pan Pizza, Café Uno
Wimpy International Ltd	Wimpy, Dr Beaks
Harry Ramsden's PLC	Harry Ramsden's, Henry Higgins
Star Burger Ltd	Starburger
Fast Food Systems Ltd	Southern Fried Chicken
Spud-u-Like Ltd	Spud-u-Like
Prêt à Manger (Europe) Ltd	Prêt à Manger
Dixy Fried Chicken Ltd	Dixy Fried Chicken
Favourite Fried Chicken Ltd	Favourite Fried Chicken
Compass Group PLC	Upper Crust, Taste, Café Ritazza, Shopgap, O'Briens, The Reef, Le Croissant
Delice de France	Delice de France
Greggs PLC	Greggs, Bakers Oven
New Convent Garden Soup Company	'Soup' bars
FLS Group	Delifrance

Source: Key Note statistics (2000) and Bozec (2001).

in 1999. Together McDonald's and Burger King had 73 per cent of the market in 1999. Table 4.3 provides the market shares of each of the main competitor brands.

Greggs is the largest retail baker in the UK but growth in fast-food bakery units has largely been underpinned by the development of sandwich chains such as Prêt à Manger, Delifrance, and Subway. In February 2001 McDonald's bought a 33 per cent stake in Prêt à Manger. Reaction to the deal amongst Prêt à Manger employees was apparently hostile, probably because of concerns about the potential effect on the product and working conditions (Clark, 2001). Subway is one of the world's largest fast-food bakery chains operating 14,165 units in seventy-two countries but as yet only has a relatively small presence in the UK with thirty or so units, but it also intends to expand considerably over the next few years. Chained fast-food chicken has lost market share to the burger chains, its share falling from 33 per cent to 27 per cent from 1995 to 1999. Until Wimpy introduced its new chicken chain Dr Beaks in late 1999, KFC was the only global player in the UK chained chicken market. Other chains such as Favourite and Southern Fried have a lower profile tending to operate in less prestigious

Table 4.2 Leading fast-food and takeaway brands by number of outlets (1999)

Organization	Number of outlets
Burger chains	
McDonald's	1016
Burger King	608
Wimpy International	283
Pizza chains	
Pizza Hut	430
Pizza Express#	256
Perfect Pizza	206
Domino's Pizza	201
Deep Pan Pizza	59
Pizza Go Go	48
Chicken chains	
KFC	480
Southern Fried Chicken	450
Favourite Fried Chicken	91
Dixy Fried Chicken	36
Nando's Chickenland	16
Other	
Greggs	1084
Prêt à Manger	90
Harry Ramsden's *	82
Delifrance	35
Spud-u-Like	33
Subway	31

Source: Key Note statistics (2000); Bozec (2001).

Notes
* Includes 22 Henry Higgins takeaway outlets.
# Company-owned restaurants only, excludes foreign franchise operations.

locations and have lower turnovers. Chained fish fast-food outlets have a negligible presence – Henry Higgins until 1999 part of the Harry Ramsden's group (which has a total of eighty-two outlets) is the only chain operator of any note. Ice cream chains are dominated by the Haagen Daz Cafés owned by the Diageo (Pilsbury Group). Other ice cream outlets such as Ben and Jerry's and Baskin Robins have only a small presence. Other types of chained fast-food outlets do not have a significant presence in the UK – Tricon's Taco Bell, for example, tried and failed to establish itself. Pizza Hut is the brand leader in the UK pizza market and is a joint venture between Whitbread PLC and Tricon Global Restaurants. In recent years its upmarket rivals Pizza Express and Ask Central have hit Pizza Hut hard. These types of

Table 4.3 Value of market shares of chained fast-food companies 1999 (excluding pizza operations)

Brand	Global brand owner and national operator(s)	Percentage share
McDonald's	McDonald's Restaurants (and various franchisees)	52.0
Burger King	Diageo (Burger King, Gowrings, Compass Group)	21.0
KFC	Tricon Global Restaurants (KFC Great Britain, Sutcliffe Catering, Compass Group)	10.2
Prêt à Manger	Prêt à Manger	1.8
Wimpy	Wimpy	1.8
Haagen-Dazs Café	Diageo (Pilsbury)	0.7
Others		12.5

Source: *Euromonitor* (2000: 103).

restaurant tend not to be included in statistics on fast-food companies because, although they are chained restaurants, they are somewhat closer to traditional restaurants in their mode of operation.

Labour relations in the UK fast-food industry

Whilst unions have enjoyed some success in continental Europe in achieving union recognition and/or the imposition of collective agreements on fast-food operations there (Royle, 2000, 2002), the picture in the Anglo-Saxon countries (the US, Canada, Ireland and the UK) is quite different. As Chapters 2 and 3 illustrate, although there have been some small scale sporadic and partly successful attempts to gain union recognition in the US and Canada most have been short lived and have not resulted in collective agreements. The situation in the UK is, if anything, even worse. Although UK unions have been able to represent small numbers of workers or individuals in isolated incidents, usually involving unfair dismissal cases, no union recognition has ever been achieved.

The Fourth Workplace Employment Relations Survey (WERS) (Cully *et al.*, 1999) suggests that the trend towards non-unionism is increasing in the UK and especially among young workers and new businesses and especially in the service sector. Lucas (1996) suggests that even when wages councils still existed in the UK, voluntary collective bargaining was rare in the hospitality industry. The increasingly anti-union climate in the 1980s and early 1990s has encouraged UK employers to withhold or withdraw union recognition, discouraged employees from joining unions and posed difficulties for recruitment.

There are three main trade unions who have been active in trying to recruit members and gain recognition in UK fast-food industry: USDAW, the TGWU, and the GMB. Union officials at these unions all tell a similar story; union recruitment was very difficult and recognition virtually impossible. USDAW for example, had once targeted McDonald's for recruitment. In the early 1990s USDAW had written to McDonald's headquarters in London asking if they could have some talks about 'talks'; the answer was a simple 'no'. Up to now there has been no coordinated approach between the three unions. GMB representatives stated that they were increasingly trying to target more part-time members. In the mid-1990s the GMB appears to have had some success in recruiting a small number of McDonald's employees. Under its '10p per week' membership scheme the GMB recruited a number of student employees; this had been achieved by canvassing at universities and further education colleges. However, the numbers were small and with high turnover rates the overall impact has not been significant.

One recent case at a Pizza Express outlet – a chained operation located somewhere between traditional restaurants and fast-food operations – illustrates these issues clearly. It involved a dispute about the minimum wage. Shortly after the minimum wage was introduced at £3.60 for those aged 21 or over, the management of the company declared that the £3.10 per hour would not be increased to £3.60. Management argued that this was because employees' pay was to be restructured to include their tips (something which is common practice in the US). Pizza Express argued that their employees received around 90 pence per hour in tips and therefore the 'real' hourly rate received by employees was around £4.00 per hour. Incensed by this action, most of the workers in the company's flagship restaurant in Manchester joined the union USDAW and sought their advice. The media got hold of the story and eventually the company, presumably concerned about bad publicity, backed down and agreed to pay the minimum wage exclusive of tips. USDAW tried to use the incident to enter other Pizza Express restaurants and encourage workers to join in the hope of trying to force the company into recognizing the union. However, management refused the unions access to their premises and the attempt failed.

Since that time the numbers of union members in the restaurant at the centre of the dispute have gradually dwindled as labour turnover has taken its toll. Union officials occasionally visit the restaurant *incognito* to try to encourage other workers to become members but they have had little success. The company also used the incident to establish a 'company forum', a kind of consultative council that is supposed to represent employees' interests. However, USDAW officials claim that the forum was really established to try to sidestep the role of the union, since it seems that none of the employee representatives are union members.

Although the new recognition procedures in the 1999 Employment Act are now in force the union doubts that they will be of any use in this sector. It suggests that if a claim for recognition were made on the basis of one restaurant the company would claim that the whole chain should be the 'bargaining unit'. In this scenario it would be very difficult to achieve the required 40 per cent of workers in all the company's restaurants. This is especially so with hostile management attitudes and young, transient and inexperienced workers, who often have little knowledge or experience of unions.

Another problem for workers in this sector is the use of 'flexible' working practices that have sometimes been taken to extremes. One case, which hit the headlines in 1995, involved a Burger King employee, a student who was paid just £1 for a five hour shift. Along with other staff, the student was told to clock off and remain available for work (unpaid) when the restaurant was quiet and only to clock on again when the restaurant became busy. The end result was that he did not earn enough to buy one of the company's 'whoppers', which at that time cost £1.89. Although he worked for Burger King for three weeks, he never once earned over £6. In one instance this employee had been clocked off almost immediately after he had arrived at the restaurant. The *Today* newspaper, reporting the incident (Lowrie, 1995), suggests that this is also common practice in Burger King restaurants across Britain. Although this is not illegal per se, it is certainly morally questionable and something trade unions would clearly try to eradicate if they were given the opportunity to do so.

Union membership is very poor in the UK fast-food industry and, as yet, no collective agreements exist in any of the fast-food companies in the UK. The TGWU has a few members in some restaurants at the Deep Pan Pizza Company and its offshoot 'Ask Central'. USDAW has some members at Pizza Express and in bakery outlets and motorway service stations. In most cases it appears that the unions have given up on this sector despite the introduction of the 1999 Employment Relations Act. The TGWU for example are targeting most of their resources in the hotel sector where success is more likely and unions, in the past, have had a reasonable recruitment record, despite high levels of labour turnover. The following sections focus in more detail on employee relations at McDonald's UK.

The McDonald's Corporation

Worth over $40 billion in 2000 McDonald's is not just the largest food-service system in the world (serving 45 million customers a day), but it is something of a phenomenon in its own right, forming the basis for Ritzer's (1996) *The McDonaldization of Society*. In 2000 McDonald's was employing around 2 million people in over 28,000 restaurants in 118 countries worldwide. In 1996 it replaced Coca-Cola as the world's top brand and it is continuing to expand at a breath-taking rate; it plans to open between 2,500 and 3,200 new restaurants every year, the equivalent of one new restaurant every four hours. If this rate of expansion can be achieved the corporation will have more than doubled in size in the space of 10 years to well over 50,000 restaurants by 2010. The US has a smaller population than the EU, yet US citizens have between three and four times as many McDonald's restaurants per head compared to their European counterparts. Of course McDonald's has been increasingly involved in the acquisition of other companies in recent years. In the UK the purchase of the Aroma coffee chain and more recently Prêt à Manger may signal a new corporate strategy. In any case the relatively small number of restaurants in Europe compared with that in the US suggests that the European market is likely to experience a lot more expansion in future, although McDonald's is already the market leader in most European countries. In 1999 McDonald's employed over 200,000 people in the seventeen countries of the European Economic Area (EEA) in over 3,700 restaurants. McDonald's first came to Europe in 1971, it opened its first restaurant in Holland and then Germany later in the same year. Restaurants were then opened in Sweden in 1973, Austria and Ireland in 1977, Belgium in 1978, France in 1979, Denmark in 1981, Spain in 1982, Norway in 1983, Finland in 1984 and Italy in 1985. McDonald's came to the UK in 1974 and was originally set up as a joint venture with an existing individual McDonald's franchisee from the US. In the early 1980s the franchise operator involved decided to sell back his restaurants to the corporation. This is one of the main reasons why the proportion of McDonald's franchises is lower than in most other countries at around 30 per cent. The corporation now has well over 1,000 restaurants and well over 50,000 employees in the UK, a similar number to that in Germany.

Structure and hierarchy at McDonald's

The hierarchy in McDonald's restaurants in the fourteen countries examined in Royle (2000) appears to be remarkably similar and furthermore where differences do exist they appear to have a minimal impact on the corporation's basic American operating system. Figure 4.1 illustrates the basic restaurant hierarchy in the UK.

The majority of employees are called the 'crew' and in fact this term appears to have been universally accepted, we have yet to find a country where this term is not in use. The term 'crew' was apparently used by the brothers right from the beginning of their 'Speedee Service System' in 1948 in which they trained their twelve-man 'crew' to work like a 'crack drill team' (Love, 1995: 16). The idea that the employees should be trained like the military was also promoted by one of Ray Kroc's early franchisees, Sandy Agate who opened his first restaurant in Waukegan near the Great Lakes. Agate carefully selected the crew, preferring mostly Navy chefs from the nearby Naval Training Centre. Love (1995: 82) states: 'During

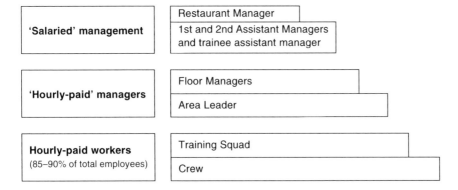

Figure 4.1 Job titles and hierarchy in the restaurants

Source: Royle (2000)

peak periods, Agate barked out production orders as a skipper might order sailors to their battle stations.' Crew jobs are fragmented into different stations, e.g. working on the till, cleaning tables and emptying bins, garnishing burgers, monitoring fries, bread machines or the grill. Again this goes back to the McDonald brother's early system. Love states that as the brothers refined their techniques members of the crew became specialists:

> There were three grill men who did nothing but grill hamburgers; two shake men, who did nothing but make milk shakes; two fry men who specialized in making French fries . . . three countermen who did nothing but fill orders. . . .
>
> (Love, 1995: 18)

Although some flexibility across different jobs is called for in theory, in practice management often use the term 'stars in their places' to indicate that rotation is often undesirable because it interferes with efficiency, so kitchen workers usually remain in the kitchen and till workers remain on the till. 'Training squad' as they are called in the UK or 'crew trainers' as they are called in Germany, France and most other European countries, train other crew. They are supposed to know all the stations and monitor the work of normal crew and, as mentioned earlier, they are supposed to do this with the use of an operation checklist (OCL – see Figure 4.2).

When training squad are 18 or over and are able to work enough hours they can be promoted to area leader (*Vorarbeiter* in Germany and Austria; *Responsable de Zone* in France; *Ayundante de área* in Spain). Further promotions would take them to floor manager and then shift-running floor manager (*Schichtführer* [G]; *Assistente de turno* [Sp]). In the Netherlands and France these more senior floor managers are usually known as 'swing managers' just as in the US (Royle, 2000). These floor managers are, in effect, hourly-paid

PREPARATION AND TOASTING	Possible	Actual
1 Buns are selected using FIFO	3	
2 Empty as well as full bin trays are stacked where they are not a hazard and sorted according to colour code	2	
3 Trays of buns are stacked so that buns are not crushed	3	
4 Appropriate bun board used and toaster set at 420°F (±5°F)	3	
5 Bun trays are flat, clean and dry	3	
6 Macs/Regulars: Buns person directs grill person to achieve perfect timing and coordination. Buns are never pre-staged in toasters	3	
7 a. Regular bun crowns or Big Mac club and heel sections: placed in toaster immediately on call from production person b. Quarter bun crowns: placed in toaster immediately after 30 seconds duty timer sounds	3	
8 a. Regulars and Quarters: when buzzer sounds, toaster handle is lifted immediately and heels are placed in toaster before crowns are removed b. Big Macs: when buzzer sounds, toaster handle is lifted immediately and crowns are placed in toaster before clubs are lifted out using a spatula, and placed on tray with heels. Tray is placed on dressing table	3	
9 Bun surface is caramelised to a uniform golden brown	3	
10 Bun is not crushed by excessive compression or damage in any other way	3	
11 Bun person keeps up with product demand	3	
12 Good communication and teamwork exist (i.e., 3 C's Communication, Cooperation and Coordination)		

GENERAL

	Possible	Actual
1 Uniform is neat and clean (wearing apron). Name badge is worn	3	
2 Hands are washed before commencing work on this station	3	
3 Clean white/blue border cloths are used and kept in the appropriate pan	2	
4 Only countable waste is placed in the red bin	1	

OVERALL GRADE

(A) × .75 =	(C)
(B) × .25 =	(D)
OVERALL = C&D	

Pass = 90%

TOTAL (pass = 40)	44
SCORE (A)	100%

COMMENTS

_____

_____

Figure 4.2 An example of an Observation Check List (OCL) used for the toasting and preparation of buns

and usually part-time workers and some are qualified to run a shift by themselves, to distribute cash-register drawers full of money and to deal with customer complaints; but they are not salaried employees. They can be mistaken for salaried managers, because they usually wear a blue or white shirt or blouse with tie or bow and black trousers, whereas the crew and training squad usually wear some kind of T-shirt. The salaried managers are the restaurant manager and first, second and trainee assistant managers. They are employed on a permanent contract and are usually only appointed by regional management. Regional management normally determines promotion to salaried management positions in franchise operations, but franchisees can and do 'poach' existing salaried managers employed in company-owned restaurants. Promotion is dependent on employees passing the McDonald's training courses which managers from a number of European countries state is without exception based on the same format as in the US (Royle, 2000). Salaried managers enjoy greater employment security, benefits and monthly salaries. However, the issue of 'hourly-paid' versus 'monthly-paid' workers is not always that helpful. In some countries where collective agreements apply – as in Italy for example – employees' pay is calculated on a monthly basis even if they work only a few hours per week.

McWork: it's idiot-proof

Virtually all aspects of the business are highly standardized and rigorously monitored. Assembly-line techniques are used to produce and serve identical products, standardization and higher productivity ensured through new technology and the systematic planning of each job, broken down into the smallest of steps. When planning the plan, the equipment layout and the scheduling of restaurants, McDonald's industrial engineers measure in seconds of time using computerized time study methods to reduce workers' movements to a minimum and hence speed up production. Workers' skills are eliminated and the work is labour intensive with the machinery making the cooking decisions. Lights and buzzers tell workers when to turn burgers or take fries out of the fat. Computerized cash registers do most of the thinking for till and window workers, separating the hand and the brain in classic scientific management style.

The modern ketchup dispensers are little changed from the McDonald brothers' days. They squirt a measured amount of ketchup or mustard on each burger. Workers learn a routinized job in one day. For example to prepare and bag French-fries, workers follow nineteen carefully calculated steps, the French-fry scoop lets workers fill a bag and set it down in one continuous motion and helps them gauge the proper serving size. All the jobs can be learnt with no previous experience or the minimum of training. Operations are monitored and controlled using the *Operations and Training Manual*, or the 'Bible' as some McDonald's managers call it. It is over 700 pages in length and extremely comprehensive. It includes full colour photographs, which, amongst other things, illustrate the correct placement for ketchup and mustard in the preferred five-point 'flower' pattern and determine the correct size of pickles to be placed on each type of hamburger. Rules and procedures cover everything, eliminating decision-making for workers and, as one respondent put it, makes the job 'virtually idiot-proof'. When the assembly line output of burgers slackens because the restaurant is quiet it does not mean that the workers are allowed to take a break. Ray Kroc was obsessed with cleanliness; he insisted that his staff should be constantly cleaning areas that no one else would even think about, with the cleaning cloth becoming an essential tool for every crew member. As Kroc frequently reminded his staff (Love, 1995: 143): 'If you've got time to lean, you've got time to clean.' So although the work can be easily learnt, it would be a mistake to think that it is easy. A UK assistant manager emphasized the intense and hard nature of the work:

> Many people are not prepared to do the work that it entails. You've got to be a very strong-minded person to be able to handle it. A lot of people who think, 'oh this will be so easy', they totally underestimate it . . . it's often students who can't hack it. They don't want to work that hard for the money.

Moreover the work is not just for the ordinary crew who do the bulk of the work, but also for the managers. One UK crew member stated:

> It is very stressful especially for the managers. I don't think I could work here full-time. The stress of trying to keep the happy face of McDonald's, that's what you've got to keep, or try to, even if you're having a bad day with the restaurant manager on your back, you've still got to be nice to customers. It can be difficult.

The majority of workers work part-time, so some may only do one full (eight hour) shift per week or a few hours over a few days. However, if the restaurant is busy or short-staffed workers are frequently asked to stay and work longer hours. In some cases employees may end up working ten hours or more, in fact it can be much longer. In all European countries hourly-paid employees are supposed to get rest breaks; in some countries where collective agreements apply these breaks may be longer or more frequent than those laid down in the law. However, as reported elsewhere (Royle, 2000), despite more stringent European regulation, workers from several countries reported that when the restaurant is busy, breaks are cut short, workers have to get permission to leave the floor and managers are often reluctant to let employees go when their contracted hours are finished. In these situations workers admitted that they sometimes inadvertently helped management by 'controlling themselves', staying on longer so as not to 'let their colleagues down'.

Although there are rules and tight procedures for everything and managers, usually working alongside, closely monitor the work, workers do sometimes find short cuts, especially when the restaurant is busy and when working within the system cannot cope with demand. UK employees referred to some of their male colleagues as 'cowboys', because these workers find shortcuts in work procedures, in exactly the same way as assembly-line workers in other industries, in order to create some porosity in an otherwise hectic schedule. One UK floor manager stated:

> Yeah, some of the lads, the 'cowboys' have figured out how to save time on cleaning, missing out some of the steps but getting the same results. Or sometimes they make more burgers than are required by the shift leader on the wrap and call station, so that they get a short break.

Sometimes the system itself fails, such as when mustard and ketchup dispensers clog up and then too little or no sauce is placed on the burger. In addition some workers have reported more deviant forms of behaviour that might be akin to physical sabotage. One example was what some young male employees called 'sweating competitions'. The hot kitchen conditions were used to see who could sweat the most over the products, apparently as a way of relieving the frustration or boredom or as a way of seeking revenge on unpopular managers or the customer. Nor is this the only example; one worker reported that he purposely did not wash his hands after a visit to the toilet whilst others would apply their nasal fluid onto the products as a way of getting back at customers and managers. Pickles are sometimes missed off the burger, sometimes food falls on the floor, and if the manager isn't watching it sometimes ends up with the customer. Buns, burgers and fries are taken out before the buzzer has buzzed and sometimes fries are kept longer than the regulation seven minutes. In some cases it appears that managers adopt an 'indulgency pattern' (Gouldner, 1964), as when restaurants are short-staffed managers may turn a blind eye to some of these behaviours providing that customer demand is met.

Managing McWork

Management in fast-food enterprises pursue a management approach that focuses on isolated individuals and concentrates on their needs and wants, which suggests that job satisfaction can be attained through adequate leadership. With this view job satisfaction is not attained through good pay and working conditions but through the less tangible area of psychological needs. A good manager is one who will solve the problem of employee discontent through adequate 'communication'. This is strongly reflected in the advice given to McDonald's managers in the UK basic training course:

Employees who understand what is going on and who feel part of restaurant life, develop a sense of loyalty and pride. As a result they work harmoniously with management.

When asked how they motivated employees UK managers at restaurant and senior management level stressed the importance of good communication. Managers are encouraged to apply and concentrate on 'motivators' such as 'achievement', 'responsibility', 'growth' and 'recognition'. This may take the form of 'employee of the month' awards, day trips and cash bonuses, or by encouraging workers to strive for promotion and take on responsibility. One UK training squad employee commented:

Really we're all brainwashed by their little procedures and incentives, they offer little carrots like the 'stars' and little pay rises or going for promotion to training squad.

On the one hand the striving for promotion locks managers' and employees' loyalty into the system; on the other, it may offer real opportunities for advancement which may be hard to come by for those with poor academic backgrounds. Managers are encouraged to discount the importance of 'hygiene' factors (Herzberg's, 1966), such as pay and conditions of work. Training reinforces the view that pay and conditions do not really matter, what does really matter is their 'positive' management style and leadership. A good manager will therefore 'solve' the problem of worker resistance or discontent through good communication or 'McParticipation' (Royle, 2000). In this scenario the 3 C's: coordination, cooperation and communication are the basis of the solutions to all problems. McDonald's management training materials point out that the failure to provide adequate communication, the correct management style, adequate praise and recognition, adequate staffing levels and correct handling of holiday entitlements and pay details are the reasons workers becoming resistant to the management prerogative. Sadly this one-sided communication process and the 'representation gap' (Towers, 1997) that this produces is also a common feature amongst other UK employers. Cully *et al.* (1999) conclude in the 1998 WER survey that there was an enormous gap between the percentage of workplace management who said they consulted their employees and the percentage of employees who agreed with them.

Identification with the restaurant and other crew members is fostered through the creation of a new form of collective. If 'us and them' is still recognized it is reinterpreted to mean 'us' as the management and crew and 'them' as the customer. Workers are encouraged to think of themselves as part of a team and managers are encouraged to equate restaurant management with coaching a team. The result of this form of 'teamwork' seems to be that individuals are often loath to be seen by their peers as making extra work for other people by not doing their share. Even the more resentful employees who had what management depict as 'negative' attitudes would still work hard to keep the respect of their peers. Many of the workers' and managers' comments reflected the strongly paternalistic nature of the employment relationship which management worked to foster. However, it would be wrong to assume that the manager's task of keeping workers happy is an easy one, i.e. to provide workers with feelings of achievement and recognition while they are themselves tightly controlled by their seniors and the system. Their freedom of action is also curtailed by stringent scheduling rules, and the needs of the restaurant that must come before those of the individuals. The carefully planned approach to managing the workforce, which requires managers to show consideration and give praise and recognition, simply breaks down under the reality of meeting extremely difficult targets. One ex-restaurant manager for example, reports that there have been some instances where salaried assistant managers have deliberately altered (electronically) the hours that employees have worked in order to reduce the level of labour costs on their shift in order to portray themselves in a 'good light' so as to improve their promotion prospects. The competitive climate for promotion amongst management within the restaurant also means many hours of unpaid work and more responsibility. This includes the restaurant manager who will often have to put in longer hours than anyone else. It was not uncommon for restaurant managers in this study to regularly work from 6 a.m. to 6 p.m. However, rather than this resulting in good management it tends to result in unreasonable expectations and poor morale as one floor manager commented:

> The main problem is crew morale. There is always somebody upset. People really take it out on others here and it can be very nasty. Managers just have the wrong attitude to other people, they can be very autocratic. [Salaried] managers work such long hours and they expect everyone else to do the same, it breeds a culture . . . even when we're not busy there is an atmosphere in the restaurant which you can cut with a knife.

Although all restaurants are closely monitored and the head offices are very keen to train managers in developing the right leadership style, the ultimate emphasis is not on how the employees are managed but first and foremost on the profitability of the restaurant and its QSC (quality, service and cleanliness). One UK floor manager commented:

> They have inspections but they focus more on cleanliness, appearance and profitability. In a full field inspection you'll have people here all night. It will be spotless, hygiene is always a very high standard, but problems of crew morale are only considered if profitability or QSC are affected.

McDonald's and its labour relations

Chapters 2 and 3 illustrate that the strictly non-union policy that McDonald's normally operates in Canada and the US has not been problematic in the UK. By the 1980s when the corporation really began to employ significant numbers of workers, British trade unions were finding life difficult under the new neo-liberal government of Mrs Thatcher. In a context of huge increases in unemployment and a government actively undermining the position of unions, it is hardly surprising that McDonald's had few problems in operating its usual non-union system. As we saw in the previous chapter, despite the fact that British unions have been trying to target part-time workers and students in recent years union membership in the UK fast-food sector is at zero or close to it. McDonald's the market leader has continually refused to recognize UK trade unions. Sid Nicholson ex-personnel chief in the UK stated in an interview with the *Daily Mirror* industrial editor in 1986 (Vidal, 1997: 233): 'We will never negotiate wages and conditions with a union and we discourage our staff from joining.'

The corporation's tradition of anti-unionism is well recorded (Love, 1995; Dowling *et al.*, 1994; Royle, 2000). John Cooke, McDonald's US labour relations chief in the 1960s and 1970s, was technically employed to 'educate' US employees about unions, which translated in practice to keeping the unions out (Love, 1995). He organized 'flying squads' of experienced McDonald's store managers who were dispatched to a restaurant on the same day that there was a known attempt to organize it. He trained managers on how to deal with employees and union representatives. As Cooke himself made clear, 'unions are inimical to what we stand for and how we operate' (Love, 1995: 397). McDonald's ran into trouble in the American courts in the mid-1970s in San Francisco for using lie detectors to weed out trade union sympathisers. Indeed he suggests that the practice only stopped because new laws made this practice illegal in the US. Vidal (1997: 231) also quotes a memo from Cooke to top McDonald's executives that stated: 'I think [the union] was effective in terms of reaching the public with the information that we do use polygraph tests in a Gestapo-type manner.'

Modern recruitment methods have become more subtle. Ex-managers report that workers only need ask about their rights to breaks, sick pay or holidays to be excluded from a job at McDonald's. Such individuals are seen as 'non-conformist trouble-makers' who may show an unhealthy interest in their rights and be sympathetic to union representation. McDonald's anti-unionism was also a finding of Britain's longest running civil court case, the 'McLibel' trial. Vidal (1997: 313–14) states: 'The judge finds "as a fact" that McDonald's is "strongly antipathetic" to any idea of unionization of crew in their restaurants.' This may be one reason that union membership is so low. The chief executive of the McDonald's Corporation until 1998, Michael Quinlan, has also stated:

McDonald's is basically a non-union company and intends to stay that way . . . I do not feel unionisation has interfered with employees' loyalty to McDonald's, or to the company's philosophy of service and employee motivation . . . unions do not bring much to the equation.

(BNA, 1991: 66)

This attitude may be symptomatic of a more general anti-union stance found in the US. Union membership in the US is reckoned to be the lowest in the Western world and union avoidance in the US is deep-rooted with considerable investment in coercion against trade unionists, especially in the private sector (Towers, 1997). These practices have prompted human rights organizations to publish case studies of many human rights violations in the workplace (Human Rights Watch, 2000).

Explaining low union membership

The often geographically dispersed, small unit, temporary, part-time and low skills base of the jobs in the wider hospitality industry have typically fostered high levels of labour turnover. These factors together with the employment of ethnic minorities and young and female employees make union organization very difficult. Union organization in the wider hospitality industry has always been low in both the UK and the US and often reflects the 'Bleak House' of industrial relations: highly 'individualized' employee relations, resulting in high dismissal rates, accidents and absenteeism, high labour turnover, large numbers of grievance procedures and low pay (Lucas, 1996). However, unions themselves may also be somewhat to blame. Perhaps because of these difficulties unions have not always been willing to focus adequate resources on recruitment in this industry. The fast-food 'portion' of this sector is at the vanguard of this form of 'atypical' work. In fact this kind of work is no longer atypical but increasingly represents 'typical' work for a growing sector of the labour market. The following sections draw on findings from McDonald's in an attempt to explain why unions have had no success in organizing workers in the UK fast-food sector.

The problems of union organizing

The earlier analysis suggests that negative management attitudes towards unionization are part of the explanation. We have already suggested that the 'basic assumptions' (Schein, 1984) of the management in most fast-food companies remain strongly grounded in anti-unionism. But to what extent are these assumptions transmitted and internalized by senior-level and restaurant management at McDonald's? In fact whether values are internalized or not may be irrelevant in practice, what matters most is that managers are aware of corporate values and conduct their behaviour accordingly. Interviews with UK and other European McDonald's management do suggest that corporate values are transmitted across societal borders to management at senior and restaurant level (Royle, 2000). The following comments from UK senior and restaurant managers suggest that either managers are aware of corporate values or have internalized these values themselves:

> Unionization has risen its ugly head over the years, but you know, we feel that we don't need unions. I think we've seen that the unions' power within business has been eroded quite considerably over the last 15 years. We've managed to get rid of them.
>
> (Senior UK manager)

> Unions can cause problems if they get out of control, I don't think they need to get any stronger. Unions should be there as an advisory function, I would like to think that there would be no need for them in the future. But I can't see it, because not everyone is as honest as the managers in this restaurant, so I think there will always be a need for them. We don't need them in this restaurant because we do things right, manage them right.
>
> (1st assistant manager)

> I think unions have an important role to play, but in the restaurant where it's only one on one there's no need for them. I've never thought of joining a union, never been in a union, my initial feeling is, it's not worth bothering.
>
> (Shift-running floor manager)

In the UK salaried managers typically had no personal experience of unions and appeared to be poorly informed about their current strength relative to employers and their wider role in society. UK managers typically saw UK trade unions as powerful and dangerous and there appeared to be very little concrete knowledge of the changes in union legislation introduced in the 1980s and 1990s. The following comments by young UK salaried managers were typical:

> I think they've got too much power at the moment, nobody wins strikes, they are getting their members over a barrel. I must admit, my knowledge is very limited, I didn't know about the changes in legislation on unions.

> It's as if they have the power to say right we're on strike, it's as if they have control over employers.

> I think they are more political than they used to be. I think they lobby for a lot more than their predecessors did. I think they are a lot stronger than they were. They've got all these lawyers looking for loop-holes now, that

they never used to and outside help. They've got a lot of money and a lot of backing, so they can do a lot of damage. That's the main reason why I'm against them. Well not against them, but I think they can do a lot of unnecessary damage.

One comment made by a UK restaurant manager unwittingly reflected previous events in Germany (see Chapter 5). He suggested that unions could perhaps play a useful role in improving McDonald's public image by representing workers over pay. However, he also made it clear that this might lead to insupportable rises in labour costs that would be unacceptable:

> The company is not interested in unions, it is its own boss. The company has got its own ideals and doesn't want an outside organization stepping in. The only issue I think unions could get involved in is pay, because it might improve its image with the public and its employees. The only trouble with that is it might get out of hand.

One UK restaurant manager also commented:

> Well we must take on the role of the trade union and protect the employees. It comes back to the motivation thing, if we protect them and look after their interests they are going to be motivated. There's no need for trade unions at McDonald's because we are two organizations in one. I can't see a problem with having no unions in society if each business had a philosophy of looking after their employees like McDonald's; but then, that's Utopia isn't it?

These responses suggest that regardless of societal differences the McDonald's corporate culture is quite effective in moulding the required responses of management. Willmott (1993) argues that strong corporate cultures 'exclude and eliminate' other values, such as in this case the acceptance of unions. The emphasis placed on the importance of 'good' management suggests a moral tone. Willmott suggests that the extent to which individuals may be willing to internalize these norms and values may depend on their assessment of its moral character. The McDonald's 'culture' appears to be one that encourages managers to see unions as an unwarranted interference, which will 'destroy' the corporation and the 'good' management practice they carry out.

Union organizing, franchises and small units

As we have already argued in the introduction to this book the high proportion of McDonald's franchise operations in some countries (some 65 per cent of its restaurants in Europe and as high as 90 per cent in some countries) is not an obstacle to maintaining control and the consistency of its operations across societal borders. Franchisees are motivated by profits not a wage. They pay much more attention to the fine details of the operation and may be much better at eradicating waste and keeping labour costs low. In this sense franchisees provide the corporation with highly motivated 'managers' of small business operations yet paradoxically retaining tight control over them. Franchisees foster the kind of paternalistic relations that allow them to keep a close eye on the activities of their employees. One UK franchisee stated: 'I like people to tell me every little incident in detail that goes on because if there is a problem I can react to it.'

Abbott (1993) makes the point that large organizations find it more difficult to stop unionization because of the distance between senior managers and employees, whilst small operations make it more difficult for unions to recruit members. Indeed this has also been evident in a number of other studies (Rainnie, 1989; Holliday, 1995). Abbott (1993) suggests that the majority of small business owners in the UK often comment that they do see the need for unions in society in general, but see no need for unions in *their* businesses. Typically, he suggests, this was because they believed they were good employers. Abbott (1993) also suggests that small businesses would interpret any interest in union involvement by their employees as a failure of management. This was also strongly reflected in the responses of McDonald's UK franchisees:

> I don't think they are necessary. If crew wanted to join a union I would feel disappointed, because it would mean that I had failed in my efforts to look after them. I'd feel I'd not been doing my job properly. I think because of the damage other employers have done to some employees unions will stay popular, I don't think they will die off overnight in those old industries. Fast-food is a new breed.

In addition franchisees are well aware that inviting unions into restaurants would not sit well with the values of the corporation. They are unlikely to do anything that might attract the corporation's criticism and risk losing their licence or the chance to add additional restaurants in the future. McDonald's have the best of both worlds, willing 'partners' in sharing the costs and risks of development and highly obedient and motivated operators spreading the corporate message and leaving little room for union involvement.

Workforce characteristics and workers' attitudes

In most countries the majority of McDonald's workers are very young, many are still at school and many are students. Young workers have very little previous job experience. If they have worked before it is often in similar kinds of low-skilled work. Many of the young employees only work for 'pocket money', do not intend to stay long with McDonald's and therefore tend to have highly instrumental attitudes. In addition they often have very little knowledge of trade unions and often do not see their relevance. In addition to hostile management attitudes towards unions this makes union recruitment of young workers extremely difficult. The following comments from a young UK McDonald's worker was typical: 'The company see it as big happy family sort of company. I think some people would join a union if there was a choice but I wouldn't bother.'

In the UK in particular a majority of young workers were simply not well informed about the current status of unions, union roles or priorities or what services unions may be able to provide for them. Not one of the UK interview respondents within the restaurants at any level could say which union would be responsible for the fast-food industry, or knew which union they should approach if they had wanted to. The following comments from UK workers were typical:

> I just don't know enough about them, I tend to associate unions with strikes but I don't know a lot about it.

> I don't know, I've never really thought about unions, it's not something I think about. I don't know really, don't know what they do. I've never been told or given anything about unions.

However, in sharp contrast to the statements made by managers and despite the lack of awareness about unions, a majority of workers interviewed in the UK seemed to have a reasonably positive view of trade unions:

> Unions are important. They play an important role in limiting the power of employers and stop employees being exploited.

> They are there to serve the rights of the workers, which I think is a good thing, but I've not thought of joining one.

Even in the UK, where something like 70 per cent of the McDonald's work-force is under 21, there is often a core of older workers who tend to stay with the company over the long term, in some cases 5 years or more. First, those who restaurant managers described as having been 'washed-up' in the labour market because of poor qualifications and a lack of other opportunities, and second, 'coasters', those who could move on to better jobs but did not, perhaps owing to indecision or fear of change. As the study on McDonald's in Europe (Royle, 2000) also indicates, in other countries like Finland, Spain and Italy workers tend to stay longer because there is so much high unemployment amongst younger workers.

Of course McDonald's may also offer an opportunity for some to make a real career with the company, especially while it continues to expand at such a fast rate. A Norwegian union official described these workers as 'career collaborators'. However, as the chapter on Germany indicates, it is not always young workers who are employed at McDonald's. In Germany, McDonald's is able to take advantage of a huge and ready supply of foreign workers, many East Europeans who are desperate for work in the West and cannot find work elsewhere. Overall the 'acquiescent' nature of the workforce makes it very difficult to organize workers. Those workers who really need the job are not likely to go against managerial wishes and join a trade union if they think their job will be threatened. In many cases workers just don't know about their rights or that a union is there for them. For many young workers it may not seem relevant or worth the effort or cost of the membership fees.

Basic pay in fast-food

Before the imposition of the minimum wage McDonald's employees beginning work in the regions under 18 started on £3.25 per hour and those over 18 started on £3.50 per hour. In January 1998 McDonald's UK increased its rates of pay for the first time in several years and this was almost certainly in anticipation of the minimum wage legislation which came into force on 1 April 1999. When first introduced the national minimum wage provided a minimum rate of £3.60 per hour for those aged 21 and over, and £3.00 between 18 and 21.[1] There is no minimum wage for those under 18. In the UK McDonald's has three separate pay 'scales' for inner London, outer London and the provinces and it has both under-18 and over-18 starting rates. In fact McDonald's increased its UK pay rates again by a flat rate of 10 pence on 28 March 1999 to bring the over-18 starting rate to £3.60 outside London. Something like 70 per cent of McDonald's UK employees are under 21, and approximately 30 per cent are under 18. In October 1999 McDonald's was the last of the leading fast-food chains to remove the youth rate for under 18s. The fact that there is no minimum wage for under-18s and there was only a £3 minimum for 18 to 21s made the minimum wage legislation look rather disappointing. After all 16- and 17-year-old workers work just as hard as those aged 18 or 21 in operations like fast-food, and yet until October 1999 they were still receiving only £3.35 per hour outside London. In theory workers can earn more if they 'perform' well, but this largely depends on pleasing management and staying with the company over the longer term so for the vast majority of workers it is the basic starting wage that is most relevant. Nevertheless even the original minimum wage of £3.60 (1999) for older workers probably had a positive impact on overall wage levels. Statistics from the Low Pay Network Survey suggest that when the UK system of 'wages councils' was abolished in 1993, employers quickly reduced overall pay rates (Quiney, 1994). McDonald's UK also took advantage of this situation by removing paid time off for public holidays.

Table 4.4 Minimum rates for front of house staff, 2000

Outlets	Minimum rates per hour (£)*
Prêt à Manger	4.50
Starbucks	4.20
Roadchef (motorways)	4.08
Compass roadside (motorway services)	4.06
Three Cooks	3.86
Sarah's restaurants	3.86
KFC (Tricon)	3.80
McDonald's	3.75
Burger King	3.70
City centre restaurants (Deep Pan Pizza, Café Uno)	3.70
Pizza Express	3.70
Select Service Partner (Upper Crust, le Croissant)	3.70
Costa Coffee (Whitbread)	3.70
Bass Leisure Retail	3.70

Source: IDS (2001).

Note
* Starting rates outside London.

In 2000 McDonald's increased its minimum rate outside London to £3.75, once again probably in response to the small increase in the minimum wage for that year of £3.70. Recent figures from IDS (2001) suggest that McDonald's does not pay the lowest wages in the sector: it actually appears somewhere in the middle compared with other companies (see Table 4.4). However, its dominance in the market place undoubtedly has a constraining effect on wages amongst its competitors. The evidence at the McLibel trial also confirms this. Vidal (1997: 312) states that the judge commented that: 'the British McDonald's operation pays low wages and it depresses wages for other workers in the industry'.

Finally, although most companies in both the fast-food and broader hospitality sectors have minimum rates at or above the national minimum wage of £3.70, many also have rates of pay for working inside London where cost of living is much higher. For example KFC, McDonald's and Starbucks pay higher rates inside London. In jobs that involve travel or are difficult to get to such as motorway service stations and airports, companies like Prêt à Manger, Compass Roadside and Roadchef all pay higher rates of pay. For example Prêt à Manger pays a starting rate of £5.55 per hour for new starters at Heathrow airport. It may be interesting to note whether or not McDonald's stake in Prêt à Manger will eventually influence this policy.

Conclusion

The UK fast-food sector is, as in many other countries, expanding rapidly and becoming an increasingly important feature of modern employment. Although the majority of outlets in the sector are independent operations, it is the chain operations often owned by large multinationals which are the most profitable and which are driving growth. It is a highly competitive industry and labour costs are a large percentage of the overall costs of the business. It is hardly surprising therefore that there is likely to be a continual and persistent downward pressure on wages and conditions in this sector.

The unique features of the chained fast-food sector are a combination of generally low skilled work and high labour turnover, combined with what we have termed elsewhere an 'acquiescent' workforce (Royle, 2000). The analysis provided in this chapter arguably illustrates the typical attitudes of both workers and managers at McDonald's and gives us some insights into the difficulties trade unions face in trying to gain a foothold in this sector in the UK. With the combination of the above features and the consistently non-union approach of employers, it is hardly surprising that unions have had no real success in either gaining recognition, acquiring significant numbers of members, or establishing collective agreements in this sector. Some may argue that the poor conditions and low pay in this sector do not matter because they mostly affect young workers who will eventually move on elsewhere. However, this is an over-simplification. First, many individuals who work in fast-food are not young and without experience; there is often a core of workers in every fast-food operation who are older and more experienced, but who have been 'washed-up' in the labour market either because of poor academic achievement, racial discrimination or a lack of self-confidence. In any case, youth and inexperience are not a self-evident justification for discrimination in terms of representation rights, pay and conditions.

Furthermore, the limitations of the new statutory procedure under the 1999 Employment Relations Act retain, in large measure, the freedom of employers to avoid unions (Milne, 1998). Nor is the Act likely to change things in the fast-food sector. While it halts the tide of anti-union legislation introduced by successive Conservative governments from 1980 to 1993, it clearly has serious weaknesses as far as the unions are concerned (Towers, 1999a). For example, there are obvious problems in the determination of the appropriate 'bargaining unit' in an industry where large numbers of small units and franchises are the norm. In such conditions it may well be impossible for unions to organize for an election on a restaurant-by-restaurant basis. Partly because fast-food employers like McDonald's would be likely to use the legislation to insist that all their 700 or so company-owned restaurants in the UK become the 'bargaining unit.' Furthermore, gaining recognition in individual franchises is likely to encounter all the usual problems of organizing in small units with patriarchal management styles. The problems for unions are also compounded by a combination of the best legal advice available to employers, entrenched anti-union attitudes among management and indifference amongst some employees. Some commentators argue that the new Act is a move towards the US recognition model, which is in itself seen as partly responsible for the decreasing level of unionization (Adams, 1999). In conclusion, the new statutory recognition procedure envisaged in the Act is very unlikely to offer opportunities for union growth or collective agreements in fast-food.

The problems of workers in the fast-food sector look set to continue. Additionally, in many cases many employees will blame their immediate superiors rather than see the corporations' systems as being responsible for their bad treatment. Satisfaction, resistance and consent are in a state of flux, but the all-powerful 'system' and the one-sided nature of the 'communication' processes usually found in these companies means that grievances and complaints are often waived aside or sometimes forgotten in the rush to satisfy the customer. Given the way in which the employment relationship is managed in many fast-food operations and given that there is an asymmetry of power in the employment relationship, it would appear that the only way in which these employees are likely to improve their conditions of work is through independent union representation. But even with current legislation this outcome seems as unlikely as ever in the UK fast-food sector.

Note

1 The over-18 rate for the national minimum wage was increased in 2000 to £3.70 per hour and was increased to £4.10 in 2001. The Labour government is pledged to further increases.

5   Undermining the system?

Labour relations in the German
fast-food industry

Tony Royle

As early as the 1930s, the Germany economy was already being described as
the 'locomotive of Europe', indeed the recognition of its importance was
explicit in the postwar settlement and the 1950 Schumann Plan that laid
the foundations for the European Community (Swann, 1988). The German
economic miracle that followed continued up until the oil crisis of the
early 1970s. Although growth in the German economy has since slowed, it
remains central to the development of the European economy and productivity levels have remained high. More recently, despite increasing global competition and the absorption of the previously communist Eastern German
states, Germany has retained its dominant economic position in Europe
alongside increasing political influence. It has been suggested that the
German industrial relations system is one of the most important elements
in the success of the German economy; widely praised for its containment
of industrial conflict and for promoting a cooperative and highly skilled
workforce (Lane, 1989, 1994; Turner, 1998).

When compared with the UK or US industrial relations systems, the
German system can be seen as being at the 'opposite end of the spectrum'
as far as workers' statutory rights are concerned. For example, the
German system provides workers with statutory rights to representation
through works councils at the workplace, and through supervisory boards
at boardroom level in larger firms. The system is highly juridified, providing
a clear framework of rights and responsibilities for both management and
employees. Collective bargaining is normally carried out at sectoral level
between employers' federations and trade unions, although some company-
level bargaining, which is increasing, also takes place in larger firms.

In the 1960s and 1970s the system was criticized by some activists and
academics, who claimed that it suppressed industrial militancy and class conflict. As trade unions have come under continuing attack in a number of
industrialized countries since the 1980s, these criticisms are rarely voiced
today. The fact that German trade unions and the German system of
employee representation have survived relatively intact may have brought
about a realization of the system's advantages. In recent years some concerns
about German productivity have led some commentators to suggest that

the German system could no longer cope with increased demands from employers for more 'flexibility' (Sauga *et al.*, 1996; Flecker and Schulten, 1999; Barber, 1999). In other words increasing levels of economic activity are pressuring managers to seek radical changes in established forms of industrial relations, threatening the existing system. In fact union density has fallen in recent years and German unions have been merging into a smaller number of very large unions in order to strengthen their position. There has been a decline in the numbers of workers covered by sectoral-level bargaining and an increase in company-level agreements. However, in 1999 72.8 per cent of workers in West Germany and 57 per cent in East Germany were covered by collective agreements. Furthermore, an additional 13 per cent of workers in the West and an additional 22 per cent in the East were covered by provisions that largely adhere to collective agreements (*EIRR*, 2001a). This has been accompanied by an increase in more flexible approaches to collective bargaining, in particular the increased use of 'open clauses'.[1] There seems little doubt that under the current neo-liberal climate and increasing globalization, and some changes already under way in German capitalism, the German economy is likely to remain under continued pressure to become more 'Anglo-Saxon' and to ditch some aspects of its highly regulated industrial relations system. Nevertheless, perhaps because it does offer some room for flexibility, the German industrial relations system is still relatively intact. Indeed, in July 2001, the German government strengthened employee rights in its statutory co-determination system (Atkins, 2000; *EIRR*, 2001b).

Ferner and Edwards (1995) argue that Germany's strong institutional arrangements and legislative underpinning remain something of a 'test case' for multinational corporations (MNCs). This chapter therefore raises a number of questions. How do foreign-owned MNCs and the larger national fast-food employers respond to the imposition of sectoral level bargaining and statutory forms of workers' representation? Have MNCs affected the way in which collective bargaining is carried out or statutory worker representation operates in this sector? How effective is the German system of statutory employee representation in protecting workers' rights in practice? This chapter largely focuses on the McDonald's Corporation's labour relations practices in Germany but we also provide some preliminary findings on the activities of other MNCs and larger national players in this sector.

Like Chapter 4 this chapter is based on an ongoing study involving qualitative interviews and documentary research in a number of European countries. Interviews are still under way with management, employees, international trade union federations, national trade union officials and employer associations. The findings presented here are based on almost 100 interviews conducted over a seven-year period in Germany. This chapter provides some of the preliminary findings on multinationals such as PepsiCo/Tricon (KFC, Pizza Hut), Whitbread (Churrasco, Maredo), Burger King and McDonald's, and a number of large national competitors such as Nordsee, Blockhaus and Dinea. However, the bulk of the chapter focuses on McDonald's in Germany, not only because it dominates the sector in terms of sales and its influence on the sector is substantial but also because its employee relations practices clearly illustrate the problems that such MNCs create for trade unions and independent employee representation.

Industrial relations in Germany

According to Jacobi *et al.* (1998) the 'German model' is based on four principles. First, and most importantly, it has a dual structure of interest representation: employee representation at board and workplace level is separated from the collective bargaining system. Collective bargaining interests are generalized and quantitative, whilst representation at the workplace is more qualitative and specialized. Second, the extensive legal basis of the dual system operates on the basis of free collective bargaining as well as a works council system, established in 1952. Additionally there are other laws detailing regulation of labour conflicts and industrial relations at the workplace. For example works councils have no right to strike, but they do have extensive rights to information, consultation and co-determination. The third principle is the extent to which the institutions of collective representation (unions and works councils) cover their constituencies. In fact both works councils and unions can make decisions in the name of the entire workforce with little formal obligation to seek any endorsement. This is supported by law. Although German employers' federations do not have the support of the law as such, they effectively represent most employers by virtue of the strength of their organizations. The fourth and final principle is the centralization of collective bargaining and the coordination of policies at sectoral level. Previously based on craft and occupational lines, German unions were reorganized after 1945 on an industry basis. Employer organizations also tend to organize in the same way. For example, each year the biggest trade union, *IG Metall*, negotiates with the employers' federation for the metalworking industry, *Gesamtmetall*. However, some very large companies negotiate directly with the relevant industry union.

Most German unions are affiliated to the German Trade Union Federation, the DGB (*Deutsche Gewerkschaftsbund*), by far the largest and most important federation. Until recently there were also three other union federations: the DAG (German Union of Salaried Employees); DBB (German Civil Service Federation); and CGB (Federation of Christian Trade Unions). In the early 1990s there were sixteen trade unions affiliated to the DGB. By 2001, however, due to a number of mergers, this had been reduced to six. The most important merger of recent times is the merger between the service sector unions (but excluding food, drink and tobacco) to form the new service workers union, Ver.Di. The union representing most restaurant workers, the food, catering, drink and tobacco union, the NGG (*Nahrung*

Genuss Gaststätten), chose not to take part in the new service sector union because they were concerned that such a large union would lose touch with its membership and would no longer be able to adequately represent the distinct needs of its different members.

The role of the state, both federal and Länder, is limited to the provision of a legal framework for industrial relations including largely procedural rules that have been permanently developed and defined by decisions of the labour courts. The high degree of juridification in the German system is widely considered to be an important source of its stability (Flecker and Schulten, 1999). Collective agreements negotiated at sectoral level are legally binding, and take precedence over any works agreements (Schnabel, 1998). Collective bargaining at sectoral level, although declining somewhat in recent years, is still the norm in Germany. The Works Constitution Act stipulates that management and works councils (*Betriebsräte*) are not normally allowed to conclude works agreements on collective bargaining issues, because these are dealt with by trade unions and employers; the only exception to this is the 'open clauses' mentioned earlier. The system does not cover all German companies. Smaller companies may not be part of the appropriate employers' association and some larger companies, like Siemens, go it alone.

The German system of co-determination

As we have already suggested, the German model of co-determination is based on *indirect* participation with elected worker representatives and formalized institutions, with rights supported in law. As far as private business is concerned, three main pieces of legislation cover this area. The 1952/ 1972 Works Constitution Act, which concentrates on two issues: first, co-determination at the workplace through various forms of works councils; and second, one form of co-determination at board level for limited liability companies with over 500 employees. The 1951 (Montan) Co-determination Act only relates to the coal and steel industries, whilst the 1976 Co-determination Act is concerned with board level participation in companies with over 2,000 employees.

Since the introduction of the 1972 and 1976 Acts, distinguishing between the two forms of co-determination at board level and at the workplace has become more difficult in practice. The 1972 Act stipulates that where there are two or more works councils in the same business employees can establish a 'central' works council at company level, called a *Gesamt-betriebsrat* (GBR). In addition, a works council serving a group of companies, called a *Konzernbetriebsrat* (KBR), can be formed at concern level, where it is requested by the works councils of subsidiaries employing at least 75 per cent of the group's workforce (Müller-Jentsch, 1995). This can be rather confusing because the works councillors represented on the GBR or KBR are also quite likely to be the same representatives on the supervisory board (*Aufsichtsrat*). It is important to be able to differentiate between these types of works council and other institutions in this system: labour directors on the management board (*Vorstand*); and worker representatives on supervisory boards (*Aufsichtsrat*). What follows is a brief analysis of these institutions.

The 1952/72 legislation provides for *drittelparität* on the supervisory board, in other words three from nine of its members are employee representatives. The 1976 Act, however, allows for equal numbers of employee and shareholder representatives on the supervisory board. Although the 1976 Act has provoked the most opposition from employers, it does not really give the employee side complete parity, because one of their members must be of managerial status and he/she can usually be relied upon to vote with the shareholder representatives. Both the 1951 (Montan) Act and the 1976 Act provide for a labour director on the executive board, but under the 1976 Act the labour director is appointed by management.

The 1952/72 Works Constitution Act provides for a works council in all businesses with five or more employees aged 18 or over. Separate elections are held for blue-collar and white-collar workers. The works council cannot call a strike but it can sue management for any alleged breach of rights. The council must meet with management every four weeks and the law grants the councils a broad range of rights to information, consultation and co-determination. Works councils can make proposals to the employer and in some areas where works councils have co-determination rights the employer cannot make decisions against the wishes of the works council. Disputes are settled either by the labour court or by the arbitration of a committee composed of employer and works council representatives with a neutral chair. Works councils have co-determination rights over economic, employment and social issues, although these rights are strongest in the social area and weakest in the economic sphere. For example co-determination in economic issues is limited to the development of a 'social plan' where changes in the workplace (such as closure) produce major disadvantages for the workforce. In terms of social issues, works councils have amongst other things the right to positively determine: disciplinary rules; starting and finishing times; breaks; temporary changes in working time; holiday arrangements; setting of bonuses and targets; principles used for the payment of wages and salaries; the type of data held on employees; selection of employees; workplace training; and the introduction of cameras or similar devices used to measure or check work.

In addition, in any business or unit with 200 employees or more, a works council member can be released from his or her normal duties to work full time on works council business; these councillors are known as *freizustellende*. The number of these full-time works councillors increases in proportion with the size of the organization, for example a company with approximately 50,000 employees could have 32 works councillors being paid to work full time on council matters (Müller-Jentsch, 1995; Jacobi *et al.*, 1998; *EIRR*, 2001b). The 2001 amendments have enhanced employee rights particularly in the areas of employment security and training, in effect extending co-determination rights and providing new rights to make proposals in some areas (*EIRR*, 2001b). Works councillors also enjoy protection against dismissal. Works council members can only be dismissed on exceptional grounds and only when the works council or the labour court agrees. In theory at least, these rights give employees considerable scope for influence over the management of the business. We now move on to examine the German fast-food industry.

The German fast-food industry

The Germans are sometimes seen as being almost as underdeveloped as the British in matters gastronomic. Their cuisine, with its *Sauerkraut* and dumplings, its fat pink *Wurst* and steaming knuckles of pork, may be regarded as tasty and wholesome but also coarse and monotonous. This image is perhaps a little unfair: Germany produces some 200 different types of bread and almost as many sorts of *Wurst*, and in recent years there has been much interest in fine foods. Of course the difficulty of incorporating new foreign words into the German language may itself be partly responsible for this poor image. As Ardagh (1987: 184) points out: 'Who fancies moussaka when it is called: "Exotisches gericht mit geschnetzelten Schweinsfilet spitzen überbacken"?'

For centuries the Germans were of course famous for their hefty appetites; the fat faced, beer bellied Bavarian, two litre tankard in hand before a plate piled high with *Wurst* or dumplings, was a stock cartoon character and not far from reality. In pre-war days poverty often dictated diets, and potatoes, bread and cakes were staple items of nutrition. In the 1950s, this pattern changed dramatically, as sheer greed steadily replaced subsistence eating: the *Wirtschaftswunder* period was equally that of the notorious *Fresswelle* (wave of guzzling), when a newly rich nation reacted against the deprivations of wartime by tucking in more avidly than ever before – and this time to a far richer diet. This continued until the 1970s when dire warnings about obesity and health brought about a change in diets towards healthier foods, physical fitness campaigns and spas offering cures for overweight children (Ardagh, 1987).

The *Wurst* or sausage still rules supreme in Germany as the national dish analagous to British fish and chips and the American hamburger. It is still a common feature in most German towns and cities and found at many a street corner hot dog stall. Nevertheless 'foreign' foods, such as kebabs, pizzas and hamburgers, have enjoyed increasing popularity over the last 30 years. Its not clear exactly when the 'Hamburger' was invented, some suggest that it developed from the staple diet of Russian sailors in the port city of Hamburg as a sandwich made from scraps of raw beef. Others claim that it was created at the St Louis World Exposition in 1904 (Love, 1995: 208).

Whatever its origins it is clear that, much as in other countries, fast-food giants like McDonald's have, as elsewhere, very successfully introduced the hamburger and other 'non-German' foods into the German diet since they established themselves in the early 1970s.

The market and main employers

The 100 largest companies in the broader German food-service sector had turnover amounting to approximately £4,800 million in 1999. Companies described as purely 'fast-food' (that is excluding airport catering, trains, motorways, retail catering, full service restaurants and leisure catering) accounted for almost half of all this turnover, with the largest twenty-seven fast-food companies accounting for £2,200 million (see Table 5.1). The seven largest fast-food employers in Germany in order of sales are McDonald's, Burger King, Nordsee, PepsiCo/Tricon (Pizza Hut, Nudel-macher, KFC), Esso, Kamps and Kochlöffel. McDonald's took the lion's share of turnover of all these fast-food companies in 1999 with just over £1,400 million. However, placing some companies in the category of 'fast-food', 'travel catering', 'retail catering', 'leisure catering' or 'full-service restaurants' is not always that helpful. Indeed, as we discussed in Chapter 1, many of the offerings of travel catering and leisure catering companies are hard to distinguish from other forms of fast-food in practice.

We present our findings in two parts: first, we present a detailed analysis of the McDonald's Corporation and its labour relations practices in Germany; and then move on to present some preliminary findings on the other main employers in the sector.

McDonald's in Germany

As we have seen, McDonald's dominates the German fast-food market and even tops the larger German food service sector in terms of turnover. McDonald's came to Germany in 1971 and has enjoyed rapid expansion since that time. By the beginning of 2000 it already had over 1,000 restaurants and well over 50,000 employees. Despite the fact that German unions generally appear to have a high level of acceptance amongst the German workforce and German employers (Lane, 1989; Eberwein and Tholen, 1990; Lecher and Naumann, 1994) McDonald's early approach to unions and statutory forms of worker representation was hostile. In a letter to the NGG, for example, the then President of McDonald's Germany, Walter Rettenwender, stated that works councils and collective agreements with unions would 'seriously handicap the development potential of the McDonald's system' (*Der Spiegel*, 1981: 75). By the late 1980s McDonald's was increasingly facing a barrage of criticism; it had refused continued requests by the unions to negotiate a collective agreement and had not

Table 5.1 Largest companies with fast-food and food service operations in Germany by turnover (1999)

Company	Turnover (DM millions)	Restaurants
McDonald's	4235	1008
LSG/Sky Chef	1348	40*
Tank and Raststätten	957	370
Mitropa	625	639
Burger King	525	223
Nordsee	461	302
DINEA	450	290
Mövenpick	301	50
Karstadt	293	150
Tricon (Pizza Hut)	213	113
Whitbread (Churrasco/Moredo)	198	69
Stockheim	194	24
Gate Gourmet	170	12
Wienerwald	165	131
Block House	146	39
Le Buffet	110	50
Kochlöffel	107	108
Total	7,283	

Source: Foodservice (2000: 21).

Notes
In this table we have taken the term fast-food in the broadest possible terms, including motorway service station, retail sector restaurants and airport restaurants, but excluding hotels, pubs, cafés and what could be termed the 'leisure' sector. This also highlights the problem of accurately defining what should or should not be considered to be 'fast-food'. The growth of service operations is increasing rapidly and crossing over into existing sectors with similar limited menu offerings and increasingly Taylorized production systems.
* Forty restaurants in airports. LSG also owns one third of Tank and Rast but still makes most of its money from airline catering; it now has 34 per cent of the world market in this sector.

joined an employers' association. In particular the unions criticized the company over its pay levels, conditions of employment and its actions regarding the election of works councils. Indeed one article in the prominent journal *Der Spiegel* (1981) suggested that working conditions at McDonald's were like that in the 'Wild West'.

Things finally came to a head when Günter Walraff (1985) published his book *Ganz Unten*. He had spent a number of years working undercover as an investigative journalist disguised as a Turkish immigrant in a number of large German companies, which included McDonald's. He made a number of damaging statements about the company, one of which was based on a leaked management circular, which detailed the recommended recruitment procedure for store managers. This explicitly instructed that anyone who might show any interest in joining a trade union should not be hired. If the applicant did show some interest in unions, the circular stated that:

> after a few more questions the interview should be terminated as quickly as possible, tell the applicant he will receive a reply in a few days . . . of course the applicant should in no circumstances be employed.
>
> (Walraff, 1985: 80)

The company later distanced itself from this statement, stating that its source had been one over-zealous manager and in no way represented company policy. However, recent findings from McDonald's activities in Germany and other European countries suggest that employees only have to ask questions about their rights to holiday pay, breaks, holidays and other conditions of employment and in many cases they will not be hired either (Royle, 2000). This unwanted publicity seems to have been the final straw for McDonald's; it appears that its increasing concerns about its public image led the corporation to consider a shift in policy. Sometime in the mid-1980s three American managers were sent to Germany to make a decision about whether or not the company should negotiate with the NGG and accept a collective agreement. Union officials argue that the corporation's major concern was to balance the effect of the involvement of trade unions on labour costs with effect on public image and therefore sales. The result was that in conjunction with other fast-food employers McDonald's established a new employers' federation, the BdS (*Bundesverband der Systemgastronomie*) and began negotiations with the NGG for a collective agreement.

McDonald's could have joined DEHOGA (German Hotel and Guesthouses Employers' Federation), which already represented a wide range of employers in the hospitality industry. However, McDonald's had not enjoyed a good relationship with DEHOGA; the fact that McDonald's were frequently being 'dragged through the mud' by the unions over their labour relations had not endeared the company to other DEHOGA employers. An NGG official states that in the mid-1980s the chairman of DEHOGA, a hotel owner, had openly denounced the company, deriding them as 'chip fryers and meatball roasters'. It took three to four years before the first collective agreement finally came into effect in 1989. It may be the case that McDonald's interests could be better represented away from hotel employers, and that it wanted to position itself as a clear leader in its own sector, not merely in terms of sales, but to be seen as setting 'high standards'. Before 1989 McDonald's had usually paid a small amount above the collectively agreed minimum wage agreed by DEHOGA. Individual employer associations also have other advantages; the BdS may have been established in order to provide a lobbying vehicle. Since the first agreement in 1989 the corporation's *official* policy towards unions appears to have changed. They are no longer outspokenly anti-union in Germany.

However, it is questionable whether the corporation's basic approach towards unions has really changed at all. NGG representatives made it clear that they did not see any change in the underlying anti-union stance of the company. One NGG official stated:

> on the outside the company appears to be friendly to unions, but when it comes down to it they're as hard as nails, exactly as before. No influence is to be allowed in, on the inside the union is kept out. It's two sides of the same coin. They do it so that they can say they are not against unions, to stop public criticism. Within the company they make propaganda against the union and the works councils. They use the old tactics just as they have before to avoid either the councils or union membership in the stores.

Co-determination

Although the corporation is involved in negotiating collective agreements through the BdS it is in the area of worker representation that conflict still rages. The typical McDonald's store has between 50 and 100 employees, so in theory there could be a works council in every McDonald's store in Germany. Similarly with well over 50,000 employees the corporation would normally be expected to have a supervisory board under either the 1972 or the 1976 legislation and a company-level works council (GBR) or a concern-level works council (KBR). In 1982 there were only two works councils from some 160 stores but by December 1995 there were only 27 from nearly 600 stores and currently about 50 works councils in more than 1,000 restaurants. There is no supervisory board, and only in the late 1990s was a GBR established which in any case represents only about 15 per cent of McDonald's restaurants in Germany. How can we account for this?

The supervisory board

In Germany McDonald's has adopted a legal form which splits the company up into approximately 65 per cent franchises, 15 per cent 'company' stores and 20 per cent in seven holding companies called *Anver* companies. *Anver* restaurants (*Anver Gewerbe- und Mietgesellschaft GmbH*) are legally separate companies. However, in practice they are 100 per cent owned and controlled subsidiaries of the corporation. In Germany they are split into six groups of outlets under the titles of *Anver* South, Southwest, Southeast, North, Northwest and West. However, these geographic distinctions bear only a slight resemblance to the actual location of the restaurants themselves. The proportion of franchise restaurants at around 65 per cent is a little lower than the corporation's world-wide average which is currently at about 75 per cent. As we have argued in the introduction and elsewhere

(Royle, 2000), although franchise operations are legally separate entities they are de facto subsidiaries of the McDonald's Corporation. If anything the McDonald's franchise system provides for very tight controls over all important aspects of employee relations. The *Anver* holding companies are also legally separate companies. However, as the NGG point out, these companies are 100 per cent owned and run by McDonald's Germany, with the German McDonald's president registered in every case as managing director. However, the result is that the workforce of 50,000 is broken up into smaller groups of 'separate' employees. In addition the 1952/72 and 1976 Acts do not apply to McDonald's because it has retained US registration in the State of Delaware. McDonald's Germany is a limited liability company (*Gesellschaft mit beschrankte Haftung* – GmbH) but it is an American GmbH and not a German GmbH. The imperatives of company law appear to outweigh those of labour law in this case. McDonald's can only be considered to fall under the 1952/72 legislation as a qualifying company if it has the appropriate legal form. Union officials suggest that this arrangement was planned well before the company came to Germany in 1971. This would not be all that surprising because American law journals are full of warnings that emphasize the need for US MNCs to prepare for the 'horrors' of heavy regulation involved in European markets (Dowling *et al.*, 1994; Honig and Dowling, 1994). These include specific warnings about Germany (Honig and Dowling, 1994: 8): 'The German corporate form you choose will affect your worker participation obligations.' The company appears to have taken advantage of these legislative loopholes in that neither parity nor one-third representation in a supervisory board can be applied. We can now examine the issue of the works council.

Works councils

Theoretically at least, the only requirement for the establishment of a works council is that five or more employees request it. So why are there so few works councils at McDonald's, especially when many stores have an average of 50 to 100 employees? Part of the answer probably lies in the nature of the work. McDonald's is a large collection of small units with predominantly part-time working and relatively high labour turnover. This creates difficulties in terms of the organization of workers and reduces 'solidarity' amongst the workforce. Another issue is the characteristics of the workforce. Employees who are not dependent on the company for their livelihood and those who do not intend to stay very long may have little interest in a works council (e.g. second income earners and some students). In addition the German McDonald's workforce is made up of a large number of foreign workers, economic migrants from the old Eastern Bloc (*Aussiedler*) and guest workers (*Gastarbeiter*) predominantly from Turkey and Greece. Indeed *Aussiedler* and *Gastarbeiter* account for between 50 and 90 per cent of the workforce in McDonald's' German stores. Foreign workers tend to be marginalized in the labour market because of language and qualifications problems and they often have no or very limited knowledge of their rights as employees. Unions have criticized American MNCs in the past for excessive use of migrant or guest workers, which is said to create a more pacified workforce and helps to keep labour costs down (De Vos, 1981). In recent years McDonald's has been taking advantage of the huge pool of foreign workers on its borders. It has been advertising in post-communist countries promising careers and high wages for those willing to come and work for McDonald's in Germany. This has also led to some rather dubious practices with workers being accommodated in managers' houses or in some cases housed temporarily in the rest-rooms or basement of the restaurants themselves. In this scenario workers are constantly at the beck and call of management, especially as they rely on management to sign and support their work permit applications.

Most foreign workers interviewed in this study had never heard of works councils and had very little knowledge of their rights in this area. Interestingly, in restaurants where no works council was established only a small number of employees of any sort had any idea that works councils actually existed in other German McDonald's outlets. Of course some employees had been involved in works councils before, knew about their rights in this area, and had in some cases tried to establish them at McDonald's. However, the above-mentioned combination of factors tends to undermine the impetus for collective action, making it difficult to instigate and sustain the necessary procedures for the election of a works council. Both this and other studies (Kotthoff, 1994; Rudolph and Wasserman, 1995) suggest that if management is against works councils they can make life very difficult for them. A combination of prompt responses to employee complaints and harassment of 'ring leaders' is often enough to stop any works council election.

There is clear evidence in this case that McDonald's does not welcome works councils. This is perhaps not that surprising, first because McDonald's management views participation not as power sharing in decision-making, but as communication and involvement, usually of the kind '*downward communication* and *upward problem-solving*' identified by Marchington (1995). This is typified by what we have termed elsewhere as 'McParticipation': suggestion schemes; crew meetings; crew trainer meetings and RAP (Real Approach to Problems) sessions (Royle, 2000). Second, German works councils often open the door to union involvement.

However, managers did not always condemn the system outright. One franchise operator said he did not see anything wrong with the works council in principle, but that if people were treated well they would not ask for one. He said it was really the company that did not understand the works council legislation, and that they had experienced some terrible trouble over this 'in the past':

> The Americans don't understand works councils, they think works councils are trade unions, trade unions are communists and communists must be fought. That's the attitude the company brought to Germany. They don't understand the Works Constitution Act.

Nevertheless, the view that works councils are inappropriate was widely reflected in management and franchise responses. Where works councils had been established, managers tended to explain this away as bad management or students causing trouble. One German store manager stated: 'Works councils? Oh, that's just students playing games, causing trouble, they don't work in the McDonald's system.' Management respondents also suggested that the small number of works councils was due to good management and a lack of interest amongst the workforce. There may be some truth in this but a more in-depth analysis suggests that there has been a continuing management effort to delay and discourage any attempt to elect works councils.

'Commando Mueller' and the 'flying squads'

According to Duve (1987), the NGG's and works council respondents' attempts to elect the first works councils were strongly opposed by the company. They state that in the early days the main response from the company was the use of a management 'flying squad' of trouble-shooters who specialized in dealing with employees who wanted a works council. These trouble-shooters were sent from head office to find out who the 'activists' were, and one way or another to stop the election if possible. One well known figure frequently involved in these activities was referred to by union activists as 'Commando Mueller' who was well known for his zeal and 'efficiency' in dealing with 'troublemakers'.

A very similar practice was widely used by the company in the US to deter unions from getting established (Love, 1995). According to Duve (1987) and works councillors, company trouble-shooters would first try to identify who was involved and question them about their requests for works councils. Respondents suggest that if persuasion did not halt the process then jobs would sometimes be changed to more unpleasant duties. Duve (1987) and respondents also suggest that threats of dismissal or actual dismissals would follow. This is particularly surprising in the German context because German employees enjoy considerable protection from labour courts in cases of wrongful dismissal. The problem with court action is that it takes too long; by the time re-instatement is offered employees may no longer be interested. In several cases employees were simply paid to leave their jobs before court action was taken, and the amounts involved were not significant for such a large MNC (Duve, 1987).

According to interviewees and Duve (1987) many other tactics were put into use during the 1980s: refusing to recognize works council nominees;

disallowing meetings on work premises; delaying works meetings so a vote could not be taken; temporary closure of stores or selling-off of stores into different ownership through franchise or *Anver*, sometimes dismissing the workforce and then re-opening later with new or 'loyal' employees; the offering of money to employees to leave; and the altering of opening hours to 'hive off' undesirable employees who could only work particular shifts. Works council respondents suggest that since the mid-1980s the way in which the company responds to works councils has changed. Aware that they could no longer confront the issue of works councils head on, senior management now take a more subtle approach.

'Avoidance strategies'

The more recent and more subtle 'avoidance strategies' are evident in a thirty-page document distributed by McDonald's Germany's head office. It was distributed sometime after June 1994 to store managers, and is called *Practical Help in Dealing with Works Councils*. The clear message which comes across in the document is that employees' attempts to establish works councils are seen as a serious problem and a failure of management. It states that the reactions of managers to any such initiative must be carefully handled, and head office in Munich must make all the major decisions:

> A works council representative from another restaurant visits your store . . . how do you behave? . . . information about the visit must be sent immediately to headquarters personnel operations . . . any further measures will not be taken by operations but only by headquarters.
>
> (Ibid.: 8)

Addressed to store management the document states:

> you must never talk with union representatives without first having authority from head office . . . [and] . . . never give employees the impression that you are against the trade unions or the works council. The incentive to lead someone to do something is much greater than you think.
>
> (Ibid.: 8)

Lane (1989) reminds us that the legislation on German co-determination is only enabling legislation. This is clearly reflected in McDonald's newer strategy towards works councils: emphasized in bold type at the bottom of one page of this document is this reminder: 'Only the will of the workforce can create a works council not the law itself' (ibid.: 10).

For those managers already having to deal with a works council, the document states that conflict should be avoided, works councillors must be managed and handled appropriately, integrated into the business, and given appropriate work to do; for example: helping with 'McDonald's worker of the month'; sorting out shifts and holidays; Christmas celebrations; and taking care of the crew rest rooms. Both NGG and works councils respondents stated that if the works council is established then management should attempt to either sideline it or coopt it as a part of the personnel function. This, they suggest, is because management do not accept the notion that works councils should impinge on management decision-making. As already suggested, participation at McDonald's is viewed predominantly as communication.

According to NGG, works council respondents and *Der Spiegel* (1997), a more recent management response to the establishment of a works council is the offer of cash compensation to works councillors and their supporters in return for their giving up their jobs. Alternatively if they can be persuaded to see the 'problem' from management's point of view, individuals may be offered promotions or other incentives for giving up their interest in the works council. This 'buy-out' strategy may also take advantage of individuals' opportunistic natures. Some people may decide that they can gain a much larger financial benefit from 'selling-out' their participation rights and employment with the company, than by staying and supporting the works council.

Once again 'solidarity' may be undermined. Some respondents suggested that some works councillors (particularly students) behaved exactly in this manner, using the 'threat' of establishing a company-level council (GBR) to 'bribe' the company into giving them financial compensation. It was suggested that after they had been taken on what respondents called the '*Kumpel-tour*' (a 'buddy-buddy' trip involving various social invitations) some individuals lost all interest in any collective cause. This situation also causes a good deal of conflict and distrust between works councillors and is a source of frustration for the NGG because, they argue, it has the effect of undermining the solidarity of works councillors and their attempts to build a cohesive joint strategy.

As the above analysis suggests, even where works councils are established, the corporation's ability to take advantage of weaknesses in the legislation makes their work difficult. Both NGG and works council respondents state that works councillors are not being paid for their work on council business, because often management will not recognize council work as an 'authorized' activity. In addition managers are refusing to provide proper office facilities; under the 1972 Act councillors should be provided with stationery, access to phones and appropriate space to work in. As already suggested, even where councillors are paid for their time on council business this is also compounded by management's attempts to coopt the council on to management, passing on personnel work which is not their responsibility or by trying to undermine their position with the rest of the workforce.

An additional concern for the employee side in this study is that the existing works councils have been unable to gain access and influence at board level. Despite rights provided under the 1972 Act, the small number of individual works councils have not as yet acquired detailed financial information about the company, or had any influence over corporate decision-making. The NGG has been trying to gain some effective influence by establishing a company-level works council (GBR) for a number of years.

The Company-Level Works Council (GBR)

Neither the company-level works council (GBR) nor the concern-level works council (KBR) are deemed to be higher organs than the works council, but they are regarded as competent in dealing with matters affecting the whole company and which individual works councils are unable to settle within their establishments or subsidiaries. The GBR is supposed to meet at least once a year, along with its additional works committee members and make a report of its activities. At this meeting the employer

> shall make a report on staff questions and social affairs in the company and on the financial position of and trends in the company, in as far as there is no risk of a disclosure of trade or business secrets.
> (Part 1, paragraph 53 (2), Works Constitution Act 1972)

Early attempts to create a GBR were strongly opposed by management. The NGG argue that it is no coincidence that the company created its first *Anver* company around 1986/1987, at the same time that works councillors first tried to establish a GBR. These attempts failed because, in order to establish a GBR, two or more works councils are required in the 'same' company. The creation of the first *Anver* effectively transferred ownership of the relevant McDonald's store with a works council to a 'different owner'. McDonald's Germany therefore no longer had two works councils in the 'same' company. Both NGG and works council respondents argue that this transfer of ownership has been vital in *delaying* the establishment a GBR at McDonald's.

However, in 1995, after the quick election of six works councils in Cologne, a GBR was established on 20 February 1995. This rapid increase in the numbers of works councils had not allowed the company enough time to transfer ownership of any of these stores. Respondents suggest that the establishment of the new works councils and the GBR were partly because of renewed organizational activity by the NGG but also because of the determination of employees who stated they had a 'mission' to establish their rights. The chairman of the GBR, a law student, said that he had been incensed by the way in which a colleague had been sacked and this had given him the incentive to push for the election of a works council in his store.

Management were unable to stop the GBR being established, but according to respondents they still refused to acknowledge its existence, suggesting that it was 'unconstitutional'. The union viewed this response as an attempt to 'starve out' the GBR through non-recognition. The company refused to pay GBR members (who had been elected from the works councils) for any time spent on either works council or GBR activities and refused to give access to any meaningful information. The NGG and GBR representatives tried to arrange meetings with board-level management, but had little success. Works councillors state that senior management would not answer telephone calls, dates for meetings would be agreed but would then be postponed or cancelled at short notice. On one occasion a meeting was held, but only junior management were present. These managers made it clear that they had no authority to make decisions or any agreements with the union or GBR representatives.

Salaried white-collar representatives (*leitende Angestellte*), salaried managers (2nd assistant or above) are also supposed to attend GBR meetings, but none ever did attend these first meetings. *Leitende Angestellte* have voting rights on the GBR but only in proportion to the number of employees that they represent. This usually means that the block votes of salaried managers is much smaller than the employee vote; this would be particularly so at McDonald's with its very small proportion of salaried managers. Works councillors stated that salaried managers had been forbidden to attend any GBR meeting by senior management. Since 1989 *leitende Angestellte* have also had the right to establish their own committee (*Sprecherausschuß*), but no such committee has been established.

According to the 1972 Act a finance committee (*Wirtschaftsauschuß*) can be created in any company with over 100 permanent employees. It is a key feature of the legislation because it allows access to detailed information about a company's financial performance. It usually consists of between three and seven members, all of whom must be employees, and at least one of whom should be a works council member. This committee is appointed by the works council, although where a GBR or KBR has been established these bodies would appoint the committee members. This committee is supposed to meet once per month and these meetings must be attended by the employer or his/her representatives.

An early attempt had been made to establish this committee in one of the larger German restaurants (over 120 employees) in the early 1990s but this failed. In that instance the restaurant already had a works council, but this restaurant was an *Anver* company. Restaurant management stated that they would not recognize this committee nor provide information of any kind. The case went to the local labour court who eventually decided that in this case a GBR must first be established before any finance committee could be established. Now that the GBR was formally established the employee side had thought that in view of the previous court ruling the company would have to recognize the finance committee and hand over the information requested. However, the company continued to refuse to recognize these rights and would not hand over any meaningful information. As the GBR chairman reported in July 1995:

at the meeting (at which the senior manager did not appear) the manager presented us with a shiny folder with some nice coloured graphs of statistics, which told us nothing, it was just another delaying tactic.

The 'buy-out'

Even if the GBR were recognized by management it could only represent approximately 15 per cent of the total restaurants in Germany. Franchise and *Anver* restaurants would not be represented. The fact that there is no supervisory board means that representation at board level could only come through a company-level works council or concern-level works council (KBR). In theory a KBR could provide representation for all McDonald's restaurants in Germany. However, this would be fraught with difficulty not just because of the holding company (*Anver*) restaurants but also because franchise operators would almost certainly instigate an avalanche of legal claims arguing that a KBR should not apply to them.

Up to the summer of 1995 the NGG remained fairly optimistic that some further progress could be made. It was hoped that recognition for the GBR and some form of cooperation with senior management would soon come about. The employee side could resort to the labour court if the company continued to stall; it seemed likely that any court decision would find in favour of the employee side. The corporation would then be forced to recognize and deal with the GBR. The major fear was that any court case would be a long process, during which time council representatives may be bought off, sell out, or simply lose interest. In fact these fears were fully justified. At a hotel in Cologne on 23 November 1995, all ten works councils' representatives and supporters from Cologne were invited to a meeting with the chairman of the BdS. In that meeting eight of the ten works councils were bought out. Forty-six employees signed agreements to leave their jobs at McDonald's in return for cash compensation. The leavers were paid around DM 5,000 (£2,220) and in one case as much as DM 90,000 (£40,000). The NGG secretary stated that this was a major setback but not a total surprise: 'A functioning GBR would have been unpleasant for McDonald's, because it would have been able to look at the internal balance sheet and wage payments of the firm' (Langenhuisen, 1995: 36).

The NGG appears to have no answer to the corporation's ultimate weapon: the 'buy-out'. The GBR was dissolved and the numbers of works councils was now reduced to twenty-seven. If the GBR had survived and received recognition from a court ruling, the question remains as to how effective the works council structure would have been without the real consent of the corporation. As Kotthoff (1994) argues: without a 'moral community' amongst management it is doubtful that the GBR would be able to effectively influence company policy; works councils would probably remain, as Kotthoff puts it, 'isolated'.

Since 1995 a number of new works councils have been established, but according to *Der Spiegel* the corporation is still buying out these works councils with compensation payments as soon as they are put in place. The article goes on to quote an NGG official who states:

> It's raining compensation payments . . . the works council chairman of the Frankfurt Kaiserstraße restaurant has been offered DM100,000 for the cancellation of his employment contract.
>
> (*Der Spiegel*, 1997: 139)

Indeed in one case recently reported in *Stern* magazine (1999), a restaurant manager was allegedly demoted to assistant manager for allowing his workers to elect a works council in his restaurant in 1997. It is also interesting to note that no works councils have been established in the old East German states. Union officials state McDonald's workers in the new federal states are not familiar with the works council legislation and because there is still so much unemployment in the East, they are much more afraid of upsetting management.

Nevertheless in the 'West' the conflict over works councils continues. Five franchise restaurants in Dortmund appear to be a 'thorn in the eye' of the corporation, all five have works councils and about 200 of the 240 workers employed in them are union members. A new franchisee took over the five restaurants at the end of 1997 and according to NGG officials has been trying to get rid of the works councils ever since. This franchisee has allegedly made a number of offensive and outspoken comments about the workers involved in these works councils, a matter which was also reported in the press (*Stern*, 1999).

In 1998 it appeared that the corporation had decided to opt for a new tactic in the war against works councils. Instead of buying out workers to stop the election of a GBR the corporation now appeared to be trying to capture the mechanism for a management sponsored agenda. This came to light when there appeared to be two separate groups claiming to be the 'real' GBR to represent McDonald's German workers. After years of trying to block or nullify the union-supported GBR, McDonald's Germany had now decided to establish its 'own' GBR. The case went to the labour court but, despite a court ruling that suggested that the corporation had acted illegally, it also specified that the GBR election would have to be re-held. After what NGG officials described as more 'underhand' tactics the corporation managed to get their preferred candidates elected in the majority of key posts in the new GBR. This outcome also had serious implications for the European Works Council (Royle, 2000).

These kinds of activity appear to be on the increase rather than subsiding. Union officials state that in 1999 in particular the few existing works councils have been put under enormous pressure from management. A union-supported works council chairman in Wiesbaden was allegedly offered DM200,000 (almost £70,000) to leave McDonald's. He refused and, according to the same sources, McDonald's management have since tried to block his works council activities by various means. An article in *Stern* magazine also states that the chairman of McDonald's Germany wrote a letter in September 1999 to the chairman of the employers' association (BdS) Thomas Heyll regarding this stubborn works council. *Stern* (1999) suggests that Heyll is well known for his 'rough stuff' when it comes to dealing with trade unions. In the letter, Raupeter in James Bond-like terms grants the licence to dismiss (Stern, 1999: 128): 'With regard to this matter you are authorized to carry out every necessary measure within individual employment contract and works council law.'

The conflict over effective worker representation at McDonald's Germany looks as though it is likely to continue. The NGG are still trying to encourage grass roots support for the establishment of more 'free' works councils in the hope that they will eventually gain more seats on the GBR, but this is likely to be a long and difficult struggle. Whether the recent amendments to the Works Constitution Act will change this situation remains to be seen. On a more general note these findings also emphasize the fact that works councils, like any other institution, are dependent on the action of individuals and the attitudes of the parties involved. Indeed Kotthoff (1994) in his 20-year study of German works councils makes exactly this point.

Preliminary findings from the broader fast-food sector

Fast-food employers and the employers in the broader German food service sector such as train catering and airline food are currently organized in four different ways. Most of the multinational corporations including McDonald's, Burger King, PepsiCo/Tricon-Pizza Hut, Nudelmacher and KFC and Häagen-Dazs and a number of large national food retailers such as Dinea (department store restaurant catering) and Train-Catering (a subsidiary of Mitropa) are members of the German fast-food employers' federation (BdS). Some others like Churrasco, Maredo (Whitbread), Wienerwald and Blockhaus have signed national agreements with the German Hotel, Guest House and Restaurant Federation (DEHOGA) since 1997. The remainder either sign regional collective agreements with DEHOGA or are not members of any employers' federation and sign company-level agreements, for example, Mitropa. Most employees in the fast-food sector are represented by the NGG. However, the workers employed by Nordsee are represented both by the DAG salaried or white-collar workers' union and the NGG. The BdS established by McDonald's in the late 1980s has had an increasing influence over the way in which bargaining relationships and arrangements have developed since that time. The collective agreements within the BdS are, according to NGG officials, more complex than agreements in other industries and those agreed by DEHOGA. Union and works council representatives argue that this also makes the agreements more difficult to monitor, and harder for the many numbers of foreign workers to understand. There have also been some instances where companies have threatened to pull out of DEHOGA or company-level agreements and join the BdS if they did not get what they wanted in bargaining rounds.

In fact in 1999 McDonald's took this approach a step further by threatening to 'de-recognize' the NGG as bargaining partner and negotiate solely with a 'yellow' union called *Ganymed*. This union falls under the umbrella of a union with a 'Nazi' history, the German Association of Commercial and Industrial Employees (DHV). The DHV is affiliated to the CGB, the Christian Federation of Trade Unions, which in total has fewer than 300,000 members (Jacobi *et al.*, 1998). The *Ganymed* union is extremely small, having around 1,500 members and being administered by five staff in an office in Bonn. McDonald's representatives threatened that if the NGG did not accept a pay offer of 1.5 per cent per year (for three years) it would no longer negotiate with them, but would conclude a deal with *Ganymed*. The NGG organized workers to demonstrate outside McDonald's restaurants to complain about low pay and in the end McDonald's dropped its threat. Nevertheless, this example illustrates the problems that the NGG has had in trying to raise basic wage levels in this sector, and the effect that large corporations can have on industry-level bargaining outcomes.

It appears that with the help of the DHV, McDonald's has also been able to place employer-backed candidates on the workers' side of the bipartite body that administers the accident insurance fund for workers in the food and HRC sectors. Since the postwar period, the NGG has proposed a list of candidates to represent the employees to sit on that body every year. In 1999 the NGG agreed to the participation of other candidates proposed by the DHV, only to learn as the election was in process that the signatures legally required for participation in the election had been gathered at the instigation of McDonald's Germany. Of the 1,700 signatures collected for the list, most were McDonald's employees; the NGG alleges that the company had sent directives to local managers instructing them to gather signatures. NGG officials state that in effect McDonald's has now created a seat on the employees' side, thereby destroying the legal principle of administrative parity between employers and employees.

Co-determination in the sector

As we have already seen, undermining or avoiding works councils has been a continuous feature at McDonald's. However, it is not all that unusual in some other firms in the sector, indeed it appears to be particularly common amongst other Anglo-Saxon corporations such as PepsiCo/ Tricon (Pizza Hut, KFC), Burger King and to some extent the British

Whitbread subsidiaries Churrasco and Maredo. Although Burger King, for example, does have a *Stadtbetriebsrat* covering some of the Burger King restaurants in Berlin, there are very few works councils elsewhere. According to Burger King workers in Berlin their works council, which only represents Berlin's company-owned restaurants, is constantly under threat from Burger King management.

Industrial relations in most German-owned firms appear to be somewhat less antagonistic; in most cases the large national players have by and large accepted the role of both trade unions and works councils. For example the NGG enjoyed good relations with Maredo while it was under German ownership and before it was taken over by (the British) Whitbread group. Since the takeover relations with management at both Maredo and Whitbread's other subsidiary, Churrasco, have been difficult. Despite having a very active company-level works council at Churrasco the NGG suggest that they have had to fight over every point of law to achieve anything for their members since the takeover.

Nordsee, famous for its seafood products, changed ownership from Unilever to become part of the German APAX group in 1995. In 1997 the company began restructuring Nordsee to bring it more into line with other fast-food operations and the result has been that many skilled and long-term workers have left the company. A new collective agreement has been negotiated to reflect this re-organization. There are approximately twelve large works councils representing all Nordsee workers in the 350 or so restaurants; these are organized on the basis of twelve districts based within three regions, 'north', 'middle' and 'south' Germany. Works councillors report that by and large the company has not tried to obstruct works council business. The original Unilever management at Nordsee appear to have decided early on to take a strategic and pragmatic approach to works councils. Rather than waiting for workers and unions to request their own structure they proposed the current structure in which they 'voluntarily' allowed some works council members to be paid to work full time (*freigestellt*) on works council business. This structure has not altered under the APAX management. In theory the unions and workers could argue for another structure based around the regional areas and not the smaller districts, which could provide them with a larger number of *freigestellt* workers. It seems likely that APAX would be well aware of this and have perhaps decided not to propose any changes, in case a more 'onerous' works council structure is imposed upon them through a labour court decision.

Dinea, a large retail company, has a number of in-store fast-food catering operations. According to NGG officials there is a strong system of over 100 works councils and a very effective company-level works council. However, the management at Dinea may have more in common with those at Nordsee and do not have the same kind of fast-food 'heritage' as management at McDonald's or Burger King. However, German companies, such as the steakhouse chain Blockhaus, have adopted anti-union strategies and have actively avoided and undermined works councils. There are also examples of British companies where a more union friendly approach has been adopted. A catering subsidiary of the British Compass Group, Eurest, apparently works cooperatively with both works councils and unions.

Supervisory boards do not exist at Burger King or at Tricon (KFC, Pizza Hut). It seems that, like McDonald's, Tricon has also taken advantage of the 1954 American–German trade agreement. Where supervisory boards do exist in other firms they seem to vary in effectiveness as far as representing worker's interests are concerned, depending on the type of legislative underpinning. For example supervisory boards such as those at Churrasco and Le Buffet (providing only one-third representation under the 1952 Works Constitution Act) are far less effective than those with 'parity' representation as at Mitropa and Dinea, which are established under the 1976 Co-determination Act. But this outcome is also likely to be a feature of management attitudes as much as it is about the particular form of supervisory board in question.

However, even where relations have tended to be more cooperative amongst German owned firms – those which were not originally considered to be fast-food in the purest sense, e.g. companies normally owned by retailers or other kinds of consortia – both workers and trade union officials raised concerns that this approach was changing. In the cases of both Nordsee and Maredo it appears that increasing standardization of production is being accompanied by a reduction of skills and the removal of older and more experienced workers. Works councillors state that as this process is taking place management appear to be showing increasing signs of reluctance to take the work of works councils and supervisory boards seriously. While this has not yet become serious it may be a sign of things to come. In both cases these changes appear to be taking place after a change in ownership, but it appears to be the move towards more standarized procedures that is driving these potentially less cooperative relations.

Monitoring pay and conditions in the sector

NGG officials state that since the establishment of the BdS and other collective agreements negotiated after the early 1990s, some improvements have been achieved in pay and the broader conditions of work for most employees. Nevertheless, there remain two main problems: first, that in comparison with similar skills and jobs with similar work intensity in other sectors, pay for the majority of fast-food employees is still low; and second, the absence of works councils in most restaurants in companies like Burger King, McDonald's, Pizza Hut and other companies means that there is no mechanism in place to ensure that collective agreements are properly applied. The research suggests that in a number of fast-food companies collective agreements are not being properly observed, not only in terms of paying people according to the appropriate wage grouping and miscalculation of pay, but also in terms of their entitlements in areas such as correct calculation of holiday pay, sick pay, inadequate notice over shift changes and other leave entitlements. Employees are often unaware of their rights to various allowance or pay structures unless these are brought to their attention and are otherwise dependent on the goodwill of management.

Conclusions

It is clear from the above analysis that determined companies can operate to some extent independently of the German industrial relations system, but so far, these are mostly foreign companies. McDonald's, for example, after 18 years of operations, finally accepted regular collective bargaining rounds with unions. However, this change in approach was more to do with improving the corporation's public image, and little to do with any real desire to adapt to the German system, or accept unions as a 'pluralist' principle. Although the Anglo-Saxon MNCs McDonald's, Burger King and KFC have been unable to avoid collective bargaining, they still resist co-determination and unions at restaurant level. The fast-food employers' federation established by these same companies, the BdS, allows them to influence terms and conditions that more closely reflect their own needs and perspectives, rather than those of the wider hotel and restaurant sector. This may be part of a further fragmentation of collective bargaining in Germany, but it also concentrates 'fast-food bargaining power' under the leadership of McDonald's amongst a small number of MNCs and other companies. The conflict over works councils looks set to continue, with McDonald's so far successfully capturing the company-level works council and restricting the establishment of works councils to just a small number of restaurants. As we have seen, the small number of works councils established means there is little effective monitoring of working conditions at restaurant level. The findings suggest that in the absence of some form of union presence in the restaurants breaches of collective agreements are likely to continue.

Even highly juridified systems like that in Germany may be unable to adequately restrain the activities of MNCs if they are fundamentally opposed to the notion of collective bargaining and statutory worker representation in principle. Whilst not denying the importance of legislation, workers' rights still depend in part on the willingness of the employer to bargain 'in good faith'. This is because employers can find ways to turn legislation to their advantage. In the US, for example, the New Deal legislation, which was first introduced in the 1930s, was intended to promote collective bargaining; however, over time it has actually succeeded in encouraging the opposite (Towers, 1997). Seeking redress from the German labour courts is also no guarantee of success. Cases can take many months to come to court; the self-confidence and 'solidarity' of workers are undermined over time; and many individuals settle out of court, something which it appears powerful

MNCs can easily afford to do and prefer. Even when some individuals are reinstated they are unlikely to return, making the establishment of works councils and the sustaining of union membership very difficult.

The German system itself continues to be the subject of a good deal of debate. The breakdown of formerly rigid sector-wide regional collective agreements has been driven by high levels of unemployment and achieved by employers gaining concessions from works councils at plant level. Much has been said about the adaptability and the strength of the German system (Ferner and Hyman, 1998; Kotthoff, 1994; Lane, 1994; Sadowski *et al.*, 1995), but over recent years some authors have become less optimistic about its future (Streeck, 1997; Flecker and Schulten, 1999). These claims may be somewhat overdone. This analysis suggests that although foreign MNCs are continually undermining the effectiveness of the system and in some cases bringing it to a standstill, many employers still seem to accept and work with the system. The system itself may not be on the verge of collapse, but it may be the very fact that determined companies can get around important parts of the legislation that aids the survival of the system. In other words, a building that bends with the wind is more likely to stay intact during a hurricane. However, the adaptability of the system may be a double-edged sword for workers. On the hand it provides workers with rights to representation, but on the other hand its 'flexibility' may in part be dependent on undermining workers' terms and conditions.

The findings do suggest, however, that Anglo-Saxon based MNCs in this sector are more likely to adopt non-union and/or works council avoidance strategies than German firms. Many German employers seem to accept and work with the system. However, the 'country of origin' effect does not provide all the answers as far as employment policies are concerned, because some German companies such as Blockhaus have also adopted strong anti-union policies. This suggests that one needs to examine carefully not only the type of operation concerned, but also the current and past ownership of companies, the type of workforce, and the behaviour and attitudes of individual managers. As for McDonald's, it looks set to continue to dominate and set the agenda for the German fast-food sector in the short and medium term. However, whether increasing numbers of German companies will begin to emulate the labour relations practices of their Anglo-Saxon competitors, in the hope of increasing their market share, is hard to determine at present. In the meantime the drive for more 'efficiencies' and more standarized procedures looks set to continue, placing pay and conditions under increasing pressure, in a situation in which, compared with other German industries, pay and conditions are already poor (Royle, 2000). Furthermore, the larger fast-food competitors like McDonald's look set to continue their resistance to co-determination, suggesting that workers' rights to independent representation are likely to come under increasing threat in the future. Whether this will change with the recent amendments to the Works Constitution Act remains to be seen.

Note

1 'Open clauses' were introduced in the 1990s as an attempt to ensure the survival of
the sectoral model of bargaining. They allow companies to delay or waive part or
all of sectorally agreed provisions, usually concerning pay and bonus payments, if
companies can prove that they are in economic difficulties.

6 Consensus and confrontation

Fast-food in the Netherlands

*Jos Benders, Sonja Bekker and
Birthe Mol*

More than ten years after the Dutch social partners concluded the now
famous *Accoord of Wassenaar* (1982), the term *poldermodel* was coined to
describe the achievements of the cooperation of the framework on socio-
economic policy between unions, employers' organizations and the government. The *Accoord* fits a more general pattern: relative to most other
countries, consensus is a prevailing approach in the Netherlands, as
d'Iribarne (1989) stressed in his comparative study of factories in the
United States of America, France and the Netherlands. The *Accoord*
sought to limit wage rises and regulate the supply and demand of labour,
but Visser and Hemerijck (1997) also stress that a third element should not
be overlooked: the fact that the elaborate social security system was also
reformed, and in fact, downsized.

From a theoretical perspective, it becomes interesting to investigate what
happens when a multinational from a country with confrontational labour
relations traditions establishes subsidiaries in the Netherlands (cf. Pot,
2000). Pfeffer (1994) presses for American managers to abandon their hostile
attitudes towards unions. Not for nothing did Lawrence (1996: 95) describe
the American industrial relations scene as 'interest-driven pugnacity'. Yet
obviously, such attitudes are not necessarily exported. In this respect,
Cooke (1997) studied the influence of industrial relations factors on US
foreign direct investment. He found that the level of investment was nega-
tively related to high levels of union penetration, centralized collective
bargaining structures, restrictions to layoffs, and pervasive contract exten-
sion policies. However, it was positively related to high levels of education
and policies requiring works councils.

It is often assumed that American managers, more than colleagues from
other countries, are inclined to adopt hostile attitudes towards forms of
statutory employee representation. That may be understandable in adversarial contexts but becomes problematic in environments where cooperation
is the norm. Specifically, importing 'American' norms for dealing with
(generally cooperative) Dutch employee representatives is likely to create
friction and hostility. Explaining such features as *werkoverleg* (regular work
meetings), the *ondernemingsraad* (works council), and the level of detail in

collective labour agreements to foreign bosses can be a very demanding task for Dutch personnel managers. This is illustrated by a remark made by a Dutch HRM manager of a plant acquired by an American company: 'You have to explain to them that works council members are not horrible people, and that you can cooperate with them.' Even more telling, though again anecdotal, is the statement made by the former Director of Social Affairs, De Leij, of the main Dutch employers' organization VNO-NCW: 'We do not want American circumstances here.'

Against this background, the purpose of this chapter is to investigate how industrial relations evolved in one particular American multinational, McDonald's, in the Netherlands. The chapter is based on interviews with managers, employees, and union and company representatives, and on documents from various sources, ranging from company and union PR material, published statistics and popular media (cf. Mol, 1996).

As we explain in the following section, McDonald's is by far the most prominent multinational operating in the sector. Subsequently we present a sketch of the Dutch industrial relations system, followed by a case study of McDonald's in the Netherlands. We end with some conclusions and a discussion.

Fast-food *à la neérlandaise*

If one product is typical of the Dutch fast-food sector, it is *friet* or French fries; the Belgians claim that this product originates in their country, but the French dispute this. In any case, its international expansion may have started with British and American soldiers acquiring a taste for friet during World War I. This was probably in the French-speaking part, which may explain the adjective 'French' in the English word for friet (Zuiderveld, 1995: 13–15). What is uncontested is friet's popularity in the Netherlands. The traditional '*frietkramen*' (typical stand-alone, often wooden cabins of friet sellers) have now largely been replaced by more permanent housings, and even the word *frietkramen* is falling into disuse in favour of more contemporary words such as 'snackbars' and *cafetaria*, yet such outlets still form the backbone of the Dutch fast-food sector.

Most snackbars are run by their owners, often as a family business with just one location. There are a few chains, most of them regional. The only national player is Febo, which operated sixty-plus locations in 2000. Another important initiative in this market segment is called '*kwalitaria*', a contraction of '*kwaliteit*' (quality) and *cafetaria*. When satisfying certain quality conditions certain snack bars can be certified as 'Foundation Acknowledged *Cafetarias*', signalling to customers that they observe high quality standards. This stamp of approval foundation was an initiative of the employers' association for hotels, restaurants and bars (*IJsfrica* of the *Koninklijk Horeca Nederland*).

In 1999, the number of '*spijsverstrekkers*' (a generic word for different kinds of food suppliers in the hospitality industry) was 10,151. These generated cumulative sales of approximately Euro 2 billion (from a gross national product of Euro 374 billion in 1999). The *bedrijfschap* (an organization to represent the sector and promote its interests) distinguishes between *shoarma* bars, snackbars/*cafetaria* and fast-food restaurants. In 1999, there were 273 fast-food restaurants (Bedrijfschap Horeca en Catering, 2000). Although there are no precise data on how these are distributed over different firms, it is clear that McDonald's dominates this market. In 1998 they operated a total of 177 restaurants and this increased to 190 in 1999 and to 203 by September 2000. Of these, twenty-three were company-owned and 180 were operated by eighty-one franchise-holders. In total, McDonald's employs over 15,000 people in the Netherlands. For comparison: Burger King, which considers itself to be in the top four of its sector had nineteen restaurants (2000), employing about 1,000 staff. Febo and Kwalitaria, which are snackbars/*cafetaria* were listed as numbers two and three after Burger King. Other American chains on the Dutch market are Applebee's, Pizza Hut, Domino's Pizza and Kentucky Fried Chicken. Pizza Hut has started opening outlets within railway stations, which appear to be rather successful. The Belgian hamburger chain Quick entered the Netherlands in 1996, operated four restaurants in 1997, had to close two restaurants in 1998 due to insufficient performance, and decided to retreat from the Dutch market in January 2000, allegedly due to 'heavy competition from McDonald's'. About a week later, McDonald's opened its two hundredth restaurant and announced its ambition to open a further fifty within the next three years.

The 1990s were clearly successful for McDonald's. The prospects for the sector as a whole seem promising as well. The Dutch economy has been flourishing ever since 1993, and the number of people who prepare full meals at home has declined. Alternatives such as delivery services, pre-cooked microwave meals and eating out are gaining ground as well. This growth slowed in 1996 when shops and supermarkets were legally allowed to extend their business hours. Regardless of changes in the fortunes of the economy McDonald's has continued to expand at its own rate and has continued to open one or two restaurants per month. We now provide an outline of the Dutch industrial relations system.

Industrial relations in the Netherlands

As pointed out in the introduction 'consensus' may easily become a caricature for Dutch society. Even if correct as an overall characterization, it must be understood in relative terms. Dutch employers and employees do not always live together peacefully, and strikes occur in the Netherlands like anywhere else. Yet throughout recent history, the incidence of strikes in the Netherlands, as measured by the number of days lost due to strikes, was well below the average for all industrialized countries. Scholars of Dutch industrial relations do, however, identify the 1970s as a period in which 'conflicts' were more common (Windmuller *et al.*, 1990: 226–41), although in this era too, the Dutch may have appeared consensual to foreign observers.

An important moment for the development of postwar industrial relations was the agreement of representatives of both parties during the war that employees were to be given strong representation in national advisory bodies in exchange for not interfering with internal organizational policies (Windmuller *et al.*, 1990). The call for employee participation found one expression in the Law of Works Councils of 1950, which, as in other European countries, arose from the widely felt need for cooperation in the rebuilding of postwar economies and societies. Part of the government's economic policy was a strict wage policy enforced by law, which kept wages at a modest level. For most of this period this policy was supported by employers and unions alike, yet strains occurred when labour markets tightened towards the closing of the decade. In 1959, the government relaxed its wage policy and three years later it was abolished. Wages rose quickly during the 1960s. The character of Dutch industrial relations became more radical, and open conflicts between employers and employees were relatively common in the late 1960s and 1970s. There was also an increase in the tendency towards decentralization, unions were focusing on national policies and neglecting local level organization. The call for democratization manifested itself in setting up *bedrijvenwerk*: union representation within companies to deal with organization-specific matters. In the 1970s economic conditions deteriorated leading to increasing unemployment. Unions increasingly stressed the need to curb this development.

In retrospect, the *Accoord of Wassenaar* of November 1982 was the turning point. The government, unions and employers' organizations agreed on a national policy to keep wage rises moderate in exchange for active policies to increase the number of jobs. These policies included collective working time reduction, stimulating part-time work (Delsen and Jacobs, 1999) and a stress on enhancing 'employability' through education. Unlike the 1950s when the government tightly controlled wages, the policy was now implemented through collective labour agreements (CLAs). At the same time, the government with the consent of the 'social partners' (unions and employers' organizations) began to cut expenditure and reform the social security system.

It took at least a decade before the benefits of what was to become known as the *poldermodel* emerged. The sustained national consensus about macroeconomic policy eventually gained international recognition. Refraining from substantial wage demands meant that unions had to concentrate on other items to further their members' interests. Action points were found, among other things, in issues such as enhancing job opportunities for people with a weak position in the labour market, such as the long-term unemployed and ethnic minorities. Measures were proposed and taken to encourage women to take part in the labour market. The stimulus given to part-time work has been an important and particularly successful policy. Although no Dutch scholar of industrial relations has done so, one may characterize the period that started with the 1982 *Wassenaar Accoord* as a return to the harmony that prevailed in the 1950s. Once again, however, labour market scarcities have returned and the period of limited wage increases appears to be ending.

Turning to collective labour agreements, these are negotiated between employee representatives, generally sectoral unions, on the one hand and on the other either employers' associations or individual companies. Company-level agreements are not so common, but are becoming more prevalent. The general tendency is to leave the details of agreements to lower levels of the bargaining structure. For instance, the Horeca CLA signed in September 2000 leaves it to employee representatives and employers to negotiate the compensation for working on Sundays. An important feature of Dutch CLAs is that the Minister of Social Affairs and Employment generally declares them 'collectively binding', i.e. the CLA also applies to employers who are not members of an employers' association. This puts unions in a strong position: even if few employees are union members, the union still represents all employees in a sector.

Currently, many smaller sectoral associations exist next to the central and large employers' association, the *Verbond van Nederlandse Ondernemers-Nederlands Christelijk Werkgeversverbond* (VNO-NCW). VNO-NCW is a powerful player in the Dutch field and primarily represents large companies and other employers' associations. The sectoral associations concentrate on representing their members in negotiations for collective labour agreements and may or may not be active in stimulating sector-specific developments such as providing vocational training programmes, promoting collective marketing campaigns, organizing study trips, lobbying, research and development, and disseminating technological and organizational knowledge. As mentioned above, *Koninklijk Horeca Nederland* represents employers in the Horeca. In September 2000, the organization had some 17,500 members, mostly small and medium-sized enterprises. Its members employ about 80 per cent of all Horeca personnel.

There are two main forms of employee representation: unions and works councils (*ondernemingsraden*). The main Horeca union is the *FNV Horeca-bond* with some 28,100 members (January 2000) (Centraal Bureau voor de Statistiek, 2001). Horeca employees may also join the *vakgroep CNV Horeca* of the CNV Bedrijvenbond, which is part of the protestant federal union CNV. With an estimated 15 per cent, the trade union density in the sector is low and below the national average (1999) of about 27 per cent. Part of this can be explained by the large numbers of flexible and part-time staff, among whom the density is about three times as low as among full-time permanent staff (Centraal Bureau voor de Statistiek, 2000).

Works councils have several statutory rights which apply to different issues: the information right, the consultation right, the advisory right, and the approval right. On some issues, management is obliged to inform and consult the works council, on others its advice or even approval must be asked. For instance, rules on personnel assessment and reward systems cannot be implemented without a works council written approval. In case of disagreement, management (approval right) or the works council (advisory right) may take the initiative to go to court. Legally, a works council is compulsory if an establishment has 50 or more employees.

In the Horeca, an establishment can be defined as a single restaurant but also as a collective of restaurants owned by a legal entity or individual. Employers have 'in principle' fulfilled their legal obligations if no candidates for works council positions can be found. The existence of two representative bodies for employees may lead to antagonistic relations between both (Nagelkerke and De Nijs, 1998). Whereas there have been cases where both bodies contested each other's responsibilities and the works council may even practically become a substitute for union representation (Van Lier, 2000), such cases appear exceptional, as Nagelkerke and De Nijs (1998) pointed out in their review of Dutch research. Typically again for Dutch society, cooperation is the norm and open conflicts seldom occur. Where works councils exist union members tend to be well represented, and unions provide educational and consultation services for works councillors. Works councils are probably the unions' main mechanism to be kept informed about what goes on within companies and, as such, in many cases are a useful substitute for the failure of workplace representation mechanisms introduced in the 1960s. CLAs are losing their significance as a general sectoral framework, leaving the details to be negotiated at lower levels. Consequently, the 1997 revision of the Law on Works Councils gives works councils the right to abolish company-level CLAs.

McDonald's in the Netherlands

Both Love (1995) and Royle (2000) stress the significance of the franchising system for McDonald's mode of operation and expansion. The founder of the corporation, Ray Kroc was constantly seeking to gain more control of his franchisees and paid meticulous attention to working out and enforcing very detailed operating procedures. By means of a number of control mechanisms, the company ensures that its detailed operating procedures are complied with, and any infringement can result in the franchisee losing the licence. Whilst franchisees are allowed to suggest new product developments and put forward other ideas, any changes of substance have to be authorized by the corporation.

McDonald's opened its first restaurant in the Netherlands in Zaandam, a little north of Amsterdam, in 1971. The Dutch branch was a 50–50 joint venture with Albert Heijn, a prominent supermarket chain in the Dutch market. Rather than following the American practice of putting operations-oriented managers in charge, the new company relied on a consultant experienced in international markets but without knowledge of the fast-food system. In commercial terms the start was not a very successful one: Love describes it as: 'a series of small mistakes that added up to a long-term disaster' (1995: 418). Initially, it began by opening restaurants in suburbs. In the US, this made sense as downtown areas had deteriorated and those who could afford it had moved into suburban areas. In the Netherlands as in other European countries, however, shops and public life are concentrated in the inner cities. These suburban locations were not sustainable and the Dutch director pressed for restaurants to be opened in shopping areas to make the public acquainted with the new phenomenon. In addition to the issue of locations, the menu was adapted heavily to Dutch taste, even eliminating menu items characteristic of the company. Yet it took the Dutch subsidiary 12 years before it became profitable. Nevertheless, after a long period of slow growth, the number of restaurants increased rapidly. Of the 203 restaurants established by 2000, 181 are operated as franchises, the remainder being either company-owned (McOpCo) restaurants or joint-ventures. As we mentioned earlier McDonald's now employs over 15,000 people in the Netherlands.

Operations management

As might have been expected, the Dutch restaurants follow the original American operations and training manual closely. Managers and employees are required to use the standardized procedures. As one manager stated: 'The standards are there. You accept them. It was proven that they are the best. Furthermore, you know in advance that you are to work according to these standards.' Or in the words of an employee: 'Working with so many standards is simply necessary. It can't be otherwise. In that case it wouldn't work as it should.'

However, as in many occupations managers sometimes find ways to get around some of these elaborate procedures; for example hamburgers are sometimes kept longer than they should be. There have also been some minor adaptations of the American procedures to better fit in with Dutch culture. For example there are deviations from the prescribed counter service system. Managers allow employees to drop the so-called 'reminder sale' which tends to irritate Dutch customers. One assistant-manager remarked that the reminder sale was 'just for foreigners'.

Furthermore, a 'Total Quality Management' programme launched in 1994 in the Netherlands marginally revised the counter service system: customer satisfaction is now apparently more important than an over-strict adherence to standard procedures. For instance, operators still have to greet the customer as a first step of the counter service, but the sentence for doing so is no longer prescribed. Additionally, the TQM programme is meant to 'empower' workers but in practical terms has little effect other than to allow workers to make up their own greetings to customers. As in other countries (Royle, 2000) the company has also conducted limited experiments with 'self-directed teams' and more 'self discretion' in some aspects of the jobs.

Another adaptation is the introduction of 'hazard analysis of critical control points'. This 'HACCP' involves daily hygiene checks. It is compulsory in the European Union as of 1996, but was adopted earlier by McDonald's (Deijen, 1995). As elsewhere there have been some modifications to suit the menu to Dutch taste and market. This includes the addition of the 'vegetable burger' ('approved by the Dutch Association of Vegetarians', according to company information) to the menu in 1993, which like other product developments had to be approved by the US headquarters. In 1999 the *kroket*, a fried meat-based snack, was temporarily offered, but was later incorporated in the regular menu. Such small adaptations to local tastes are customary for McDonald's around the globe and may involve setting up new standardized procedures (Royle, 2000).

Personnel management

Corporate headquarters provides the franchisees with a handbook for personnel management. This contains guidelines rather than directions. It is hence left to the individual franchisee whether or not to comply with it. However, franchisees were found to stick less to the rules than managers of company-owned restaurants, for example failing to complete paper work for staff appraisals.

Management training is still essentially based on an American programme, although this was partly remodelled under a modular training system developed in the Netherlands. More recently, a new programme was introduced and on 16 November 2000 a Dutch training centre was opened similar to that in Germany and the UK. However, some senior managers are still sent to the 'Hamburger University' in the US for training meetings and conferences.

Working at McDonald's requires no formal educational skills. A tidy physical appearance is required but not a perfect command of Dutch (Feiter, 1996). Recruitment for crew is handled locally, and according to the corporate personnel director a restaurant's staff will 'reflect the composition of the local environment' (Feiter, 1996: 22), thus sending a signal to local customers that the restaurant belongs to their neighbourhood. Consequently, one will find 'blonde Frisians' in rural Friesland (north of the Netherlands), and representatives from many different ethnic minorities in Amsterdam.

On age discrimination the sectoral agreement which covers McDonald's stipulates that a minimum wage applies for workers up to the age of 22.5 years after which they have to be paid at a higher rate. It is perhaps not surprising therefore that McDonald's prefers to employ workers under that age. One McDonald's manager stated in 1996: 'The general policy at McDonald's is that a person is no longer interesting over the age of 22.5 [years].'

However, restaurants may employ some older employees in tight labour market conditions. But there are obvious differences between restaurants. An employee of a restaurant that had been taken over stated:

> you sensed that they really just wanted very young employees. Older persons became too expensive, and were teased away. Or contracts were only renewed for a limited period, after which one was fired.

Recently, high economic growth rates have intensified tightness in labour markets in many sectors, and the fast-food industry is no exception to this. The outcome is that some restaurant owners have been forced to pay higher wages than the minimum CLA rate and the policy of substituting younger for older workers is increasingly harder to realize. In addition though the personnel handbook pays a good deal of attention to procedures for hiring and firing staff, this reflects the protective nature of Dutch labour legislation.

Turnover rates in the fast-food industry are high, and in 1998, one out of every three employees was a newcomer to the sector. In this way, the 'age problem' resolves itself automatically. In addition, so-called 'help staff' (generally quite young employees, who are however employed on a regular basis) often work during holiday periods and weekends. The much contested 'zero hour-contracts' (contracts stating that employees are to work at short notice but which do not guarantee a minimum number of hours of work) are not allowed in the CLA and contracts must have a minimum of 18 hours per month. 'On-call staff' are not used at McDonald's (Mulder, 1997). The large use of temporary and part-time staff possibly leads to some segmentation between full-time, 'core' staff and other personnel.

Apparently, little use is made of the handbook's sample advertisements for personnel, as there are many applications anyway. In addition, recruitment takes place via existing employees, a procedure recommended by the handbook. The ways of introducing a new employee vary and may range from a restaurant tour to a special introduction programme. 'Crew trainers' train newcomers and training is supposed to take place by means of 'Station Observation Checklists' (SOCs) and (American) instruction videos. Managers stated that they used job rotation as much as possible, but in practice rarely moved employees around all the stations. Not only do managers prefer experienced workers to stay on certain positions because they are good at their jobs but also because some employees prefer this. The SOCs can also be used for checking whether or not individual employees are meeting the standards. According to the handbook, every employee's performance should be evaluated on a monthly basis by means of the

SOCs, but in practice this was sporadic and hardly occurred at all in franchise operations.

Officially, the employee with the highest score on the monthly SOC-based evaluation becomes the 'employee of the month', and his/her picture is displayed in the restaurant. Opinions about this system vary: most Dutch restaurants do not seem to bother with this, perhaps because the selected employees fear being ridiculed by the rest of the staff; in some cases the staff objected to it because it was seen as too 'American' and/or at odds with working as a team. It appears that other activities that are seen as typically American are not used at all such as organizing 'Family Days' and counselling. The managers interviewed had not even heard of 'counselling', although the practice is mentioned in the personnel handbook. 'Counselling' involves checking on employees who are under-performing. Managers stated that the standardization of these procedures was 'unnecessary'. Badges containing names and stickers with information on the number of stations an employee can work on are used, but with little enthusiasm as employees appeared not to like them.

Once a year, every restaurant is submitted to personnel audit, which includes checks on matters such as: personnel administration; rostering, including job rotation and compliance with legal and other rules; personnel evaluations; the quality of the local management; absenteeism policies; compliance with legal requirements such as the Labour Environment Act and the Act on Works Councils; employee facilities; organization of crew meetings, rap sessions and crew opinion surveys. In practice, however, the importance attached to these items appears to differ. Overall, one can conclude that personnel management guidelines allow for some limited variation between restaurants. Where variations are permitted such variation appears to be closely determined by local conditions and profit margins. In addition, some guidelines are seen as too 'American' and/or inadequately take into account local conditions.

Employee relations

On several occasions, the former chairman of the confederate union FNV, Mr Johan Stekelenburg, has called McDonald's a model for other companies to follow. In an advertising appendix of a national newspaper, Stekelenburg is quoted about McDonald's personnel policy:

> Everything the FNV holds as desirable, McDonald's actually does. They stimulate part-time work, hiring women and representatives of ethnic minorities and offer schooling and training.

This statement may seem surprising given its source and appears to be in stark contrast with McDonald's industrial relations record in other countries. Stekelenburg's statement has to be seen in the light of union policy after the 1982 *Accoord*. For more than a decade after signing the *Accoord*, the unions saw part-time work (and working time reduction) as the main means to resolve the unemployment problem. The policy on part-time work was effective: as of 1980 the proportion of part-time workers in the Netherlands increased. In 2000, 70 per cent of all Horeca staff worked for less than 38 hours a week – a full-time job in the Netherlands (Bedrijfschap Horeca en Catering, 2000: 9).

Another union aim was and is to enhance job opportunities for people with poor qualifications and a weak position in the labour market, which includes women and ethnic minorities. This union policy placed McDonald's in an ideal position. McDonald's can use part-timers to cover peaks in the work-load, and part-time jobs are attractive to women with household respons-ibilities. Furthermore, as working at McDonald's requires little formal skill, job opportunities were created for those with few formal qualifications, and the percentage of ethnic minorities is relatively high in this group. In December 2000, the company was awarded a prize for its multicultural personnel policy by the *Stichting van de Arbeid*, a national bipartite body where consultations on industrial relations take place. Some 30 per cent of McDonald's staff are from ethnic minorities. Ethnic minorities conprise 35 per cent of 'managers'; on the surface at least this might suggest that career opportunities are good, but the term 'managers' also includes floor managers who are either full-time or part-time non-salaried staff. The com-pany personnel director claimed not to pursue a special policy with respect to minorities, stating that: 'We feel that we won a prize in a game that we never played' (Nobis, 2000: 28). This statement well illustrates that McDonald's rapid growth automatically met with the union's approval as it provided lots of part-time jobs and jobs for ethnic minorities.

The above does not mean that the union is happy with everything McDonald's does, nor that the good relationship has always existed. Around 1980 there was a large conflict between some of McDonald's franchisees on the one hand and the organization Catholic Working Youth and the union on the other. In January 1974, a law on minimum wage levels for youth had become effective, but for the remainder of the decade a considerable number of employers were still paid below statutory levels. In addition, franchisees were criticized for long working hours and not paying supplements for working on Sundays. Employees complaining about such matters were often badgered so that they would quit. In 1979 and 1980 this led to actions to inform young employees about the law, and later to lawsuits against the violators (Blom *et al.*, 1985). As of 1984, when the chain started to make its first profits, McDonald's Netherlands was pressured to comply with the sectoral CLA. Sector CLAs are generally 'collectively binding': all employers in the sector must comply, even if they have not taken part in negotiations. The unions held talks with McDonald's management to urge them to comply with the Horeca CLA. A difficulty for the unions was that few employees wanted to undertake industrial or legal action against their employer.

Only around 1990 and possibly connected to a global guideline (Dowling *et al.*, 1994), McDonald's adopted a more proactive attitude: the company began consulting with the unions on issues such as the quality of working life and career opportunities. In that year, the company offered its help to a national committee on 'Social Renewal' by creating jobs for, and providing training to, persons who are difficult to employ (*Financieel Dagblad*, 1990), but no national policy emerged (Krikke, 1994).

With respect to such issues, McDonald's and the union apparently agree that there is room for improvement. Disposing of employees aged over 22.5 years obviously does not generate enthusiasm with the unions or the employees directly affected. When there are frictions between the union and McDonald's it tends to be at restaurant level and especially with franchisees. There are occasional complaints from individual employees; low union membership makes it difficult to get a good overview of the incidence and severity of such complaints. In addition, there are restaurants who forbid employees to talk to journalists (Van Casteren, 1997). More seriously, the number of works councils is low: there are now ten restaurant-level works councils within some of the franchise operations, and a company-level works council for head office staff and the company-owned restaurants was recently established. In theory at least, works councils are compulsory when establishments have fifty employees or more who work a minimum of one-third of a regular working week, i.e. about 12.5 hours a week. In the legal sense an 'establishment' may be one individual restaurant or composed of several restaurants which are jointly owned by the same franchisee or company. Employers have 'in principle' fulfilled their legal obligations if no candidates for works council positions can be found. McDonald's maintains that due to the small average size of restaurants (as a rough estimate: dividing 15,000 employees by 200 restaurants generates an average size of about 75 persons) and the large number of part-timers most restaurants are not required to have a works council.

The FNV Horecabond, however, did not agree with McDonald's figures and started an action in the autumn of 1997 to promote the establishment of works councils at McDonald's restaurants (Mulder, 1997). Three years later in 2000, FNV Horecabond was still working on this policy, negotiating with McDonald's headquarters. Furthermore, empirical research on other companies persistently finds that roughly 30 per cent of smaller establishments in general do not have works councils in the Netherlands (Van der Burgh and Kriek, 1992; Slomp, 1995; Huijgen and Benders, 1998). This percentage is probably considerably higher in the restaurant sector, so that the low number of works councils at McDonald's may not be exceptional. Whether or not a works council exists will probably to a large extent depend on the attitudes of individual restaurant managers/owners, and also on the willingness of employees to participate in a works council. As

Royle (2000) indicates, there have been three or four works councils at McDonald's Netherlands in the past and franchisees are not necessarily always against organized labour. As one union representative even stated (interview 1996): 'occasionally, we get a phone call from a franchise-holder that some person [an employee] standing next to him wants to join the union.'

Overall, however, works councils at McDonald's have had a somewhat troublesome past. The company-level works council was only established on 8 April 1999, at the initiative of the HRM director, earlier attempts having failed because they did not get the support of corporate management. Managerial attitudes towards works councils had not been positive, yet this apparently has now changed. The company now fulfils its legal obligation as far as the small number of its own restaurants is concerned, with the works council acting as a kind of communication channel between employees and management. When signs of discontent are picked up, proposals to resolve problems are presented to management; however, if there are no union representatives in each of the company restaurants some issues may not be uncovered. Interestingly, the company-level works council has problems in retaining a sufficient number of members: in February 2001, only five of the original eleven members were still in office. Works council members often have above-average ambition and leave to find better jobs. For example, in that month three student members graduated and two other members found jobs outside the company. Replacements are hard to find, given the high percentage of part-timers and the low educational level of many employees. None of the current members of the works council is a union member, but works council members called the FNV to help them fill the vacant positions. The company-level works council employs a secretary, and meets alternately at a company restaurant and at the head office.

The current relationship between the McDonald's Dutch headquarters and the unions appears to be good. Dutch headquarters urges restaurant managers to obey legal regulations and the sectoral Collective Labour Agreement. McDonald's existing control systems appear to ensure that its standards, including those on industrial relations, are largely kept. It could be argued that the company compares favourably to other companies in the restaurant sector (cf. Bello, 1987; Braam, 1994). Of course McDonald's current stance is certainly not free from well-understood self-interest. Franchisees are urged to conform to the Collective Labour Agreement, because the company wishes to avoid bad publicity and damage to its public image. In an interview in 2000, the newly appointed director of McDonald's Netherlands stressed the importance of good contacts with a leading national environmental action group, with the consumers' organization, and with the unions. Following a meeting in January 2001, a key union official stated that 'no future problems were expected'. The maintenance of proper industrial relations can be seen as part of a broader philosophy to keep good working relationships with external parties and possibly a concern for the company's public image.

The present good relationships between McDonald's Netherlands and the unions can be explained by the interplay of a number of factors. The bad macro-economic conditions at the beginning of the 1980s and their ideological background led Dutch unions to support moderate wage increases, part-time jobs, and the integration of ethnic minorities and women in the workplace. At the same time McDonald's Netherlands started to make profits, which alleviates the pressure to keep costs to an absolute minimum, and somewhat later McDonald's seems to have become more sensitive to its public image, in which fear of negative publicity plays a role.

Conclusions

The findings about McDonald's in the Netherlands can be interpreted in different ways. One may argue that in the course of time, the company changed its policies towards unions and employee representatives from the predominantly hostile towards the fairly cooperative. As such this foreign multinational could be seen as over time making some adaptations to the norms and values of this particular host country. However, this conclusion would be too straightforward. It suggests a more or less gradual and automatic adaptation to local conditions. A number of qualifications must be made, however.

In the first place, the Dutch industrial relations scene has known its periods of conflict as well: the 1970s especially, the decade in which McDonald's first entered the Netherlands, can be characterized as such. McDonald's market approach was experimental and its relationship with unions strained. The latter stayed so for the larger part of the 1980s, but ultimately the company and the unions started negotiating. This fits with the overall relaxation of Dutch industrial relations after the signing of the *Accoord of Wassenaar*. Both parties' approaches could perhaps be seen as representative of the general trend at the time. The impact of the Dutch societal framework has arguably also meant that, over time, management felt no need for union avoidance strategies in any case sectoral agreements automatically applied to McDonald's whether it signed up to them or not. Indeed, given the generally cooperative attitudes in Dutch society in general and in industrial relations in particular, such a policy would appear foolish. This might have been different, of course, if Dutch unions had not agreed upon and stuck to leaving decisions on work organization as a managerial prerogative – where works councils would normally be active. Such union interference could conceivably lead to clashes with McDonald's strict policies on operations management and quality control.

In the second place, in the 1980s McDonald's types of job matched perfectly with the unions' strategies of redistributing work and encouraging employment for women and ethnic minorities. The company simply happened to offer the kinds of job that the unions felt were needed at the time. However, Stekelenburg would certainly not have praised McDonald's if its overall attitudes toward unions had been contested.

In the third place, McDonald's policy change must not be mistaken for a humanitarian concern for democracy. As a caterer to mass markets, and as a subject of various pressure groups and more recently because of the tight labour market, the company has to be concerned about its public image. Certainly in a country where consensual relationships are more common, open hostility between a company and various interest groups may be detrimental to the generation of additional sales. Being already an icon for anti-American sentiments, it would be unwise to stir up the fire by conflicts with unions. Thus, however self-interested McDonald's is by opting for cooperation with unions, this appears to have been a decision made by the Dutch headquarters instead of opting for a confrontational course as they did for roughly the first 15 years of their existence in the Netherlands.

Finally, attitudes towards employee representation vary within McDonald's in the Netherlands, and have changed over time. Most restaurants are operated by franchisees, and their individual attitudes and behaviours towards their employees obviously matter. However Dutch these franchisees may be, some of them are against constraints imposed on their managerial prerogatives by employee representatives. As in Germany and in some other Dutch companies, works council avoidance certainly does occur, but this is something that, publicly at least, the Dutch headquarters does not condone. The company-level works council was only effectively established in 1999 and at the initiative of the HRM director. However, this company-level works council only represents McDonald's small number of wholly-owned restaurants and not the 90 per cent of restaurants operated by franchisees in the Netherlands. Thus, in this particular case the foreign multinational can indeed be seen to some extent to have adapted to the host country's norms. Yet the process was and is by no means automatic, complete, or free of self-interest.

Acknowledgements

The chapter has benefited from comments by Paul Abraas, Mark van Bijsterveld, Willem de Nijs, Hans Slomp, Jac van Hoof, Patrick Vermeulen, several company representatives from McDonald's Nederland, and of course the editors. We also thank the interviewees and all others who provided data.

7 To Russia with Big Macs

Labour relations in the Russian fast-food industry

Stanislav V. Shekshnia, Sheila M. Puffer and Daniel J. McCarthy

Introduction

The concept of fast-food has been almost entirely foreign in Russia with its tradition of long *zastolie*, or dining sessions, complete with tables laden with *zakusky*, or hors d'oeuvres, and drinks, accompanied by endless toasts and songs. Additionally, food shortages have been widespread within the country over much of its history, particularly during much of the communist period. How could fast-food establishments be accepted in a country where food has always been regarded, at all levels of society, as a symbol of affluence? Within this cultural setting, which seemed inimical to the success of the fast-food concept, McDonald's has become the most visible symbol of a foreign company's success in Russia, with its fifty-eight restaurants in a dozen cities, and plans for opening fifteen to twenty restaurants in the country annually (*Russian Business Monitor*, 2000). Moreover, employing more than 5,000 people, the company has remained one of the more important employers for younger Russians for the past decade (*Boston Globe*, 2000). On 31 January 2000, in fact, McDonald's celebrated the tenth anniversary of its first Moscow restaurant, which remains the largest and busiest McDonald's in the world (McDonald's Web site, 2000). Its staying power is even more striking in comparison with Kentucky Fried Chicken and Pizza Hut, which entered Russia later, exited for a short time after the country's financial crisis of mid-1998, and then re-entered (Barshay, 1993; Rubinfien, 1993). How have McDonald's policies and practices toward its labour force contributed to the company's commercial success? And to what extent have its human resource (HR) practices and policies been country-specific, or have they been driven primarily by corporate policies and culture?

To provide a context in which to view McDonald's activities and policies in Russia, the chapter begins by covering the evolution of public catering in the country from 1917 to 1990, as well as the broader economic and political contexts in which this occurred. The nascent fast-food industry in Russia after 1990 is then reviewed, emphasizing the role of McDonald's in this process, as well as the competitive developments which occurred during the decade. The chapter then focuses on managing labour at McDonald's and presents conclusions about labour relations in the Russian fast-food industry.

Much of the data for this chapter are based on interviews conducted by the first author with company managers and employees in Moscow and St Petersburg in mid-1999. Additional information about the company, its employees and employment practices during its start-up phase in Russia was drawn from an article published by the second author and her Russian co-author (Vikhanski and Puffer, 1993). Some information also came from an interview with the senior Moscow McDonald's manager conducted by the same co-author (Vikhanski, 1992). Finally, an extensive literature review of academic and practitioner publications was conducted. This yielded substantial information on the Russian fast-food industry, McDonald's operations in Russia, and labour legislation and trade union issues.

The historical context: public catering and the economy 1917–1990

The Russian empire before the Communist Revolution of 1917 was a vast territory with almost 150 million people scattered between its borders, but located primarily in the European part. Over 70 per cent of the population lived in the countryside and three out of four Russian citizens were illiterate. The economic progress of the late nineteenth and early twentieth centuries created a few pockets of relatively modern heavy industry in some major cities, and attracted hundreds of thousands of peasants to them. However, the service sector remained small and undeveloped. Public catering consisted almost exclusively of serving wealthy people at expensive restaurants and cafés. The working population ate lunch brought from home, or could sometimes afford to stop at *traktir* or cheap restaurants, with a limited menu and infamously slow service. The fare was usually a bowl of *shchee*, or hot cabbage soup, and a glass of vodka. Family dining for all classes was reserved for the home, and women and young children almost never ate out.

The 1917 Bolshevik Revolution set a course toward a collectivist society, with the development of public catering as one of the government's priorities. In the early days of the Soviet state, a primary objective was to 'liberate' women from the kitchen to work in other pursuits, with meals being prepared in industrial and other public settings. Accordingly, such catering enterprises mushroomed, the most common form being the *stolovaya*, or cafeteria, where people could get a traditional Russian lunch of soup, a hot main course, and even a limited variety of desserts. Most organizations had their own *stolovaya*, usually with subsidized prices.

The closest thing to a private fast-food operation was the *pirozhkovaya* where a variety of hot *pirozhky*, or small pies, was sold along with hot broth, tea, and coffee. Their number, however, remained limited, since many people believed that fast-food was unhealthy! This notion was supported by the state-controlled medical community, which probably shaped this popular view. In addition, the Central Planning Committee allocated one hour for a lunch break to every Soviet employee, and few people seemed to be in a rush to return to work earlier!

The concept of broad-based public catering, which saw people eating most meals outside the home, showed signs of breaking down by the late 1920s. The quality and service deteriorated and food shortages became more severe. Furthermore, the industrial base was not capable of feeding 170 million people. Also, many Russians were reluctant to give up their favourite homemade foods and the traditions of spending time with family and friends around the dinner table.

Trade unions in the former Soviet Union

After the communists incorporated the independent trade unions in the early 1920s, they created a centrally managed system of 'pocket unions' in which every industry branch had its own union with sub-branches in each enterprise. The ideally declared purpose of unions was to defend workers' rights and provide opportunities for participation in the management of production. However, Marxism/Leninism could not conceive of unions as other than being a vehicle for Communist Party member plant managers to maintain tight control of workers and to deliver the will of the Party (Grancelli, 1988; Ballot, 1995). Union membership came automatically with employment, and people working in public catering, for instance, became members of the Union of Trade and Public Catering. Unions were managed centrally by the All Union Central Council of Trade Unions. Union leaders were formally elected in open ballots, but the outcomes were predetermined, since candidates were nominated by local Communist Party officials. These organizations actually served as arms of the Communist Party in ideological terms, and were referred to by Lenin as 'a school of Communism'. Wages were determined by the central government, without collective bargaining in the USSR. However, unions administered sick pay and social funds, after centrally determined allocations to activities in each enterprise by the government. In the later years of the Soviet regime, trade unions were given more voice in controlling safety at work, and also began establishing their own technical training schools to provide training and retraining to workers and local union representatives.

Public catering as a part of the economy's service sector was regarded as a secondary industry, far less important than heavy industry and manufacturing. Accordingly, the sector had low wages. In 1986, for instance, its average monthly wage was 153 rubles compared to the national average of 195 (Narodnoe, 1987). Yet the food service industry was a relatively attractive and somewhat prestigious place to work, because of chronic food shortages throughout the 70-year communist regime. Workers had for many years experienced the problems arising from food shortages, facing near-empty shelves in food stores, and enduring the inordinately long waits in lines to purchase basic food necessities. It was common practice for workers in the food-service industry to help themselves to available food, and management often turned a blind eye to this practice. Being able to share with family and friends in a shortage-ridden environment brought status to these workers.

Russia's emerging market economy

In 1985, Mikhail Gorbachev became General Secretary of the Communist Party and emphasized the need to infuse new life into the stagnating Soviet economy. In 1987, he fostered legislation which allowed joint ventures between foreign investors and domestic cooperatives, or small private enterprises. In December 1991, he resigned as president of the Soviet Union, and the newly independent Russian Federation aspired to the prospect of political freedom and economic prosperity. A decade later, however, the results of this journey were still very mixed (Clarke, 1995; Hertz, 1997; Holden *et al.*, 1998; Puffer *et al.*, 2000; Sherghneva and Feldhoff, 2000).

Entering 2000, Russia was still the largest country in the world geographically, with a population of 146 million people, but it was declining at a rate of 0.2 per cent per year. Its GDP, which had experienced some growth in the later 1990s after years of deep decline during the earlier part of the decade, contracted again following the August 1998 financial crisis. This crisis also saw the ruble's marked devaluation against the US dollar and other foreign currencies. Russian GDP continued to shrink throughout the reform years, declining by over 40 per cent, with a 5 per cent drop in GDP as well as in industrial production during the financial crisis year of 1998 alone (*Economic Newsletter*, February 1999). In 1999 there were some improvements in the economy, with a marked increase in industrial output in virtually every month compared to the 1998 monthly figures. Such increases, boosted by much higher oil prices, raised tax revenues to a level where the 1999 consolidated budget of the Russian republic actually had a small surplus in the third quarter (*Economic Newsletter*, December 1999).

The service sector's share increased from 40 per cent of GDP in 1990 to 51 per cent in 1998, not as a result of marked growth, but because of the dramatic decline in mining and manufacturing. The hardest hit area was the military-industrial sector, which declined by almost 70 per cent during that period. Inflation, which reached over 1,000 per cent in 1992, was successfully controlled from 1996 to 1998, but soared again after the August 1998 crisis to 84 per cent for that year (*Economic Newsletter*, February 1999). In 1999, however, inflation abated somewhat, reflecting the increase in domestically produced consumer products, with an accompanying decrease in imported consumer products due to the reduced purchasing power of the ruble (Coker, 1999).

Economic problems in general had a negative impact on the nation's living standards. Retail sales, overall, were 2 per cent lower in October compared to 1999 the same month a year earlier. This was in spite of the fact that industrial production was expected to increase by over 2 per cent for the year. A dramatic negative effect of the 1998 financial crisis was the significant increase to 75 per cent of the population having incomes falling below the government's established poverty level of around $30 per month in 1999. The income of the average Russian decreased during the first 10 months of 1999 by nearly 20 per cent compared to the same period in 1998 (*Economic Newsletter*, December 1999).

At the same time, a super-rich class of 'New Russians', consisting of some entrepreneurs, corrupt government officials, and even former black-marketeers and criminals emerged. They assumed a key role in the country's political and economic life and many exhibited blatant, conspicuous consumption. In September 1999, for instance, the richest 10 per cent of the population earned 14.5 times as much as the poorest 10 per cent. Moscow clearly remained the most prosperous centre of the country with 22 per cent of its population being at the upper level standard of living during the first half of 1999, compared with 4 per cent for the country as a whole. Surprisingly, St Petersburg, the second largest city, was far below Moscow in the highest living standard category, and even below the national average (*Economic Newsletter*, December 1999).

The Russian middle class, consisting of a small group of professionals, small business owners, and corporate managers, had started to flourish in the large cities in the second half of the 1990s. However, this group was severely affected by the August 1998 financial crisis, and many individuals had to adjust their lifestyles to the limitations brought about by a devalued ruble. The economic development of the 1990s had also affected different geographic regions unevenly. In some regions, economic reforms went much further than in others. Moscow, the country's capital with a population of 10 million, accounted for over 35 per cent of all federal taxes collected, and was estimated to have attracted 70 per cent of the New Russians' money. The city, which was one of the most expensive places in the world even before the August devaluation, was by far the most attractive market in the country. Other promising cities included St Petersburg, Nizhny Novgorod, Samara, Kazan, and Sochi.

Although tangible results of the political and economic reforms in the 1990s were far less than planned, they did have a significant impact on the country's institutions. The newly adopted Russian constitution guaranteed basic human rights and liberties, including the right to private property, and established a system to protect these rights, although it did not always function well. Another major change during the period saw over 65 per cent of Russia's GDP being generated by private companies, while more than 50 per cent of the labour force became employed in the private sector. The government had privatized virtually all major industries, with the exception of power generation and gas, and had also created a system of private commercial banks.

Labour relations in the new Russia

After 1991, Russian governmental bodies began restructuring the labour market and its governing institutions, as well as passing new legislation. Three major sources for reforming labour relations were government institutions including the new constitution of 1993, labour legislation, and labour unions. The Russian constitution adopted by a public referendum in 1993 guaranteed Russian citizens the right to work in safe and healthy conditions, receive nondiscriminatory compensation, and be protected against unemployment. The practical application of these reforms was, however, slow in being accomplished, causing many problems for employers, employees, and their representatives.

Labour legislation entering the twenty-first century consisted of the Labour Code, stand-alone laws of the Russian Federation and its constituent regions, and presidential and ministerial decrees. Russia also ratified numerous conventions of the International Labour Organization (ILO), covering various aspects of labour relations. Legislation was based on what had existed during Soviet times, but this foundation was amended in 1991–1992 with the objective of reflecting the new realities of an emerging market economy. Legislation, for instance, provided the right of employees to organize in labour unions, contest management decisions, and to strike.

The Labour Code of the Russian Federation is a set of laws regulating employment. The Code was approved by the Supreme Soviet of the Communist regime in 1971 but was extensively modified in September 1992, with additional changes made throughout the 1990s. The Code regulates a wide range of employment issues such as individual and collective labour agreements, working hours and conditions, compensation and benefits, safety, discipline at work, labour unions and conflicts, and State social security. Late in the decade, the Code consisted of eighteen chapters containing 255 articles. The general tenor of the Code was pro-employee, but having been adopted under the Soviet regime, it still contained many loopholes allowing employers to circumvent its requirements. Combined with the population's limited understanding of legal issues, it is not generally regarded as an effective instrument in regulating labour relations. The need for a completely new labour code has been advocated many times both by employers and trade unions. However, the State Duma, or Lower House of the Russian Parliament, was dominated by the Communists, and successfully blocked moves in this direction.

After 1992, however, the Russian Parliament adopted a number of specific laws governing labour relations, including the 'law on employment of the Russian Federation', 'the law on resolving collective labour disputes', 'the law on trade unions, their rights and guarantees of their activity', and 'the law on foundations of safety at work'. In general, the new laws were more comprehensive and appropriate for an emerging market economy than the old Labour Code. But some of the earlier problems remained, notably the excessive dominance of the State over the interests of the social partners.

Numerous decrees and executive orders issued by the President and Council of Ministers addressed less fundamental issues of labour legislation such as 'Recruitment and employment of a foreign labour force in Russia', and 'Reimbursement of personal vehicle use for business purposes'. Still, presidential decrees have been viewed as more pro-market than the Labour Code or federal laws adopted by the conservative Duma. Also, the eighty-nine regions and autonomous republics issued their own laws and decrees that were supposed to complement and not contradict federal laws. Finally, local or municipal administrators also had the right to adopt acts regulating labour relations at their level, consistent with the existing legal frameworks of higher-level government bodies. Multiple levels of legislative and executive power, however, have contradicted each other and added complexity to the system of legal norms perhaps already overburdened with an excessive number of regulations.

The same traditions manifested themselves in the way the government organized its direct participation in labour relations. The top executive body responsible for this activity was the Ministry of Labour and Social Development. Its mandate was to promote full employment, safe working conditions, and professional training to ensure the social welfare of Russian citizens, as well as to monitor the labour market, living standards, and other important employment and social indicators. Within the Ministry, two major departments directly participated in employment relations – the Federal Employment Service and the Federal Labour Inspection Service. The Employment Service is charged with matching people to jobs and administering unemployment benefits. In its first role, the Service operates as a traditional employment agency recording applicants and job vacancies in its databases, scheduling interviews, and providing basic training such as interviewing skills and computer basics. Poorly financed and under-equipped, these employment offices deal primarily with low-skilled employees and poorly paid jobs. To receive unemployment benefit, people often have to wait in line for hours, every two weeks, to confirm their status. Thus, not surprisingly, the number of officially registered unemployed is generally thought to be only a small percentage of the real number of jobless.

The Ministry's second arm, the Federal Labour Inspection Service, operating in similar difficult circumstances as the Employment Service, is responsible for ensuring compliance with existing labour legislation. It consists of a head office in Moscow as well as offices in each of the Federation's regions, and the organization employs about 5,200 administrators who enjoy wide discretion in exercising power. They have the right to enter any enterprise at any time and receive any internal document, except those containing confidential State or commercial information. They can fine the general manager of an inspected company, and also determine what compensation an employer should pay to an employee injured at work. An inspector's decision can be disputed in court, but only after it has been implemented. The relatively small number of inspectors and the meagre salaries they receive make them easy targets for bribes, and these realities contribute to the lack of enforcement of labour relations under the organization's jurisdiction (Petrick and Rinefort, 1999).

The final level of State involvement in labour relations is the judicial system. There is no special court for labour issues at the federal level in Russia. There are district courts, city courts, regional and republic-level courts, as well as the Supreme Court of the Russian Federation. Russia has no system of representative juries, and instead courts are headed by a professional lawyer assisted by two elected jury members. During the Soviet regime, the Communist Party controlled the courts, and an employee's appeal against an employer could lead to long-lasting negative consequences for the employee. Thus, there is no real tradition of such court disputes. During the 1990s, however, the number of labour disputes brought to the courts increased significantly, but such an action is still often regarded as an unusual act of bravery or desperation. The complex system of labour legislation and other circumstances are additional factors discouraging workers from taking their disputes to court. As in other countries economic conditions also make it difficult, because very few people can afford to pay for an attorney's services. In spite of these limitations on bringing cases to court, poorly paid judges and their assistants at the district level are often sympathetic toward employees rather than employers, who are sometimes perceived as exploiters. However, large organizations can usually construct a defence unaffordable to plaintiffs, and win their cases. Finally, court decisions are still far from being free from the political influence of local administrators or business elites.

Role of Russian trade unions

The Russian trade union movement experienced some clear setbacks during the 1990s (Borisov *et al.*, 1994; Blasi and Panina, 1994). This decline was due primarily to three specific factors, in addition to fundamental political and economic changes. First, political liberalization made it possible in practice to avoid becoming a member of a union, and allowed workers to set up or join alternative trade unions rather than the traditional ones. Second, the government's decision to take the distribution of sick benefits away from the unions made union membership much less attractive, leading millions of people to stop paying union dues. Highly mobile groups of employees such as young professionals and creative people left initially, followed by other employees of all trades and demographic characteristics. Third, many employers, beginning with newly created private companies and some of those with foreign investors, made it clear that unions were not welcome in their enterprises (Borisov *et al.*, 1994).

As a result of these circumstances, the old Soviet-era union federation, which was renamed the Federation of Russia's Independent Unions, lost many members and much of its status. It did, however, preserve most of its assets, including training and research centres, recreation facilities, and real estate. After a few years of experiencing a deep identity crisis, new leadership arose within the Federation with an objective of reversing the negative trend in the union federation's membership. It also aimed to increase its influence in Russian politics by adopting a more moderate approach to labour–management relations. The new leadership began to cooperate actively with the Russian executive branch, parliament, and the International Labour Organization in monitoring labour market and employment conditions, retraining employees, and fostering more effective legislation. The leaders seemed to recognize that the creation and proliferation of competitive private companies, both domestic and foreign, served their interests by creating employment, and thus the union supported the growth of such enterprises, especially smaller ones.

In spite of its new face, however, and some changes in its approach, the Federation retained much of its old ideology and methods. It still preferred to deal with the government rather than with specific employers, and to have an impact at the macro rather than micro level. For example, the Federation actively promoted the raising of the minimum wage, controlling manager's compensation in state-owned enterprises, and creating a federal retraining programme financed by the government.

Such macro-level initiatives, however, often did not appeal to rank-and-file members who sometimes sought alternatives by creating their own independent unions. Most new unions remained single enterprise organizations, but some grew to become industry-level organizations, such as the All-Russia Miners' Union. New unions still played the traditional role of representing employees and continued to deal with collective agreements, benefits, and working conditions. Their approach was at times confrontational and some saw wildcat strikes as a legitimate tool to protect the interests of their members. Most of these unions were in traditional industries such as mining, metallurgy, and manufacturing, all of which had suffered greatly from the economic restructuring and downsizing of the 1990s, and thus retained relatively few members.

The fast-food industry in Russia since 1990

These are the labour market contexts in which foreign fast-food multinationals like McDonald's have been establishing themselves in Russia. As we have seen, on the surface at least, these historical and social conditions did not appear to be all that favourable for the modern fast-food concept. In fact McDonald's was not the first US-style restaurant. TrenMos Restaurant had been opened some years earlier by an American, Shelley Zeiger, a 20-year veteran of the Russian business scene (Zeiger, 1994). McDonald's' first restaurant, the company's largest in the world, opened its doors in January 1990, 10 years after the company's Canadian franchisee approached the Moscow City Council with a proposal to set up operations for the 1980 Moscow Olympic Games (Cohon, 1999). Paradoxically it appears that Moscovites developed a taste for McDonald's products much faster than expected, and the restaurant became an overnight success (Schlosser, 2001). Kilometre-long queues began forming and a black market even sprang up when enterprising Moscow teenagers began re-selling hot McDonald's meals at a profit to people willing to pay but with no patience to wait in line. Moscow McDonald's was a joint venture between the company's Canadian franchisee and Mosrestorantrust, the Moscow City Organization for Restaurant Management (Vikhanski and Puffer, 1993). Restaurants were at first limited to Moscow and the surrounding region, but in 1996, the company opened outlets in Nizhny Novgorod and St Petersburg, and later in Samara and Kazan. By the year 2001, McDonald's had fifty-eight restaurants in Russia, of which twenty-six were in Moscow, and the company planned to open fifteen to twenty new restaurants in Russia annually.

McDonald's and its rivals

Entering the new century, McDonald's clearly controlled the lion's share of Russia's dollar-based fast-food market. Unlike the Russian economy overall, this market had grown steadily since the early 1990s, with McDonald's expansion leading the way. Its restaurants, and later those of other fast-food companies, attracted specific groups within Russian society whose needs could not be met by the traditional, and still deteriorating, public catering industry. One group consisted of teenagers, who were greatly influenced by Western culture and lifestyles and were looking for a trendy place to eat. Young professionals were another group who had discovered McDonald's as teenagers in the 1990s, to whom time was a scarce resource. They saw such restaurants as clean and pleasant places and in which they were served quickly. Russians also began to place more importance on food that was safe to eat, and McDonald's food contained ingredients that were prepared under strict sanitary conditions. Families with children were the third group; they sought an affordable and inviting place to eat out on weekends. One young mother was noted as saying that she brought her children to McDonald's every Saturday, and that they enjoyed the food, especially the pies (Blundy, 1999). Each of these groups appeared to value the standards of cleanliness and service, and perhaps more importantly, a Western atmosphere.

McDonald's early success attracted other players to the fast-food market and many appeared to be adopting a similar strategy, but none seemed to be able to challenge the international giant's dominant position. Russia's fast-food industry in the late 1990s consisted of three types of operation. The first was McDonald's, the only remaining foreign chain with a nationally recognized trademark.[1] The second group consisted of local chains such as Rostiks, a company started by a Venezuelan entrepreneur with restaurants in Moscow and St Petersburg (Ingram, 1994). Another local chain, Russkoye Bistro, which was highly promoted by the Moscow City Council as the local answer to McDonald's, had twenty restaurants in Moscow, and others in St Petersburg called Carolls (Specter, 1995). In 1996, an American opened the New York Pizza restaurant in Novosibirsk, and by 1998 had seven locations in that Siberian city (Mulhern, 1998). The third group of fast-food operations consisted of thousands of stand-alone Russian restaurants spread across the country. Generally, none of these could compete with McDonald's. Some tried to differentiate by adding a Russian touch, such as Russkoye Bistro, whose manager was quoted as saying: 'this food is in the Russian blood' (Specter, 1995), and Rostiks, which featured a chicken flavour in its signature dishes, or house specialties. But usually, most competitors resorted to price-cutting in order to compete. Finally, unlike McDonald's, these Russian restaurants usually sold alcohol, which appealed to some customer segments. They typically offered very limited menus and food of questionable quality, and competed primarily on location and price. McDonald's, in contrast, appeared to maintain higher quality levels, despite sourcing 75 per cent of its food locally. The quality of its Russian-produced meat and pies was high enough to export to its restaurants in seventeen other countries, including Germany and Austria (*Boston Globe*, 2000).

Fast-food companies faced inflationary pressures throughout the 1990s. In the early 1990s those like McDonald's and Pizza Hut tried to keep their prices reasonable (Ostrow, 1992) even though by January 1993, for instance, the price of a Big Mac, fries, and drink was 1,100 rubles, compared to 6 rubles when the restaurant opened three years earlier (McKay, 1993). As we mentioned earlier, however, inflation reached over 1,000 per cent in 1992. The country's 1998 financial crisis hit the industry hard by forcing many restaurant customers to adjust their lifestyles. According to industry estimates, the total fast-food market lost more than half of its value. In its smaller segment, however, McDonald's improved its relative position, although sales dropped initially by 25 per cent. With the depressed economic conditions, the company took immediate marketing action and lowered prices. The price of a Big Mac hamburger was cut to the dollar-equivalent of $1.38 in 2000, down substantially from the $2.10 charged in 1990 (*Boston Globe*, 2000). The company also addressed costs by modifying its menu to include less costly traditional Russian items. In contrast, the competition continued doing business as usual, before retreating to even more limited menus and lower quality, as well as layoffs and other defensive actions. Some multinational chains left Russia, if only temporarily.

Defections such as Pizza Hut and KFC, coupled with the dramatic decrease in the ruble's purchasing power, made room for some smaller local fast-food businesses to open and grow (Coker, 1999).

Managing labour at McDonald's

Entering the year 2000, McDonald's was the only multinational corporation operating full-menu restaurants in the Russian fast-food industry. Some limited product operations such as Baskin-Robbins ice cream parlours and Coca-Cola kiosks, however, still remained in business. The dominant position enjoyed by McDonald's in Russia makes it a natural candidate for a detailed examination of its employment practices, although it should be noted that it is only part of a rapidly expanding sector. Nevertheless, as market leader and most significant employer in the sector it may be that they influence the activities of other companies. The following analysis examines the impact of the local labour market and legislative frameworks on the corporation.

McDonald's approach to managing employees in Russia appears to be an essential and integral part of its overall business strategy in the country. McDonald's managers report that the human resource strategy was outlined well before the first restaurant opened in Moscow, and changed little after that. As a joint venture, the Canadian partner was, from the outset, responsible for management methods and systems, including technology, business processes, and human resource management. All McDonald's restaurants in Russia have been wholly owned by the joint venture, which has helped to ensure uniformity of management systems. Still, it took a long time and great effort to fully implement these systems, beginning with the first two restaurants in Moscow. Early on, a significant number of local employees were trained in 'the McDonald's way of doing things', and later became 'change agents' at other company operations. This approach clearly helped them to develop their network of restaurants. Training, in fact, has always played two important roles within McDonald's: to provide employees with the skills they need to perform their jobs, as well as to inculcate them with the company culture (Vikhanski and Puffer, 1993). Although the company consistently attempted to provide employees with what it viewed as necessary skills and attitudes, its approach has been criticized by some as being too one-sided, since employees had little or no input into human resource policies and procedures.

By the beginning of 2000 McDonald's had invested $140 million in Russia (*Boston Globe*, 2000). It appeared to be following the same long-term outlook that contributed to the successful operations of multinationals in other industries (McCarthy and Puffer, 1997; Puffer *et al.*, 1998). At the same time McDonald's human resource management policies were nearly identical to those used in Canada. This practice is consistent with findings about McDonald's' emphasis on international standardization found in Europe

(Royle, 2000). This approach was sometimes called by some McDonald's employees as 'leave Russia at the entrance door' management. Even job titles preserved their Canadian names of crew, crew trainer, restaurant manager, and the like. The employment system, as in North America, utilized ten grades which defined employee job functions, training needs, compensation, and other benefits. The first four grades applied to hourly-paid workers who would generally be regarded as non-management in the West. The company's approach to hiring, training, motivation, and compensation was applied in a thorough and consistent fashion. In fact, some Russian entrepreneurs may have learned some 'valuable' lessons from McDonald's about managing human resources (Puffer *et al.*, 2000).

From the start, management was clear about the kind of people it wanted for its restaurants: young, mobile, flexible, honest, and without any previous experience in the food industry. The reason for the last criterion was that the company wanted them to be free of negative experiences such as theft, unfriendly service, and on-the-job drinking that often occurred in Russian restaurants during the communist period. Managers, however, were selected from applicants with experience in the country's food industry. The first McDonald's recruitment advertisements in Moscow newspapers attracted 27,000 candidates. From that wide selection of people, managers recruited 630 who seemed closely to fit the company's profile, and almost all those hired possessed, or were finishing, a college degree.

After a decade, recruitment of hourly paid employees was still done at the individual restaurant level, with the number of hires approved by the headquarters operations manager, who controlled headcount. Candidates usually sent in application forms they had picked up at a restaurant, or they responded to newspaper advertisements in youth or mass-market newspapers. The interviewing process had been modelled on the one used in Canada, and all restaurant managers and assistant managers were trained in the requisite skills. However, the profile of new lowest grade entrants, who were subject to a three-month probation period, changed somewhat in the later 1990s as a result of a smaller applicant pool. Although graduates were attracted to management positions very few people with a college education were interested in such jobs, and more young people without higher education were hired. Women began to predominate in most hourly-paid positions, while at the management level, men continued to be in the majority. College students and recent graduates began to constitute a significant number of crew trainers and swing managers, the highest 'non-salaried' (often part-time) positions. Still, the majority of hourly paid employees remained young, and single, and mobile. Annual employee turnover at crew level was close to 70 per cent. In the case of full-time swing managers it steadily declined to an annual level of about 10 per cent. Compared with turnover rates in other countries such as Canada and the US this is of course very low, particularly when one considers the characteristics of the workforce. However, Royle (2000) has already shown that turnover rates tend to be reflected in particular labour market conditions, such as the level of unemployment and the degree of labour market segmentation. For example, labour turnover rates at McDonald's in Germany, Italy and Austria are also much lower than in other countries. The corporation made much of these lower turnover rates on 31 January 2000 when it marked the tenth anniversary of the first Russian McDonald's in Pushkin Square: 100 original employees were recognized for their decade of service (McDonald's Web site, 2000).

The company's hiring practices in Russia might be seen as discriminatory against some social groups, such as older people, married candidates, and applicants with food industry experience. Such policies would even be seen as unacceptable in the US and even more so in relation to prevailing EU standards. McDonald's appears to be acting within existing practice and societal norms, and during its first decade in Russia, not a single suit had been filed challenging its hiring or firing decisions. However, this may be reflective of the fact that at that time both Russian labour law and litigation practice were quite underdeveloped, particularly in this area. Even under the later reforms the notion of discrimination was absent from the Russian Labour Code. Despite the positive outcomes for the company as a result of transporting its systems and policies virtually unchanged from its North American base, questions must be raised about the appropriateness of such a strategic approach for a multinational company. Although the company was operating in a manner that seemed to be consistent with the Russian legal and social environments, some of its policies would be unlawful or socially unacceptable in North America and certainly in Europe. This is especially true of its discriminatory hiring and promotion policies, although in the context of Russian society this may be seen as acceptable.

In addition the company has been criticized for its attempts to prevent the unionization of its operations, effectively denying employees the right to representation. For example McDonald's has had to deal with this issue at its food producing plant in Solntsevo near Moscow, where workers earned less than restaurant employees. Royle (2000) also reports that in 1998 McDonald's laid off workers and reduced wages, and that union officials claim that many who had signed voluntary redundancy forms did not get a pay-off. Unhappy with intensive work schedules and what they perceived as inadequate compensation and benefits, shopfloor employees attempted in 1999 to create a union to negotiate with management. For instance, workers claimed that inflation and devaluation of the ruble seriously eroded their wages (Charlton, 1999). Unions also allege that McDonald's responded immediately with a campaign of intimidation and harassment, with union supporters being threatened with loss of salary and benefits and transfer to more difficult jobs if they refused to sign papers denouncing the union. A forklift operator, for instance, stated that he had been disciplined six times in one year in the company's attempts to intimidate him and force him to quit the union (Wadhams, 2000). A union representative stated:

We have been told that if we form a union they will take away our benefits . . . they have organized our lunch breaks so that we can't get the message across to our colleagues.

(Blundy, 1999: 14)

In an official statement the chairman of McDonald's Russia denied such charges, arguing that the company respected employees' wishes and abided by local labour laws (Blundy, 1999). Royle (2000) also reports that officials at the International Trade Secretariat the IUF and the Commerce and Catering Workers Union protested to the city government and McDonald's. The government of Moscow initiated tripartite negotiations, which resulted in formal recognition of the union. However, McDonald's, in what can clearly be seen as typical American practice (Towers, 1997; Friedman *et al.*, 1994), has as yet resisted negotiations for a collective agreement. Despite continued pressure on union members, the union has begun to establish relations with workers at company-owned restaurants. Ironically the workers suggest that things were better when most managers were American (Blundy, 1999: 14): 'Nowadays they are mostly Russian and the regime is very strict and unfriendly.' Despite the corporation's denials these allegations tend to fuel concerns that multinationals frequently do not meet their own espoused values and codes of conduct, which frequently claim to 'value' employees. More widely these kinds of action can be seen by some as being inconsistent with the definition of representation as a human right as interpreted by the ILO and the European Court of Human Rights.

Though McDonald's have employment contracts with all their employees their value is limited from a labour perspective, especially for crew whose contract is largely restricted to the regulation of their compensation. They do, however, act as a written reinforcement of McDonald's management methods and culture. They emphasize employees' obligations as well as the disciplinary actions the company can take against them in cases where its rules are broken. Such contracts are consistent with existing Russian labour legislation, and penalties range from immediate dismissal in the case of theft, to reprimand and notice for minor violations such as poor service and lateness. The company has been strict in enforcing discipline, and repeated minor violations can lead to dismissal. Supervisors failing to discipline subordinates appropriately can themselves be reprimanded. The company maintains, however, that it prefers to focus on teaching and motivation rather than firing workers for contract violations. It also maintains that such penalties are necessary to guard against what it sees as 'lax' practices traditionally associated with the old Soviet food industry and to foster a strong work ethic. Although these views of the company are put forth as being in the best interests of the workforce as well as the company, this has to be seen in the context of the lack of direct representation for employees.

Russian labour law has established the maximum length of the work-week at 40 hours. McDonald's contracts, however, stipulate that full-time employees must work 157 hours a month, which means that in some weeks employees might work longer than 40 hours. The company does not pay overtime during such weeks, calling the system 'flexible working time'. The Russian Labour Code and legal practices remain quite vague in this regard, however, and no action has ever been taken against the company. McDonald's also hires part-time employees who are simultaneously pursuing full- or part-time education, but most are full-time employees with flexible work hours. The vast majority of employees are over 18 years of age because Russian labour law is extremely protective of younger workers, severely restricting their hours and working conditions. McDonald's has hired some temporary help, especially during the summer or for special events, such as the 850th anniversary of Moscow and the 200th anniversary of Pushkin's birth. These employees are given temporary contracts of up to three months and receive entry-level wages. It is doubtful that the company could pursue such flexible hiring practices if it were dealing with effective and independent unions, which may be another reason for the company's apparent opposition to trade union organization.

The compensation system, like most of the company's HR policies and practices, are a replica of the Canadian model. Employees at the first four grades are paid hourly rates fixed in local currency. Pay ranges are generally set and adjusted solely by management, but as in other countries all employees take part in the performance related pay system, which in theory is appraised by supervisors every quarter. Workers can be assigned ratings ranging from 1 to 4 with the highest grade (1) providing employees with a bonus equal to 8 per cent of their quarterly pay. Only a few employees received 1s, while as elsewhere a substandard performance (4) warrants a written notice, with three such warnings leading to dismissal. Restaurant managers, with grades of 4–6, receive semi-annual appraisals with five possible evaluation levels. The highest evaluation adds 17 per cent to monthly salaries, while the two lowest grades result in no bonus. The company utilizes geographical differences in pay levels, even though the overall compensation system is the same for all locations: Moscow has the highest pay rates, followed by St Petersburg, while all other regions have a uniform rate lower than that of these two major cities.

McDonald's' hourly-paid employees are also provided with uniforms (but not the cleaning of uniforms), some free food depending on the number of hours worked, and participation in company-sponsored events such as summer camps for children, free lunches for family members at company restaurants, and boat cruises on the Moscow or Neva rivers (Vikhanski, 1992). Additional benefits are provided for more senior-level employees, including medical and life insurance and company cars and other perks are sometimes provided for senior management.

In the area of compensation and benefits, as well as labour relations in general, McDonald's management takes the view that union representation is unnecessary, maintaining that it provides its employees with fair compensation, a healthy working environment, and opportunities for growth. In this view unions, seen as a 'third party', would only divert management's and employees' time and energy from serving customers and be contrary to the interests of the company. The company does not have a grievance procedure, since Russian law does not require such procedures, and because management has taken the stance that employees' problems can be taken care of through company communication channels.

Rather than spending time around a bargaining table, McDonald's' management has preferred to spend time and money with the objective of building clear performance and behavioural standards, involving 'communication' and social events for employees and their families. The message reinforced by these practices seems to be that, if employees show commitment and perform up to the required standard, the company will reward them with recognition, training, promotion, and compensation. The limitation of this seemingly altruistic approach, however, is clear. Management makes all the decisions with little or no input from workers, and certainly with no input from an independent organized employee group.

On the one hand management claim that the majority of company employees, who are young, 'Westernized', and often ambitious, accept this management approach. They also seem to have appreciated clear rules together with some opportunity to make a career without having connections at the top. On the other hand, however, many employees have little experience of any other style of management and this philosophy is sometimes regarded as overly 'capitalistic'. Management may find themselves being resisted by older employees, or those who might have demanding family obligations, or positive memories of their employment experience under the Soviet regime. Indeed McDonald's' management certainly are likely to continue to have difficulties with employees who would prefer to have their interests represented by independent trade union representation.

Conclusions

The Russian fast-food industry provides an interesting example of how Western management practices can be successfully applied in what might be considered to be a less than welcoming environment. Entering the year 2000, McDonald's was the only multinational company still operating in the Russian fast-food industry offering a full range of meals. Some of its rivals like KFC and Pizza Hut have for the time being withdrawn from the market. The company appeared to have imposed its North American management systems with little regard for Russian cultural and societal arrangements. The transfer of its North American human resource management system, which has been described as a 'leave Russia at the door' approach, undoubtedly has had the merit of speedily instilling McDonald's corporate culture into its Russian operations.

Yet despite its commercial success, its policies towards its employees appear to have been less than praiseworthy. The corporation clearly prefers to deal with labour issues internally, and thus avoid situations that might invite government or legal involvement into the company's employee relations. In particular McDonald's Russia has been criticized for steadfastly refusing to deal with trade unions seeking to represent its employees and has also refused the implementation of a collective agreement that would undoubtedly improve conditions and wage levels. It is also worth noting that the less than fully developed state of Russia's labour legislation and legal practices may have helped the corporation to implement its strategies in this regard. In addition there are also concerns about the way in which the corporation went about targeting young people in recruitment drives, practices which may not be acceptable in other countries where more developed labour legislation is in place. Though McDonald's is always insistent on building a strong corporate culture, it may be that a higher level of effective employee 'voice' in developing that culture would give its practices more legitimacy and allow for a much smoother transition into the Russian economy. Indeed a formal system of employee representation, independent of the company, would appear to be a necessary prerequisite, but this is something that the corporation still seems determined to oppose.

McDonald's management paradoxically maintains that it can take on the role of representing employees' interests, which it sees principally as fair compensation, reasonable working conditions, training, promotion opportunities based on merit, and social events for employees. Some aspects of the disciplinary rules may seem strict compared to 'looser' Russian standards, however the company maintains that the consistent enforcement of such rules helps establish an appropriate work ethic and stable behavioural norms, both of which it maintains are less common in many Russian companies. Overall, such actions, management maintains, make McDonald's an enjoyable place to work. Indeed the experience of working in such a successful Western corporation may be very positive for some. Nevertheless, the company faces opposition to many of its policies in practice, such as in hiring, work hours, employee evaluations and especially in terms of independent employee representation. The important point seems to be that organizations have a responsibility to treat employees with respect if they expect to gain their trust.

Acknowledgment

The authors would like to thank Gal Kollander, a Northeastern University MBA student, for his valuable research assistance in preparing this chapter.

Notes

1 PepsiCo had also set up a small number of Pizza Hut and KFC restaurants (Ostrow, 1992), but as noted earlier it temporarily exited the market after the country's 1998 financial crisis, but re-entered after a short period.

8 'McAunties' and 'McUncles'

Labour relations in Singapore's fast-food industry

Alexius A. Pereira

Introduction

The major players in the global fast-food industry are multinational corporations. This chapter focuses on one such multinational: the McDonald's Corporation. McDonald's has led the way in developing the modern fast-food industry in Singapore and is currently the market leader. We examine whether or not and if so to what extent McDonald's has been able to impose its home based labour relations practices in Singapore. It is generally accepted that the McDonald's menu, machinery, restaurant design and service system appear to be fairly standarized all over the world (Leidner, 1993; Ritzer, 1996). However, less obvious to the public eye are the company's training programmes, organizational structures and management and labour relations practices; to what extent are these matters standardized across the globe? The logic of standardization can be understood as a form of rational organizational centralization where for reasons of profit maximization, McDonald's retains control over thousands of franchises and company-owned restaurants. It does this through careful monitoring of processes and practices ensuring adherence to the corporation's system.[1] However, all global practices come up against social, economic and political structures in each society and country, where there may be unique (and sometimes incompatible) cultures, laws and practices. Royle's (2000) study suggests that, despite the diverse systems of labour relations in Europe, McDonald's has to a large extent been able to impose its host country system regardless of varying societal frameworks. In this light, this chapter analyses the case of McDonald's restaurants in Singapore in the period between 1979 and 1999.

The focus of this chapter is the employment relationship between the two main parties: the employer and the employee. It is important to stress that the employment relationship has both individual and collective dimensions. This means that the relationship is not just dependent on the social, economic and political relationships between the employer and the employee, but that there is the potential for collective relationships, where group-based relationships form the basis of trade unions or other forms of worker (and indeed employer) representation. However, employee relations are equally affected by other structures in society, including culture, laws and the economy. Therefore, this chapter will explain the implementation and evolution of McDonald's employee relations through an analysis of internal dynamics (between the employer and employee) and external structures (laws, culture and the economy).

Research for this chapter was conducted in Singapore between January and June 1997, involving in-depth face-to-face interviews with fifty crew members and twenty managers from nine McDonald's restaurants. The interviews asked the informants why they chose to join the corporation, how they were trained, their feelings about their terms and conditions of employment, and their general level of job satisfaction. Managers were asked additional questions including how they managed employees, implemented McDonald's Human Resource Management programme, and trained the crew members. The information was then supplemented with secondary data gathered from Singaporean newspaper articles between 1995 and 1999.

Employment relations in Singapore

McDonald's in Singapore provides an interesting case for the study of employee relations because the country is considered to be one of the archetypal 'developmental states' of Asia (Perry *et al.*, 1997). As such, employee relations, especially in the first two decades after national independence in 1965, have been described as conforming to the 'authoritarian corporatist' model, where 'industrial peace' was to be achieved at all costs (Deyo, 1981; Leggett, 1993a):

> The entire legal framework (for employee relations) is constructed to ensure industrial peace. Unions may only be formed under carefully stipulated rules. Their registration is at the discretion of the Labour Minister. The Government may de-register any union without stating reasons or having to justify the action in a court of law.
>
> (Deyo, 1981: 48)

An 'authoritarian corporatist' government would view politicized trade unions as being potentially able to destabilize political regimes or make economically damaging wage demands. Therefore, for the sake of industrial peace, a corporatist government would rationalize the suppression of trade union opposition. In this manner, incorporated trade unions would become the vehicle for socializing employees towards fulfilling their productionist role. Finally, where development and economic growth was dependent on foreign investment, industrialization was associated with the state's consolidation of 'authoritarian corporatism' (Deyo, 1981: 109; Leggett, 1993a: 223). In Singapore, the ruling People's Action Party government visibly demonstrated that disruptive strikes and labour unrest would not be tolerated, and marshalled state powers to stop any such action from taking place. This protected the state's programme of export-led industrialization driven by multinational corporations.

Singapore was not a 'natural' location for large-scale industrial activity; it lacked raw materials, had an extremely small indigenous market and more importantly had little industrial experience (Pereira, 2000b). In order to attract multinational corporations to locate in Singapore, Tan (1995) suggests that the government realized that its main competitive advantages were its strategic location in the Southeast Asian region and the availability of labour. Prior to 1965, the economy was plagued by frequent strikes, inter-union rivalry and political interference (Tan, 1995). Thus, the government consolidated various labour laws and policies in 1968, including the introduction of the Employment Act and the amendment of the Industrial Relations Act (Tan, 1995; Chew and Chew, 1995, 1996). The Industrial Relations Act gave more 'power' to the employer by excluding issues such as promotion, transfer, retirement, retrenchment, dismissal and work assignment, leaving them to be negotiated between the employers and employees. Also, it specified that negotiations between employers and unions were set at three years, with the hope that less frequent negotiations would reduce work stoppages and that the extended duration of the collective agreement would give a sense of certainty to the employers (Tan, 1995). Despite the 'pro-employer' bias, the state has legislated measures to provide 'basic' protection for employees. The law provided for a 44 hour working week, 7 days paid annual leave, eleven public holidays, 28 days paid sick leave, two months paid maternity leave and an overtime rate of time and a half and double time on Sundays and public holidays (Perry *et al.*, 1997: 55).

Another significant act by the government was to 'modernize' the National Trade Union Congress (NTUC). Formed in 1961, the 'new' NTUC emerged in 1969 to be the sole national union body in the country. By law, all unions had to be affiliated to the NTUC (Leggett, 1993b). Furthermore, the government placed many important members of parliament into key positions within the NTUC, including the post of Secretary General. This further strengthened the state's control over labour particularly as it had established a 'symbiotic' relationship with the government (Tan, 1995). The NTUC played an important role in the National Wages Council, a tripartite body where the government, employers and labour met annually to review the guidelines for wage changes in the country. While these guidelines were not mandatory, the government itself as the largest employer in the country usually accepted and followed the recommendations. Also, between 1970 and 1990, it was found that many large multinationals and local employers also adopted these guidelines (Chiu *et al.*, 1997).

Yet the most important state measure introduced in Singapore was to give workers the right to choose whether or not they wanted to join a union (Tan, 1995). Despite this, research has shown that union membership has been fairly high, especially in the industrial sector (Leggett, 1993a,

Table 8.1 Sector employment distribution, 1970–1995 (%)

Sector	1970	1980	1990	1994
Agriculture and mining	3.8	1.7	0.4	0.3
Manufacturing	22.1	30.1	29.1	25.6
Utilities	1.1	0.8	0.4	0.5
Construction	6.6	6.7	4.3	5.1
Commerce	23.4	21.3	25.7	24.5
Transport and communications	12.1	11.1	9.5	10.6
Finance and business services	4.0	7.4	10.9	12.0
Other services (including the Civil Service sector)	26.9	20.8	19.7	21.4

Source: Perry *et al.* (1997: 112).

1993b). However, union activism is very low, suggesting that if this were the goal of corporatism in Singapore it has been successful (see Chiu *et al.*, 1997). Subsequently, multinational corporations, particularly those that sought a 'docile' low cost workforce for manufacturing and assembly operations, flocked to Singapore and dominated the economy, eventually accounting for a quarter of both the country's output and employment since 1965, see Table 8.1.

The state's employment laws and policies were intentionally designed to regulate the labour market. More specifically, the state effectively manipulated the relative 'cost' of labour so that Singapore's wages would become globally competitive to multinational corporations. While the state appears to be overwhelmingly pro-employer in the labour relations system, it is difficult to argue that workers in Singapore have been unfavourably treated (Leggett, 1993a: 223). With the government's industrialization programme, the Singapore economy has enjoyed full employment since 1970, a labour shortage since 1975,[2] and consistent economic growth right up to the 1990s. The government has been careful to re-distribute much of the nation's wealth among the population, especially through the public housing schemes, national education programmes and social welfare schemes (particularly the use of the Central Provident Fund) (see Perry *et al.*, 1997).

This analysis highlights how employee relations in Singapore have been significantly structured by the state. The Singapore government's corporatist measures were designed to ensure a 'pro-business' environment primarily for the many multinational corporations involved in manufacturing activities. With the state's heavy emphasis on this sector, other sectors were comparatively more autonomous to determine their employment relations. One such autonomous sector was the hospitality and catering sector, under which the fast-food industry falls. Although the state's labour laws allowed employees in that sector to form and join unions, it was not mandatory (see Leggett, 1993b). This has important ramifications for McDonald's Restaurants' own employee relations, as the following sections will explain.

The McDonald's system

As suggested in the introductory section, one characteristic of a multi-national corporation is its utilization of uniform practices across the world. McDonald's Corporation believes that standardization is the most rational means of maximizing cost efficiencies. In addition, standardization has cultural functions, where the company maintains a global corporate image for marketing and advertising purposes[3] (Ritzer, 1996). McDonald's rationalization could be seen in its optimization of work processes, particularly through the use of technology. This is more than simply referring to the use of equipment and machinery, for McDonald's technology includes all processes from the preparation, cooking and serving of the food right up to the systems of financial accounting, ordering of stocks, staff planning and training. All these processes have been fine-tuned towards achieving cost and labour efficiency, and minimizing wastages (see Ritzer, 1996; Leidner, 1993). From the 1950s, McDonald's Corporation has adopted technologies in a Tayloristic and even Fordist sense, where all tasks are broken down into the simplest components. The result was a highly rational division of labour in the organization, where specific individuals from different groups in the labour market are assigned to corresponding tasks in the organization. In other words, the more complex the task, the company would recruit employees with greater levels of skills who can be found from higher segments of the labour market, and vice versa.

McDonald's Corporation's organizational structure and its use of technologies appear to influence its employment policy. McDonald's is structured into three main groups: the headquarters team, the restaurant managers and the crew members. The headquarters team refers to a small group of senior executives and managers in charge of public (community) relations, finance, personnel, human resources, training, property management and several other tasks.[4] McDonald's recruits qualified and experienced personnel to fill positions in the headquarters. As these individuals are normally found in the upper, tertiary segments of the labour market, their levels of remuneration tend to be correspondingly high. Also, their terms of employment are generally individually negotiated, usually consisting of formal employment contracts. Due to relatively short supply of such individuals, potential candidates for these positions have greater individual bargaining power with their employers. In the company, those from the headquarters team are in the most favourable position, even though they are the smallest in number. They command the highest salaries within the company, and they have decision-making and implementing powers over a wide variety of aspects, including the hiring and firing of other employees. The social status of an executive in the headquarters team is also very high but their numbers are few in comparison with the people employed in the restaurants either as managers or as crew. As the restaurant manager's task involves day-to-day management of the restaurant, McDonald's usually hires secondary school leavers to fill the post as the majority of the job's training is conducted within the restaurant itself. Restaurant managers began their careers in McDonald's as trainee managers, before rising to become second assistant manager, first assistant manager, and finally restaurant manager. The higher the managerial position, the greater the number and the complexity of tasks, including staffing, training and recruitment of crew members (and junior managers), budgeting, accounting, and maintaining discipline.

Numerically, crew members are the largest group in the organization, but are remunerated with the lowest wages. The crew's main tasks are preparing and serving the food, and cleaning the restaurant. As these tasks are relatively simplified due to the heavy rationalization of the technology, the McDonald's Corporation does not need to hire a person with a lot of education or skills. The crew face the least favourable employment conditions in comparison to the other two groups. For instance, while there might be a clear career path for the managers, the path for the crew is extremely limited and this seems to contradict the corporation's claims that many crew are promoted up the ranks into management. Thus, the status of the crew is also relatively low, occupying a marginal position in the organization; because of the nature of their tasks, McDonald's employs a significant proportion of the crew as part-timers. This is both to enhance the company's own flexibility – in the sense that the required levels of labour can be regulated to meet consumer demand – and also to keep costs down. Yet crew are extremely important to the company's own performance and operations; without sufficient numbers of crew, a restaurant could not function.

For its employment policies, McDonald's Corporation has its own 'espoused philosophy', which believes that issues of efficiency and equity can be dealt with without the need for unions (Love, 1995; Royle, 2000). The company has its own Human Resource Management programme, one which is similar to many other corporate HRM programmes, where the main objectives are to foster employee loyalty and to keep its employees 'satisfied' through 'individualizing' employee relations (Beaumont 1995: 39). In the context of McDonald's, collectivist notions about involving trade unions are seen as at best 'irrelevant' (Royle, 2000). In many HRM programmes, employers utilize a general package of measures designed to deliver workplace flexibility, employee involvement, commitment and identification with organizational objectives, the individualization of pay through knowledge or skills-based remuneration and new forms of direct communication, including team briefings and quality circles (see McGovern 1998: 21). Yet while HRM programmes supposedly seek to address employees' needs, such programmes also have the purposes of increasing productivity or efficiency (for wider discussion of HRM in employee relations see Blyton and Turnbull, 1998). At McDonald's, HRM functions are supposed to pre-empt the need for collective representation and bargaining, theoretically allowing the company to deal directly with each individual employee.

To summarize, due to its organization, centralization, use of technologies and its corporate philosophy, McDonald's has a distinct set of practices. For McDonald's, employee relations focus on its own HRM programme, where 'individualism' is preferred over 'collectivism'. Yet, in reality, individual bargaining and negotiation of employment terms and conditions is only available to the very few who are based at headquarters; otherwise, the corporation determines every aspect of the terms of employment and its broader conditions. As Royle (2000) and other contributors to this book suggest, these employee relations practices are implemented across the world in an attempt to retain uniformity and centralized corporate control. However, as suggested earlier, global practices always come up against local cultures, laws and practices. Indeed, as other authors in this volume discuss, labour law in some countries mandates that employees must be given rights to union representation. The following section now examines the implementation of McDonald's employee relations in Singapore.

McDonald's in Singapore

In Singapore, McDonald's is the biggest player in the fast-food industry. By mid-1999, there were over 100 McDonald's outlets, employing over 5,000 persons, serving 100,000 customers each day in a country where the population is around three million people (*Singapore Straits Times*, 4 July 1999). As in many developing countries, McDonald's commercial success in Singapore has been due to its highly effective marketing and advertising strategies as well as the growing youth-oriented consumer culture (Watson, 1998). It is therefore no surprise that in Singapore, McDonald's is perceived as an archetypal global corporation (Pereira, 2000a).

Before McDonald's arrived in Singapore, there already was an 'eating-out' culture, especially at 'hawker' centres. These centres usually consisted of many different food vendors, each preparing their own dishes for dining in a common area. Some of these vendors did not even have permanent stalls in the centres as they located at different centres around the island on different days of the week. Historically, the most popular hawker centres were those that only operated after sundown. For instance, the two most famous hawkers centres in pre-independence Singapore were at Telok Ayer Market and Koek Road Markets, where the hawkers only came in the evenings after the vegetable and meat sellers closed for the day. After national independence in 1965, the Singapore government intentionally built hawker centres in every one of the public housing estates, both to cater to the vendors as well as the consumers. In the 1990s, many hawker centres have 'modernized' themselves to resemble the 'food courts' that could be found in American shopping malls.

In Singapore, McDonald's Restaurants was not the first American-styled fast-food restaurant to establish operations. A & W's Restaurants and Kentucky Fried Chicken came to Singapore through a system of local franchising in the 1970s. Between these two restaurant chains, Kentucky Fried Chicken was the more successful, as chicken appeared to be more immediately palatable to Asian tastes. Yet, although A & W's fare of hot dogs and hamburgers did not sell well, their root beer and root beer floats became extremely popular with young Singaporeans. However, since McDonald's entered the Singapore market, the consumption of American-styled fast-food has increased significantly, with A & W's Restaurants – along with Burger King Restaurants and Wendy's Hamburgers that established operations in the 1980s – expanding the number of outlets. Yet, the most important event in the history of the fast-food business in Singapore was the arrival of McDonald's Restaurants.

With the award of the franchise in 1979, Robert Kwan's contract with the McDonald's Corporation stipulates that he owns the exclusive rights to the franchise in Singapore. This gives McDonald's Restaurants in Singapore a high degree of centralized control, especially in establishing the terms and conditions for employment. Kwan himself is the managing director of the headquarters team, whose corporate office is located in King Albert Park. The headquarters team was filled by experienced and highly qualified persons. Many were university graduates and most had worked as managerial-level executives prior to joining McDonald's.[5] Between 1979 and 1990, restaurant managers were mainly secondary school leavers and crew usually had low levels of educational qualifications. There were also many part-time crew, particularly youths who were still in full-time education. This pattern also appears to correspond closely with McDonald's employee recruitment practices around the globe, in which McDonald's is able to able to recruit 'acquiescent' workers in different countries regardless of variations in national labour markets (Royle, 2000).

A comparison of the employment terms and conditions for employees at all three levels in the company gives a good indication of the employment relations in McDonald's Restaurants. Terms and conditions for head-quarters team personnel are generally kept confidential by the company. However, this research found that each executive has an individually negotiated employment contract. Restaurant managers are paid a monthly wage and are employed on the basis of a 40-hour week. Full-time crew are remunerated on a hourly rate and could work for a maximum of eight hours a day for up to six days in a row. On the seventh consecutive working day, crew should be paid an overtime rate of time and a half of the hourly rate. In terms of remuneration, the crew's hourly wage rate generally has been pegged at around 10 per cent higher than Singapore's minimum wage level. Just to give an idea of the difference, in 1998, the starting salary of a new trainee manager (who often held a tertiary degree or diploma) would earn around S$1,800 per month. Full-time crew on the other hand averaged between S$800 and S$1,400, depending on the number of hours they worked. Part-time crew could work for as little as 4 hours a week up to a maximum of 40 hours a week. Also, restaurant managers were entitled to 14 days annual paid leave,[6] whereas crew would be entitled to seven days of paid annual leave. All McDonald's employees in Singapore received in-house medical benefits.[7] Crew members are also entitled to annual pay bonuses – determined by the managers of their restaurants – at the end of every 12 months of service. Restaurant managers received their annual pay bonuses – determined by headquarters – at the end of the financial year. The bonus is paid pro-rata if the manager has served less than 12 months.

In Singapore, the starting salaries for restaurant managers and crew were slightly higher than the 'market rate'. Thus, while it might appear that crew are financially disadvantaged compared to restaurant managers, the crew was in an advantageous position if compared to other jobs in the lower segments of Singapore's labour market. In addition, McDonald's offered perks and benefits to crew, many of which were 'informal'. For example, crew reported that working in a comfortable air-conditioned environment which included meals provided by the restaurant was a significant perk. The former 'perk' might not sound like much, but in hot and humid tropical Singapore, this actually was attractive to individuals who were from the lower segments of the labour market. Their alternative employment opportunities might be as cleaners, car park attendants, manual labourers or other similarly low paying jobs, which were often in uncomfortable settings. Also, having a 'meal' provided by the company appeared to be attractive to many crew members, where they would be entitled to any 'three items' from the current menu for every six hours that they worked, or two items if they worked less.

As indicated earlier, under Singapore's employment laws, employees have the right either to join a trade union or not. This allows McDonald's to carry out its own HRM programme in Singapore fostering corporate values and discouraging employee resistance. For example, Singaporean restaurant managers adopted McDonald's 'Recruitment and Retention' policies where vacancies for crew were usually advertised at individual outlets. Thus, recruitment for crew was kept within the company. In contrast, most multinational corporations cooperated with (state-sponsored) employment agencies. McDonald's in Singapore also adopted the implementation of the company's disciplinary system. For example, in the course of disciplining an employee, the company had to initially give one verbal warning followed by one written warning before dismissal could take place for non-criminal acts.[8] These practices generally were different from the disciplinary systems adopted by unionized companies in Singapore (see Tan, 1995; Leggett, 1993b).

There appears to be some evidence that McDonald's HRM programme is effective, as most of the crew who were interviewed reported that they did not feel exploited or underpaid. In fact, many were satisfied with their terms and conditions of employment. This would suggest that many accepted a relatively low level of remuneration because of their lower position in the labour market. However, another reason why many crew – especially those who work part-time – accept these terms and conditions is because of their relative transience in the company. In Singapore, as a large proportion of the part-time crew consists of students, many stopped working at the restaurant when they graduated from school or, in the case of young men, were conscripted into Singapore's national (military) service. Upon completing national service, most of these young employees sought permanent and better paying forms of work rather than returning to McDonald's. This was compounded by the fact that posts at McDonald's do not have a developmental career path. The highest level to which crew can be 'promoted' is crew leader (crew trainer or training squad in some other countries), which carried an additional stipend to the wage. However, crew leaders did not deal with managerial issues such as staffing, budgeting, quality control and accounting. Instead, they were conduits between the restaurant managers and the other crew, performing the dual role of maintaining crew discipline and representing the managers. Theoretically, crew members could possibly be promoted to the managerial level but only through the acquisition of higher educational qualifications. This research found that in Singapore very few crew members moved into the restaurant managers' tier. Those who have were reported to have enrolled in part-time educational courses to improve their qualifications.

Despite the large numbers of crew within the overall corporation, this research found that they never considered collective representation. One reason was the absence of mandatory union membership. However, another reason was because crew were fairly satisfied with their current terms and conditions and felt that McDonald's was a 'good employer'. It could be argued that McDonald's had to 'look after' its crew because without them the restaurants simply could not function. Furthermore, because McDonald's is very reliant on selling large numbers of products, it has to consider its corporate image: the company cannot risk any form of public relations disaster. Although McDonald's focused on the quality of the products (the food), it had to pre-empt any form of problems with the service (labour). The final reason why McDonald's in Singapore was willing to keep its employees satisfied was because it did not involve much financial cost.

To summarize, because of its organizational structures, management practices and its use of technologies, McDonald's Restaurants transplanted many of its global practices to Singapore, including its employee relations. This transplanting was 'aided' by Singapore's employment laws, which were generally 'pro-employer'. Furthermore, as the state did not mandate that employees had to join labour unions, this made the operation of McDonald's' own individual-based HRM programme much easier, avoiding the imposition of collective negotiation and bargaining. Despite initial fears that hamburgers would not sell well in Singapore because of the population's Asian tastes in food, this was quickly dispelled as McDonald's was doing extremely brisk business. This laid the foundation for the company's rapid expansion programme in the country after 1990.

McDonald's in the 1990s

Although McDonald's Restaurants had twenty outlets after a decade of operations in 1989, 100 outlets (including restaurants and concessions) were operational in time for the company's twentieth anniversary celebrations in July 1999.[9] Many new outlets were located in public housing estates. This expansion led to strains on the operational capacity of the restaurants because of the contracting labour market. By the mid-1990s, the pool of indigenous labour began to decline as Singapore experienced lower fertility rates (see Tables 8.2 and 8.3). Simply put, McDonald's found that new crew and restaurant managers were in short supply, particularly to fill the many new outlets it was planning. Although the Singapore government allowed 'foreign workers' for certain sectors in the economy, the fast-food industry was excluded.

In Singapore, McDonald's Restaurants had previously recruited most of its restaurant managers from the pool of 'secondary school leavers', also commonly known as 'O-Level holders'. However, due to both increasing societal pressure and the smaller numbers of young persons, the pool of people in Singapore who had the highest educational qualification of an O-Level certificate shrank dramatically. As a solution, the company began recruiting from a higher segment in the labour market, namely junior college graduates ('A-Level holders'), polytechnic diploma holders and university graduates. The result of this was a subtle shift in the company's employee relations policy. To attract these better-qualified persons, the company

Table 8.2 Singapore population growth, 1947–1980 (% average annual increase)

Years	Total growth	Natural increase
1947–1957	4.4	3.6
1957–1970	2.8	2.7
1970–1980	1.5	1.4

Sources: Singapore 1980 census (Khoo, 1983: 89).

Table 8.3 Singapore labour force growth rate, 1947–1990

Years	Persons	Male	Female
1947–1957	3.0	2.4	6.3
1957–1970	3.2	2.4	6.1
1970–1980	4.4	3.1	7.5
1980–1990	3.4	2.5	5.0

Source: Huff (1994: 293).

increased its starting salary range and began to adapt its benefits and conditions offered. The starting salary, for a trainee manager, now spanned the 'market rate' for a secondary school leaver to a university graduate. Therefore, in 1998, a trainee manager could command around S$1,800, as opposed to around S$1,000 in 1990. In addition, a trainee manager could complete the Corporate Training Programme in three months in the 1990s, as opposed to taking up to one year as it had in the past. It could be argued that the higher educational qualifications of the 1990s' trainee managers meant that they were more capable of completing the course in a quicker time; however, it was equally true that McDonald's Restaurants had to 'pump out' as many fully qualified managers as they could because of its own expansion programme. Upon passing the managerial training course, managers receive a S$250 increment, and further increments after a year's service. So as not to undermine the intra-employee relationships in the restaurants, existing (non-university graduate) managers' salaries were also raised accordingly. In financial terms, these increases in salaries could be considered negligible for the company as its business performance was still very strong.

By the mid-1990s, recognizing that the majority of their restaurant managers were graduates, the company began treating them more like 'professionals'. Although restaurant managers wore uniforms at the outlets, when they had to attended training sessions, conferences or seminars organized by McDonald's Restaurants they were required to dress as executives. This meant male managers wore a suit and tie, while women managers wore dress suits. Furthermore, McDonald's Headquarters also organized more 'management'-oriented seminars and conferences for these managers, in an attempt to 'professionalize' them. In effect restaurant managers in the 1990s had their economic and social status raised, both in response to market conditions and in order to keep them 'satisfied'. However, the task orientation for managers did not change much, which is a problem as far as these graduate managers are concerned. By the late 1990s, several managers reported that they felt that remaining at the restaurant level was not a long-term option as they felt that the job was not challenging over the long term. There was also little opportunity to move upwards into the headquarters team, although the possibility was apparently left open. Another reason behind the relatively high turnover of restaurant managers was the 'fatigue' factor. Unlike most other jobs for university graduates, the restaurant manager is required to do shift work. While it might appear to be an exciting prospect for a new trainee manager, it soon became a major complaint among graduate restaurant managers after a few years in the post. Indeed it was found that many graduate restaurant managers left McDonald's for more 'sedentary' jobs, particularly those with more 'regular' working hours. This ultimately led to a fairly high turnover rate for McDonald's graduate restaurant managers. While official figures on turnover are not available, this study suggests that very few managers remain for longer than five years.

To recruit the large numbers of crew required for the expansion, McDonald's Restaurants also had to make adjustments to its recruitment, training and management processes. By the mid-1990s, the 'traditional' pool of teenage crew members, aged between 14 and 21 years, began to dry up.[10] However, as the position of the crew was crucial to the organization, McDonald's had to find alternative employees. As mentioned earlier, students – as a group of employees – were located near the bottom of the labour market. This was both because they had few skills and also because of their temporality at the job. Due to the low position in the segmented labour market, part-time crew were generally poorly remunerated. To maintain this cost effectiveness in the 1990s, McDonald's in Singapore found another group from an equally low position in the labour market to 'replace' the students. By the late 1990s, 'older' crew members accounted for 40 per cent of all employees in McDonald's restaurants in Singapore. The 'older' crew that joined McDonald's in Singapore mainly comprised retirees and housewives.[11] In the nine McDonald's Restaurants included in this research, 328 of 557 crew members were aged 30 and over (60 per cent). This demographic structure in the company contrasted significantly with the situation in many other countries. In America, teenagers still form up to 70 per cent of the crew members (Ritzer, 1996; Royle, 2000). In the United Kingdom, only 5.49 per cent of its entire crew members are aged 30 and over (McDonald's Education Service, 1997: 9). However, as Royle (2000) points out, McDonald's employs many foreign workers in countries like Germany and Austria, making the average age of employees in those countries much older than elsewhere. This study found that older crew joined McDonald's on a part-time basis because they were either unwilling or unable to commit themselves to a full-time job. Retirees wanted to work short hours during the weekdays, while housewives chose to work during the weekday hours, preferring to be with their families in the evenings and during the weekends. As many of the new McDonald's outlets were opening in public housing estates, these older workers did not have to travel into the downtown area. These older crew eventually became affectionately known as the McAunties and McUncles in Singapore.[12]

Adapting employee relations

To accommodate these changes, McDonald's Restaurants made subtle alterations to its employee relations. First, nearly all of these older crew were allowed to choose their preferred working hours. This required the restaurant manager to restructure the restaurant's roster around these workers. For instance, the students who were working part-time were offered slots during the weekends, while the 'core' crew were redeployed in evenings and during the early breakfast slots. There were other adaptations. Restaurant managers appeared to be more patient and willing to help these older employees cope with the training modules that originated from the United States and were in English. Some of these older employees were not so fluent in the language, as they were educated before Singapore's national English-language curriculum was introduced in the mid-1960s. McDonald's HRM programme was also utilized to keep older crew 'satisfied' with their jobs. Older crew often stressed that the job needed them more than they needed the job. Many claimed that they would leave the company as soon as they were dissatisfied. They often did not cite financial rewards as the main reasons for working. Instead, many claimed that they chose to work to stay healthy, pass the time fruitfully, and to maintain social relations with others (Pereira, 2000a). Thus, as crew members were absolutely crucial to the operations of the restaurant, the onus was on management to keep these employees 'satisfied' while not affecting the company's cost efficiencies.

McDonald's HRM programme gave restaurant managers the discretion to offer various forms of perks, benefits and incentives over and above the existing ones. For instance, as a perk, restaurant managers organized day trips to theme parks such as Haw Par Villa and the border towns of Johor or Batam. These trips were targeted mainly at older crew as younger crew members generally were not interested. Instead, annual parties at disco-thèques were organized for younger employees as incentives. Older crew were also relieved of more strenuous duties, such as cleaning or cooking, at the discretion of the restaurant managers. Most were assigned counter duty, which entailed taking orders and serving the customers. Older crew were also given 'special' attention from managers, in the sense that managers regularly conducted one-to-one feedback sessions, as often as once a month. The aim of these sessions was to ensure that any problems that the older crew might have were brought to the attention of the manager. Although in theory the corporation normally operates what it calls six-monthly RAP sessions[13] in other countries (Royle, 2000) there appeared to be no official 'system' to gather feedback from younger crew outside of the employee's six-month performance review.[14]

McDonald's was able to turn a difficult economic situation in Singapore in the mid-1990s to its advantage without any apparent effect on its efficiency. It maintained its operational capacity despite the large expansion whilst carefully avoiding any public relations problems. The Singapore public would have been extremely sensitive to any exploitation of the 'aged' in Singapore, as there is a strong culture of respect for senior citizens. Interestingly, the company's corporate reputation also improved during that period. In 1995, the government began to tackle the problem of (old) age discrimination amongst employers in Singapore. During that time, there were reports that certain companies were laying-off older employees in favour of younger ones to reduce wage costs. Indeed targeting older workers turned out to be something of a public relations victory, with McDonald's being praised by the government for pioneering the recruitment of older workers (*Singapore Straits Times*, 1996a).[15] The company was also one of the key participants in the Ministry of Labour's 'Back to Work' scheme in

1996. This scheme, supported by the Singapore Productivity and Standards Board, Singapore National Employers Federation and the National Trades Union Congress, hoped to woo many of the 150,000 unemployed older persons back into employment (*Singapore Straits Times*, 1996b). One month after the launch, it was reported that most of the first 350 positions taken up by older persons were at McDonald's Restaurants, the Housing Development Board and the Ministry of Education, even though over forty companies offered posts under the scheme (*Singapore Straits Times*, 1996b). McDonald's was even hailed as a pioneer in 'progressive employment strategies' in Singapore for its 'senior citizens' programme, as executives from McDonald's headquarters were invited by the National Productivity Board and the Singapore National Employers Federation to share the company's experience at several 'Human Resource' seminars to boost the recruitment of older employees (*Singapore Straits Times*, 1996a). All these programmes and activities served to enhance McDonald's reputation despite employing older persons in what are ostensibly marginal positions.

Conclusions: has anything really changed?

While McDonald's in Singapore has made some adjustments to the social and economic changes in society, it can be argued that its global model of employee relations was maintained. In the 1990s, the terms and conditions for restaurant managers and crew members might appear to have improved over those in the 1980s, particularly with higher remuneration and better work conditions. Yet it could be argued that McDonald's made these adaptations in response to the external environment in order to maintain its operational efficiency rather than in response to internal pressure to improve employee relations. Thus, it could be proposed that if the social, economic and demographic situation had not changed, it would be highly unlikely that McDonald's would have made any changes on its own. Despite these 'improvements', certain aspects of employee relations for both the restaurant managers and the crew remain 'problematic'. Although there have been some limited attempts to 'professionalize' the post of restaurant manager, it is unlikely to improve in economic terms. McDonald's might have incorporated graduates as restaurant managers, however, the company does not appear to be able to retain them over the long-term period. The most important reason for this is the lack of a progressive career development path for these graduates. Second, it could also be that the working conditions of restaurant managers, despite the recent attempt by the company to 'professionalize' these posts, are not very attractive to graduates over the long term. As mentioned earlier, compared to other graduate jobs in the Singapore market, McDonald's restaurant managers are required to work shifts. So while the young graduate might relish working in a 'high pressure, fast moving and constantly challenging' job, many have left due to fatigue for more 'sedentary' graduate management jobs. Interestingly, while a high staff turnover might signal a serious problem of employee relations to certain companies, it might not affect McDonald's significantly as many 'fresh' graduates appear to be continuously joining the company. Thus, McDonald's was able to continue its expansion in Singapore, even during the Asian financial crisis of 1997–1999.

Similarly, McDonald's crew members, the largest group of employees in the organization, still remain marginal in the organization. This is due to the nature of their tasks, their relatively low wages, benefits and career prospects. By incorporating older employees as part-time crew, McDonald's found another group in the lower segment of the labour market to replace students. The recruitment of this marginal group is influenced by McDonald's globally oriented organizational structure, management practices and technologies employed and certainly supports Royle's (2000) concept of 'recruited acquiescence'. Any concessions made by the company – in terms of raising wages or being more receptive to older employees' needs – were still well within the company's financial abilities. In other words, the company did not have to make significant alterations to its existing operations and did not have to compromise on its efficiency in any way. Having marginal groups as older crew only gave the company greater flexibility. Should there be a downturn in demand at McDonald's, the company could reduce the number of part-time crew as required. As crew they generally have no rights to insist on being employed. In this sense, the company remains in a highly favourable and dominant position.

Yet McDonald's has not wholly exploited this dominant position. It can be argued that McDonald's, although placing efficiency as its prime objective, also appears to consider 'equity' as important. As the case of the McAunties and McUncles in Singapore demonstrates, McDonald's is careful not to fall foul of the opinion of the government or the public. In many ways, McDonald's is affected by how the public perceives the company, not only because of its size, scale and pervasiveness, but also because it, as an enterprise, deals directly with the public as consumers. As consumers, how the public views the company is (financially) important to the company. Therefore, it could be argued that the strategic adaptations of its employee relations has not adversely affected its public image or its operational efficiency. Furthermore, the costs of adaptation have been negligible and have not had a negative impact on the corporation.

In conclusion, employee relations in McDonald's Restaurants in Singapore generally adheres to its global model mainly due to the company's organizational structure, management system, and use of technology, which is complemented with the lack of state structures for mandatory unionization or employee interest representation. Furthermore, the only variation from the model, in this case the incorporation of older crew and tertiary graduates as restaurant managers in the 1990s, generally reinforces the model of recruiting employees from specific segments of the labour market rather than challenging it. This study demonstrates how McDonald's has the resources and expertise not just to adapt to, but to take advantage of the operational environment at little cost. This can be seen both in the 'high turnover' graduate restaurant managers as well as in the employment of older crew members. For the latter case, McDonald's even improved on its social standing in Singapore, both in the eyes of the state, which generally approved of McDonald's employment of older persons, and in the eyes of the public. McDonald's has been instrumental in its operations in Singapore. It has not only effectively adapted to Singapore's changing economic conditions but it has also benefited from them while retaining its dominance in the employment relationship, arising from the continued absence of any independent trade union representation.

Notes

1 For an analysis of McDonald's and its franchise system see Royle (2000). The McDonald's Corporation's headquarters is based in Oak Brook, Illinois and controls and monitors restaurants all over the world.

2 When Singapore faced a severe labour shortage, the government – in consultation with various bodies – accepted a proposal to allow restricted numbers of foreign labour to work in Singapore. In 1975, the state allowed a maximum of 12.5 per cent of the entire workforce to comprise foreign labour, rising to over 20 per cent in 1984 before stabilizing at around 18 per cent in 1994 (Tan, 1995: 49).

3 Local franchises of McDonald's Restaurants are, however, given some autonomy to incorporate 'local elements', again mainly for the purposes of marketing and advertising (see Watson, 1998).

4 It was reported that there are 84 employees based at the Headquarters, excluding Robert Kwan himself (*Singapore Straits Times*, 4 July 1999).

5 Robert Kwan was quoted as saying that all managerial staff (at the headquarters) were recruited with help from professional headhunters (*Singapore Straits Times*, 4 July 1999).

6 Restaurant managers were contracted to work five 8-hour shifts a week which does differentiate weekends or public holidays from other days. This excludes 'lower ranked' non-salaried managers, such as floor managers, who are paid at an hourly rate and tend to be part-time staff by their own choice.

7 For McDonald's Restaurants in Singapore, the company has an appointed private clinic that will see all employees at the company's cost. However, McDonald's Restaurants allows all employees to claim costs for visiting national polyclinics for minor ailments (defined as costing less than S$20 per visit – including consultation and medication).

8 'Non-criminal acts' are breaking company set rules, such as for punctuality and adherence to the company's code of conduct. Criminal acts, which include theft, could mean immediate dismissal if prosecuted by law.

9 In fact, it was reported that 108 outlets had been opened by July 1999 (*Singapore Straits Times*, 4 July 1999).

10 McDonald's was not the only institution feeling the effects of this; primary and secondary schools had to be restructured. Conscripts for mandatory national service for males at the age of 16 also fell.

11 The term 'housewife' is actually still commonly used in Singapore by the media and by this particular group of women who generally are not in any long-term full-time employment. The question of why older employees and not other

groups – such as ethnic minorities – were chosen to replace the teenagers in McDonald's Restaurants has been dealt with in another paper (Pereira, 2000a).

12 In Singapore, as in other Asian societies, the terms Aunts and Uncles are conferred on older persons regardless of whether there actually is any kin relation. The terms also are generally used in a respectful rather than derogatory manner.

13 RAP sessions: Real-Approach to Problems sessions designed to hear crew grievances.

14 This review is designed to review the performance of crew members by the restaurant managers for purposes of wage increases or disciplinary action.

15 To a lesser degree and reflecting McDonald's 'McJobs' policy in the US and elsewhere (Royle, 2000), McDonald's Restaurants have also actively hired individuals with certain disabilities such as those with speech and hearing impediments to work in Singapore.

9 Employment relations in the Australian fast-food industry

Cameron Allan, Greg J. Bamber and Nils Timo

Introduction

Researchers are increasingly focusing attention on the role of multinational enterprises (MNCs) in transmitting particular employment relations practices across national borders (Sparrow *et al.* 1994). One of the issues of concern is the extent to which national industrial relations systems impact on the diffusion of transnational employment practices and how effective national labour regulatory regimes are in moderating MNC business and employment practices (Lane, 1991) and protecting the employment conditions and rights of workers employed by MNCs (Ramsay, 1997). Fast-food MNCs are significant employers of labour around the world but until recently their working practices have had little attention from researchers.

Fast-food products are often linked to global brand names. What is fast-food? It may be defined as 'branded' convenience food cooked on the premises (not generally re-heated) for direct sale; it may be consumed on the premises or sold as 'take away' convenience food. Despite the importance of MNC activities in fast-food in Australia, little research has been conducted into how their operations have impacted on Australian employment relations and vice versa. In this chapter, reference to MNCs in the fast-food industry means mainly McDonald's and Hungry Jack's (a franchise of Burger King). A few researchers have investigated MNC fast-food operations. For example, Barron and Maxwell (1998) examined the connection between weak HRM practices and poor job satisfaction and service outcomes amongst fast-food workers. Wooden (1996) and Mangan and Johnston (1999) have examined the connection between minimum wages and employment outcomes. Reeders (1988), Munro (1992) and Timo (1996) have examined the connection between low skill and mass production of food, arguing that fast-food has adopted many of the features of a neo-Taylorist system of work organization including an anti-union ethos.

In this study, we consider evidence about employment relations and labour utilization practices of fast-food MNCs operating in Australia. Data for this study were obtained from several sources during 1998–2000, including interviews with senior executives and franchisees of Australian fast-food

MNCs and senior union officials from unions that aim to organise fast-food workers. To gain an insight into employees' experiences with unions in fast-food we conducted a survey of university students and some focus groups of students who were employed in the fast-food industry. The review of literature was amplified by cases from the industrial commissions concerning the management strategies and tactics of fast-food operators.

In this chapter, we argue that MNC fast-food operators in Australia as elsewhere operate a global systematized method of production that shapes the way in which the product is manufactured, presented and sold. We also argue that fast-food MNCs have pursued their own interests by adapting to Australia's centralized system of labour regulation enabling them to keep unions out of restaurants and to gain a competitive advantage.

The political and economic environment

Australian states were separate colonies until 1901, when they federated to become an independent country. Since federation, conservative political parties have generally dominated federal government. However, there were reformist postwar Labor governments in the 1941–49, 1972–75 and 1983–96 periods. Given its links with the unions, the Australian Labor Party (ALP) has been much more sympathetic to their interests. Despite federation, Australian states still wield power over many issues, including industrial relations legislation.

Under Section 51 of the Australian Constitution the federal government has limited industrial relations powers relating to compulsory conciliation and arbitration for the prevention and settlement of industrial disputes extending beyond the limits of any one state. Reforms implemented since the 1980s have challenged this traditional interpretation of the powers of federal governments, and provided a greater scope for the use of the Australian Constitution's 'corporations power' by allowing governments to regulate the internal affairs of larger enterprises particularly by extending bargaining relationships to include direct negotiation between employers and employees. There has long been a high degree of state intervention in the Australian labour market then, by contrast with Britain, which used to be characterized as having a voluntary approach to labour-market issues with relatively little state intervention (McCarthy, 1992).

Early Australian unions rejected the notion of compulsory arbitration, preferring collective action. However, unions changed their stance after some disastrous defeats during a wave of strikes in the early 1890s. Following federation in 1901, the Australian Parliament introduced the Conciliation and Arbitration Act 1904 that encouraged employers to recognize unions registered under the Act, and empowered these unions to make claims on behalf of all employees within their membership coverage. The advent of arbitration was a significant departure from the British traditions that had been important in Australia before the 1890s, when the foundations of

Australia's twentieth-century industrial relations system were established. The aim of compulsory arbitration was to replace the role of strikes so that wages and conditions could be decided by an independent 'industrial' umpire. Each State maintains its own industrial relations system in one form or another. At a federal level, the Australian Industrial Relations Commission (AIRC) exerts considerable influence on the determination of pay and conditions.

The development of the Australian labour movement differs from that in Britain and other industrialized market economies. There were at least three special characteristics of Australian labourism. First, the 1904 Act and its provision for compulsory arbitration was a key element of Australia's initial 'social contract' (Frenkel, 1990). A second element was a law restricting immigration, thereby limiting the supply side of the labour market. The 'white Australia' policy aimed to keep out Asians, in particular, who were seen as threatening union strength and union members' living standards. The third element involved creating a protective tariff wall against cheap imports. All political parties maintained such approaches until the post-1945 period. This tariff policy was originally designed to help create employment for an expanding population enabling industrial commissions to regulate wages in 'protected' industries without fear of being undermined by cheap imports. Contemporary social policy was more concerned with social equity than promoting efficiency and productivity. Employers' interests in protected industries anticipated the threats from international competitors. Hence they lobbied tenaciously but unsuccessfully to retain high tariff levels.

The main outputs from the industrial commissions in Australia are industrial 'awards'. Awards are legally binding on employers and employees and prescribe wage rates, job classifications, training, hours of work, overtime rates, holiday entitlements and many other issues of industrial relations. Awards can apply at occupational or industry level, or to a group of employers such as members of an employer association. Unions have a vested interest in promoting awards. Unions use awards not only to help in recruitment, but awards generally also define areas of union coverage. In the mid-1980s awards covered more than 80 per cent of Australian workers. However, continued labour deregulation and introduction of enterprise bargaining in the early 1990s have inevitably impacted on the bargaining power of employers and unions. This has reduced the jurisdiction of industrial commissions in the award-making process in favour of enterprise agreement making. By the late 1990s, enterprise-level bargaining was the major determinant of wages and conditions with the official role of awards having changed to that of providing a 'safety net' (a no-disadvantage test) for enterprise agreements. By the end of the 1990s, almost 66 per cent of Australian workers were covered by enterprise agreements.

The establishment of the legally-based arbitration system in the early twentieth century encouraged the rapid growth of unions. According to the

Australian Bureau of Statistics (ABS) there was a peak of about 65 per cent union density (according to data collected by unions) in 1953. Density since then has declined steeply and was less than 30 per cent by 1999 (ABS, 1999c) and it is predicted that density will continue to fall (Cully, 2000). Contributing factors include the relative decline in employment in manufacturing (a bastion for unions), and the strong growth in the largely non-union private-sector service. Significant growth in part-time and casual employment and in the proportion of women in the workforce are additional factors, as generally these workers are difficult to unionize.

The Australian Council of Trade Unions (ACTU), formed in 1927, is the central congress for manual and non-manual unions. Few important unions remain outside it. The ACTU's considerable influence over its affiliates was reflected at ACTU congresses and conferences throughout the 1980s and 1990s, when nearly all its executive recommendations were endorsed. Officers of the ACTU also play key roles in the presentation of union cases before industrial tribunals and in the conduct and settlement of important industrial disputes. The centralized nature of Australia's industrial relations system means that union decision-making has been centrally organized based on full time union officials, with most workplace delegates having relatively minor roles in union organizing. Most Australian unions have tended to see wage determination via arbitration as a higher priority than fostering union activism at workplace level. At the same time the introduction of enterprise bargaining since the 1990s has increased the workload and role of workplace delegates. Nevertheless, in comparison with comparable unionized workplaces in Canada, the UK and the US, local union representation at the shop floor still tends to be relatively weak. In the past in most Australian workplaces, those making decisions about employment relations have tended merely to implement the awards determined centrally either by federal or state commissions (Bamber and Davis, 2000). This generalization is particularly applicable to the private services sector, including fast-food.

The growth of casual and temporary or precarious forms of employment challenges the traditional foundations of union recruitment. Australian union structures and representational policies built around a centralized arbitral system are ill equipped to deal with the changes ushered in under decentralized workplace bargaining. This has been a particular problem for unions recruiting members in the fast-food industry where a combination of young and casual labour and a general dislike of unions by managers and franchisees has made union recruitment difficult. Union membership in the fast-food industry is very low. However, many Australian unions are trying to improve their recruitment and retention of members by adopting organizing strategies targeting workplace recruitment, and some are succeeding (Mansfield, 2000).

The election of the conservative coalition government in 1996 brought radical changes to Australia's system of industrial relations. Under the Workplace Relations Act (WRA) introduced by the new conservative

Liberal/National government in 1997, the labour market was further deregulated by the introduction of a union and a non-union tier of bargaining involving union and non-union collective agreements ('certified agreements') and a system of common law contracts ('Australian Workplace Agreements' – AWAs). The introduction of the WRA also had important implications for union membership recruitment strategies because it introduced stronger anti-strike measures, provided for 'freedom of association' and brought common law sanctions into industrial legislation, thereby threatening the right to strike.

The growth of the fast-food industry in Australia

Between 1986 and 1996, Australians consumers more than doubled their annual expenditure on fast-food. Australians typically spend about one-third of their total food expenditure on take-away food and restaurant meals as compared to the US where the proportion is almost a half. The number of meals eaten by Australians outside the home increased by 57 per cent from 2.5 billion meals in 1992 to almost 4 billion in 1996–1997. By 1998, there were 17,000 fast-food and take-away outlets. Until the mid-1980s, fast-food experienced around a 9 per cent annual growth rate. This fell to around 6.5 per cent during the 1990s as Australian consumers explored alternatives such as Asian foods and 'healthier' alternatives (Lyons, 1999).

Fast-food represents one of the fastest-growing sectors of food retailing in Australia, with a new restaurant opening approximately every week. By 1999 there were some 18,368 fast-food and take-away businesses in Australia (ABS, 1999b). Consequently, during the mid-1990s fast-food MNCs began serious discounting of their products, introducing family discounts and special packages (such as a meal up-grade for a small price increase). The price paid by consumers for a fast-food meal has not increased in real terms over the past decade. We estimate that MNC fast-food operators usually employ in total on average between 40 and 60 people per restaurant. MNC fast-food operators have also responded to the increasing popularity of their products by improving technology. For example, in 1980, it took more than three minutes to make a McDonald's hamburger, but by 1999 it took less than 40 seconds (Lyons, 1999).

Restaurant locations tend to follow the growth of urban areas. Many of them are free-standing outlets, which may have a car park alongside. Many others are co-located with shopping centres so that McDonald's, Hungry Jack's and KFC may be located within close proximity to each other. The ability to attract large numbers of consumers is paramount in decisions regarding restaurant location. The growth of shopping centres since the mid-1970s has tended to exert push and pull influences on local economies, such as pushing out smaller cafés, shops and food outlets that are near shopping centres, and pulling in fast-food operators. A recent trend is for fast-food outlets to spread to new areas such as schools, hospitals, transit centres, cinemas, petrol garages and so on.

The introduction of fast-food into Australia also coincided with major social changes. In the immediate postwar Australian culture, 'going out' tended to be limited to cinemas, clubs, pubs, dance halls, churches, take-away shops (following a British tradition of fish and chips and meat pies) or restaurants. Much entertainment was at home or with friends at BBQs (an Australian weekend tradition, perhaps analogous to the Sunday roast in the UK). The introduction of fast-food in Australia changed the way that many Australians spent their leisure time. Whilst BBQs remain an important Australian icon, going out to 'Macca's' has become increasingly typical. Fast-food restaurants have become sources of recreation and entertainment providing, for example, family days, kids' safe play areas and childrens' birthday parties. McDonald's and Hungry Jack's now designate particular employees as 'birthday party managers' responsible for organizing the fun (at no extra pay!). Fast-food restaurants have also become popular venues for meals 'on the run', enhanced through the introduction of 'drive thru's' or as meeting places for young people. These innovations have enabled fast-food operators to access a larger and mobile market. Additionally many Australians are increasingly 'time poor'. According to the ABS (1999a) there has been a shift away from the norm of a full-time job of about 35–44 hours to a greater proportion of people working at least 45 hours per week.

McDonald's is the largest fast-food MNC in Australia. It has approximately 600 restaurants employing over 65,000 young people. After the introduction of McDonald's in Australia in the late 1960s, other American companies entered the market in the early 1970s including Pizza Hut, KFC (or Kentucky Fried Chicken during earlier less dietary conscious times) and Hungry Jack's. The Australian fast-food industry is dominated by subsidiaries of American MNCs: McDonald's, Hungry Jack's, Pizza Hut, Kentucky Fried Chicken (KFC) including Taco Bell, and Australian firms such as Red Rooster and Big Rooster. Tricon (a subsidiary of PepsiCo) operates 360 Pizza Hut and 440 KFC and three Taco Bell outlets in Australia. About half of these restaurants are franchised. Big Rooster started in 1972 as a privately owned company and has fifty-one franchised outlets across Australia. In 1986 Big Rooster was purchased by the Red Rooster chain, a division of Coles Myer, Australia's largest retailing company. This was part of the company's diversification into the fast-food market. The six biggest fast-food restaurant operators are McDonald's, KFC, Pizza Hut, Hungry Jack's, Red Rooster and Domino's Pizza, holding a combined market share of about 42 per cent (Lyons, 1999; BIS Shrapnel, 1999).

Hungry Jack's is franchised from Burger King and commenced operations in 1971. For copyright reasons, Burger King was unable to use its name in Australia, and the Australian operator, Jack Cowin, used a Pillsbury pancake mix brand name known as Hungry Jack's. This was a brand name owned by Diageo, the parent company of Burger King that was available in Asia and the Pacific. The first Hungry Jack's hamburger restaurant based on the Burger King concept opened in Australia in 1971. By the mid-1990s, Hungry Jack's had 189 restaurants in Australia. During the 1990s, there was a dispute between the proprietors of Hungry Jack's in Australia and Burger King Corporation. Burger King accused the proprietor of Hungry Jack's of a failure to live up to Burger King standards. Hungry Jack's countered by claiming that Burger King Corporation unfairly wanted a part of the growing fast-food industry in Australia and was attempting to 'crowd' Hungry Jack's out of the market (Trevilyan and Lyons, 2000). By mid-1998 Burger King was operating ten restaurants including seven burger outlets in Shell service stations, as co-branded sites (Burger King, 1998). Tempers flared when Burger King unilaterally terminated its franchise agreement with Hungry Jack's in 1995. The resultant feud saw Hungry Jack's take court action against Burger King under the Trade Practices Act. The dispute was decided by the New South Wales Supreme Court in favour of Hungry Jack's with substantial damages.[1]

Fast-food MNCs rely heavily on print and electronic advertising. More than a third of their advertising expenditure is on in-store advertising and brand promotion (BIS Shrapnel, 1999) in an attempt to ensure that products are easily identifiable. Fast-food MNCs have also shaped the way in which food is grown and produced by using specialist and individual suppliers to deliver particular products (e.g. Queensland beef, Tasmanian potatoes suitable for fries) which meet the specific requirements of fast-food operators. The formation of long-term alliances and relationships with a limited number of suppliers through the use of exclusive supply contracts helps MNC operators not only to keep their costs down, but also to force suppliers to comply with their product and ingredient specifications. These arrangements also ensure that the production process is supplied on a just-in-time basis by reliable and customized components and ingredients supplied by specialist and dedicated (dependant) suppliers (Ritchie, 1990).

Employment practices in the Australian fast-food industry

In Australia, Hungry Jack's and McDonald's follow operating food preparation and marketing systems established at head office level in the US. If we take McDonald's as an example, the three pillars of its success are intensive and targeted marketing, a low-cost workforce and the 'McDonald's System'. The system encompasses a wide range of supports that aim to reduce, if not eliminate, the uncertainty of running a McDonald's restaurant. The system prescribes a series of operational procedures and tasks that focus the attention of the franchisee owner towards the goal of maximizing the income gained through sales. At the core of this global system are a series of manuals (or 'toolboxes') produced by McDonald's head office. These manuals systematically address all facets of owning and operating the business. Each manual describes in detail the procedures and tasks to be completed to control all aspects of the production and sales process (e.g. pictures of the final product, cooking times, recommended refrigeration temperatures, opening and closing procedures, cleaning, sales marketing and costing labour).

In our interviews with McDonald's managers, frequent reference was made to this 'system'. The way in which this 'system' operates and its apparent capacity to subsume national regulatory systems, cultural and ethnic differences is a key to understanding the success of MNC fast-food operators. McDonald's, for example, has attempted to adopt and adapt to local cultures such as using lamb instead of beef in India, or producing a 'Mc Oz burger' to cater for the Australian penchant for burgers with additional bacon and BBQ sauce!

Fast-food MNCs in Australia generally aim to appear to be 'good corporate citizens'. This approach encompasses massive advertising as a family friendly and happy place to eat, but also contributing socially in terms of community work, for example; through the Ronald McDonald House for children with special needs. Hungry Jack's also supports local initiatives and allows its outlets to be used to collect money for community causes. In this way, MNCs in the fast-food industry have successfully adapted to Australian local political, economic, cultural and labour regulatory conditions. McDonald's maintains that it adheres strictly to local labour laws and employs people in accordance with the award's minimum wage standard (McDonald's, 1998).

In order to ensure the compliance of their franchisees McDonald's, Hungry Jack's and KFC attempt to centralize their industrial relations by handling all grievances and union negotiations through their corporate head offices. There are two principal reasons for this strategy. First, it assists to avoid bad press and stave off close media scrutiny. Second, it ensures that franchisees do not 'go off on their own' in entering into unauthorized union negotiations (that might lead to pay increases at other stores) or encouraging union membership. MNCs also administer a centralized wages system in an attempt to ensure control and monitor labour costs. For example, Hungry Jack's provides software systems to franchisees that include relevant wage data from the applicable award enabling the proprietor to monitor wages and cost fluctuations on a store-by-store basis.

Despite such efforts, fast-food MNCs do not completely control all aspects of franchisees' operations. Franchisees have a degree of autonomy in terms of how they apply the MNC's system; social relations and managerial behaviour inevitably vary from one franchise to another, reflecting different attitudes and norms. Generally franchisees are reluctant to enter into any form of bargaining relationship, although we know of at least one franchisee who has attempted to make a *non-union* Australian Workplace Agreement (AWA) with employees. Even if it materializes into an agreement it is too early to evaluate the significance and outcomes of this attempt.

The importance of cost minimization

Underpinning the 'systematic' approach adopted by fast-food MNCs is standardization. This includes standard specifications of building design, colouring and layout. This is complemented by standardized products, uniforms and shop fit-out in order to replicate the product and customer interaction between stores and countries. The idea is that a 'Big Mac' should look and taste the same whether bought in Sydney, Southampton or San Francisco. Underlying this standardization is cost minimization and mass production. The production systems are geared towards low cost and high volume; a mark-up is only 3 or 4 per cent on a burger, but 150 per cent for fries (chips) and more than 200 per cent for ice cream and soft drinks. Thus, the main products (mainly burgers or chicken derivatives) are inexpensive and stores rely on selling additional branded products such as a large McDonald's fries instead of a regular, a large Coke and so on by way of 'upgrading' (referred to as 'up-selling'). This increases sales volume and encourages the consumer to buy additional products. Second, the cost of establishing a store and the large 'commission' paid back to the company places a considerable constraint on individual store owners to be productive and cost efficient. Labour constitutes between 30 and 40 per cent of operating costs and any labour savings that individual operators are able to achieve contribute directly to the operator's bottom line, thereby furthering cost minimization.

Another source of revenue for MNCs is from the sales of franchises. In the case of McDonald's and Hungry Jack's, the typical cost of purchasing a franchise is estimated to be £350,000–400,000; it is perhaps understandable therefore that some franchisees have taken legal action against the MNC in an attempt to protect their sales areas from further encroachment of new stores. For example, in the northern suburbs of Brisbane over the past decade, four McDonald's franchised stores have been opened within five minutes' drive from one another. The MNC's marketing response is to increase advertising in an attempt to saturate sales. Also McDonald's have appointed a franchisee *ombudsman* in an attempt to resolve differences between the company and its franchisees.

The importance of youth wages

The fast-food workforce in Australia is relatively young. For example, about 72 per cent of McDonad's employees are less than 19 years old. At Hungry Jack's, 75 per cent of employees are less than 18 years old. An analysis of age distribution of employees and wage data employed by McDonald's company-owned stores is in Table 9.1. In comparison to many other industries, work in fast-food in Australia is low paid. For example, the weekly rate of pay (as at September 1999) for a first-year (unskilled) adult employee under the *Engineering Award (Queensland)* is £146 as compared to £132

Table 9.1 Age distribution and weekly wages[1] of crew employees in McDonald's company owned stores

Age of employee	Number of employees	Level 1[2] (£)	Level 2[3] (£)	Level 3[4] (£)
21 years and over	1,675	132.23	144.11	148.99
20	870	132.23	144.11	148.99
19	1,350	112.39	122.50	126.64
18	1,947	99.17	108.10	111.74
17	2,633	85.95	93.68	96.84
16	2,976	72.72	79.26	81.95
15	2,420	72.72	79.26	81.95
Total	13,871			

Sources: Based on Macdonald's submission to Junior Rates Inquiry, October 1998.

Notes
[1] All currency conversions in this chapter were conducted at the exchange rate of 0.375 pence to the AUD$ as at 9 March 2000. Wage comparisons are based on the *Engineering Award (Queensland)* and the *Fast Food Industry Award (Queensland)* at 1 September 1998 as published in September 1999.
[2] Level 1 applies to new starters who are receiving 15 weeks on-the-job training (about 25 per cent of employees).
[3] Level 2 usually covers all other employees (about 70 per cent of employees).
[4] Level 3 applies only to those employees appointed as crew leaders (about 5 per cent of employees).

under the *Fast Food Industry Award (Queensland)*. This difference increases when comparing the 'skilled' adult rate of £174 per week under the *Engineering Award* as opposed to £144 under the *Fast Food Industry Award (Queensland)*, representing a difference of £30 per week. 'Skilled' engineering workers are also usually in receipt of 'over-award pay'.

The connection between age and low pay is also illustrated in Table 9.1. The overwhelming majority of fast-food workers are less than 18 years old. Under awards such as the *Fast Food Industry Award*, juniors earn only a proportion of the adult wage: less than 17 years of age, 55 per cent; 17–18 years of age, 65 per cent; 18–19 years of age, 75 per cent and 19–20 years of age 85 per cent. Based on the award standard of 38 hours per week, juniors may be paid less than £2 per hour.[2] Fast-food operators generally do not make 'over-award payments' nor do they provide incentive, performance or productivity based pay. Workers usually obtain a 25 per cent discount on items purchased whilst at work during their meal breaks or at the completion of their shift. Employee incentives are usually in non-monetary forms, such as employee-of-the-month schemes and badges. Supervisors and store managers may receive bonus payments. However, these 'bonus payments' seem to be limited to such fringe benefits as the company paying telephone or internet service provider accounts and petrol vouchers. In any event they usually depend upon the discretion of the storeowner.

Low skill and low pay is facilitated by a production system that enables large numbers of young people to be employed. In the case of McDonald's, its operating system manuals (as discussed above) provide a detailed account of how the production process and training is to be conducted and how worker performance is monitored and appraised. Crew (or team) performance is measured at the level of the individual through the Station Observation Checklists (SOC), one for front counter service and one for the kitchen/assembling area. The SOC is a key to achieving McDonald's Quality, Service and Cleanliness (QSC) standards. The SOC commences by checking employee hand sanitation, equipment and equipment settings. Then the SOC assesses the employee against the 'steps' of service: 'smile, greet the customer, take the order/suggestive sell or sell up, assemble the order, present the order, receive payment, thank the customer and ask for repeat business or show additional interest' (Employee Brochure, McDonald's Corporation, internal document, 1996).

The SOC includes a series of explanatory notes that employees must follow. For example, the SOC instructs employees to wash their hands for at least 20 seconds with a company supplied anti-bacterial hand wash. When greeting the customer, the employee is instructed to adopt a pleasant tone of voice, establish good eye contact and greet the customer as if a 'guest in your own home'. Once customers have made their selection and established whether it is 'dining in' or 'take away', the employee is instructed to either 'suggestive sell', for instance, 'would you like a large order of fries?' or 'would you like a drink with this?'. Once the order is assembled, the employee is instructed to check for quality (e.g. properly wrapped, served within correct holding time of not more than 10 minutes or to ensure hot beverages are capped correctly). The employee is also instructed 'if it's not right, don't serve it'. The SOC also goes on to detail how to receive the money correctly and how to follow cash procedures as well as a repertoire in relation to greeting and salutations, using terms such as 'Sir' or 'Ma'am' and finally inviting the customer back in a 'polite and sincere manner'. Employees are instructed to treat children as they treat adults, however children should receive a toy!

A permanent casual labour force

The employment relations strategies of fast-food operators centre around casual employment, with up to 90 per cent of workers engaged in this way. This is generally defined as work that is paid by the hour, irregular and from engagement to engagement with no employer commitment to continuing employment. Work is usually structured according to reasonably regular hours using a roster. Casual employment allows the store manager to vary labour costs according to demand by either increasing or decreasing the number of casuals required at any one period. As one operator put it: 'When times are quiet, we might ask an employee to go for a walk!' In addition, casual employment offers a point of entry and provides a de facto probationary period without many of the constraints associated with Australia's labour legislation. Casuals with less than six months' continuous and regular employment are not covered by laws relating to unfair dismissal. Using casual staff as ports of entry not only maintains control over staffing levels, but also allows more control over employee behaviour and discipline: if casuals do not seem to be a 'good fit' for what ever reason, they can be dropped from the work roster and quietly dismissed.

Under the award system, casuals are generally paid a 'loading' (e.g. a supplement of about 20 per cent more than the standard rates) and receive a minimum payment of 2 or 3 hours per engagement. This loading is in lieu of annual holidays or sick leave. Casual employment is induced to an extent by the goal of cost-minimization. Neither casuals nor part-timers are entitled to special weekend overtime rates (in other sectors, these may be time-and-a-half or double-time on Saturdays and Sundays). There have been allegations that managers withhold work from employees as they get older and their wage levels increase. Our research adds some supports to such assertions. More than half of those in our survey (N = 269) reported that, as employees got older, they tended to be offered progressively less and less work. Eventually, most of these older employees move on to other employment and the fast-food operators then replace these older workers with younger workers.

Skill formation and careers

Fast-food MNCs in Australia generally do not establish a separate HRM department. The personnel function is usually subsumed within broader 'operations' management, though McDonald's does have an Employee Relations Manager. Operations managers are responsible for implementing personnel practices. Corporate area managers are primarily responsible for production, quality and sales, but will also deal as appropriate with IR and staff issues at individual store level. Advertising, job descriptions, grievance handling and dismissals are typically dealt with on an ad hoc basis with head office becoming involved only if an employee issue is taken up by a union or becomes an industrial commission matter. It appears that relatively few employees have seen their job description or are aware of an employment policy manual. Awards are required by law to be 'displayed in a convenient place at work' which often means that they are posted on the notice board in full view of the store manager's office! Few employees interviewed could name the award that covered their employment, suggesting that they depend on management providing information concerning their employment conditions.

Fast-food MNCs have clear objectives and practices in relation to recruitment, selection and training. New recruits are carefully selected on the basis of personality, appearance, smile, and 'having the right attitudes'. These companies often prefer to employ students due to their capacity to work flexible hours. The students' parents may be asked to attend the 'selection interview' in an attempt to ensure the potential employee has parental support and motivation to work. In some cases (since the practice is illegal, it is hard to prove), we were told that offers of employment were subject to the new recruit completing three days 'on the job' training without pay to see if they 'are of the right stuff'. McDonald's emphasized that they do not follow such a practice.

Training and low entry barriers to work in fast-food may explain why it is attractive to young people seeking temporary work. Our research suggests that the predominant reasons for seeking employment in fast-food is the perceived ease by which jobs can be obtained and the convenience of work shifts that fit in with study. Whilst work in fast-food is generally seen as low skilled, work in the industry provides a useful social function. McDonald's maintains that:

> The work available at McDonald's is ideal for young people. No previous work experience is necessary and we provide on the job training. Young people gain competencies such as problem solving, teamwork and planning, and organizing skills. They become customer focused, self-confident and develop a strong work ethic.
>
> (McDonald's, 1998: 57)

In an attempt to gain greater legitimacy as a training provider, fast-food MNCs have linked their training programmes with broader industry training systems. Since 1992, for instance, McDonald's has offered employees access to an approved and registered 'fast-food retail' traineeship that lasts for 12 months. The purpose is to provide accredited training in return for a government subsidy for each trainee. These traineeships involve on-the-job training and articulate into other food and retail traineeships. However, whilst such training may be accredited, not all employees wish to undertake a traineeship.

Training procedures and job tasks are defined in much detail in training manuals (for example, making a hamburger occupies twenty pages, starting off on how to wash your hands and how often) that not only shows how each step of production is organized, but also illustrates precisely how the product is assembled and presented. Our experience suggests that once there is a cadre of experienced employees, there is less reliance upon the training manuals by store managers. Rather, training becomes ad hoc and exclusively dependent on 'buddy' training or 'sitting by Nellie'. This form of training serves three purposes. First, it transfers the responsibility for training to a more experienced employee who becomes responsible for mentoring and even helping the new employee. Second, it reduces the formal training cost borne by the company or franchisee. Third, it serves a behavioural function by establishing lines of authority and discipline. In one case, a McDonald's employee remarked: 'I was reprimanded for getting too friendly with the new starters. Management wanted them to be afraid of me so that they would take orders and work harder.' In addition, task allocation may also be linked to job status within a functional area as one Hungry Jack's employee stated: 'This badge means that I am the health and safety rep. I got it because I've been here the longest.'

Management career structures

Fast-food MNCs generally develop line managers by promoting from within. In McDonald's, about 80 per cent of line managers had begun work as casuals and part-time crew members. In both McDonald's and Hungry Jack's, the majority of line managers (70 per cent) are between 21 and 30 years of age. Their situation is somewhat precarious and more appropriately seen as lower-level salaried staff. For example, their salary ranges between about £10,000 and £14,000 per annum (this includes implicit allowances for overtime and weekend work). They earn slightly more than an adult employee on average wages. Line managers work extremely hard and provide fast-food 'managerial labour flexibility' by being on call at any time and working weekends and public holidays where necessary. We found that line managers bore the brunt of flexible working hours and pressures for cost minimization. They also tended to display a management style that is derived from an individualist and unitarist approach to employment relations. Individualism and local store control over staffing issues enable a range of informal work practices to develop in each store. These often involve store-specific distribution of rewards and favours according to an informal system of individual bargaining (e.g. access to days off, favourable rosters, and so on). The allocation of these 'rewards' may also engender employee loyalty and commitment.

In relation to franchisees, the situation is quite different. Franchisees are not generally promoted from within. Many do not have a fast-food background. What distinguishes them from managers is that a potential franchisee has access to significant capital to enable them to meet the high start-up costs. In the case of McDonald's, franchisees have to meet the cost of fitting out the store and are expected to contribute around 50 per cent of the equity. The company usually buys the site, constructs the building, and then leases it to the franchisee. In this way, the company maintains ownership over valuable commercial sites. In Australia, there appears to be strong demand for the ownership of a fast-food franchise. Companies like McDonald's go through a sophisticated recruitment and selection process to chose 'the right person'. This can take more than 12 months including a period of on-the-job training before individuals get into their own store. The idea is not only to maximize the success of each candidate, but also to ensure that they follow the procedures set out for franchisees.

Unions, worker representation and consultative structures

The main unions covering workers in the fast-food industry are two large and general industry unions: the Australian Liquor, Hospitality and Miscellaneous Workers Union (ALHMWU) and the Australian Workers Union (AWU). More recently the Shop, Distributive and Allied Employees' Union (SDA) covering retail and shop assistants, has moved into the area. In terms of politics, the ALHMWU has a reputation for being militant and left wing, while the AWU and SDA have both been seen as conservative and right of centre.

Whilst fast-food MNCs may be reluctant to bargain with unions, when they do engage in collective bargaining, they may pursue their industrial relations interests strongly. During the early 1970s, when fast-food MNC operators were launching their operations in Australia, they sought union cooperation in regulating the wages and conditions of employees. The strategy of fast-food operators (especially McDonald's, Hungry Jack's and KFC) was commercially driven, seeking union acquiescence to a regime of minimum wages and conditions; this was achieved by agreements with unions. In return for union recognition, employers obtained union agreement to classify all fast-food employees under the generic heading of 'kitchen hands'. Furthermore, in some cases, such as in North Queensland, these arrangements led to a closed shop under the threat that the union (AWU) might withdraw from the agreement. The outcome was that the agreement displaced industrial commission awards.

These arrangements provided fast-food MNCs and other fast-food operators with an important concession, for under the relevant contemporary commission decisions, fast-food operations were covered by café, restaurant and catering awards that had a link with the higher levels of wages paid to employees serving alcohol. The kitchen hand rate was the lowest rate of pay. In addition, as many awards excluded casuals from receiving special rates for weekend work, by employing casuals fast-food MNCs were able to avoid weekend rates. This gave MNC fast-food operators a substantial competitive advantage over cafés and restaurants. Consequently, fast-food operators were in a symbiotic relationship with unions: dependent upon them for cheaper wages and conditions, and in turn, unions relied upon these arrangements in order to access and organize workers in the fast-food industry. McDonald's, which generally has a non-union preference, has arrangements in South Australia with the SDA to remove McDonald's stores from coverage of the local café, restaurant, retail and catering awards.

In 1982, there was a breakdown in cooperation between fast-food MNCs and the ALHMWU. This was precipitated by a change in union leadership of the ALHMWU associated with an approach that was more radical in outlook. The fast-food MNCs in Queensland formed an employers' association, known as the Fast Food Industry Association. This association applied successfully for special award conditions exclusive to MNC fast-food operations. For example, in 1983 the Queensland Industrial Relations Commission made an award exclusive to MNC fast-food operators. The grounds for treating MNC fast-food operators differently was the recognition that the skills required were low and the workforce was predominantly students and there was a public interest in ensuring that young people had access to readily available work. Once the award had been made, MNCs such as McDonald's, Hungry Jack's and KFC jettisoned their cooperative arrangements with unions and pursued a vigorous non-union policy at workplace level, including terminating all of the check-off arrangements for union dues (Timo, 1996). The new bargaining strategy was that the fast-food MNCs continued to negotiate with unions at first, and, if that failed, sought arbitration at industrial commissions. The strategy did not involve employee consultation. For unions, the activities of MNC fast-food operators presented a dilemma; should unions continue to try to represent employees who were not members, or abandon the industry to employer prerogative? Mostly, unions adopted the former strategy, though their influence was rapidly waning.

During the mid-1980s, the ACTU began to reorganize union structure and membership coverage. The ACTU sought to restructure the large number of Australian unions into twenty so-called 'super unions' (ACTU, 1987). This move was to rationalize union resources to improve union recruitment strategies at workplace level. Following an ALHMWU dispute with Pizza Hut in 1989 and a perception by employees that the union was no longer interested in their welfare, employees approached the SDA for union coverage. The change in union membership can be traced to policies of the ALHMWU not to expend further energy in the fast-food industry due to the small membership, particularly in New South Wales, the largest State in terms of population and numbers of fast-food stores. The ACTU held discussions with the ALHMWU, SDA and AWU, then reorganized coverage of fast-food, giving exclusive rights to the SDA in all states, except Queensland where the coverage was divided between the SDA and AWU. The introduction of the SDA was welcomed by the fast-food employers, as it was seen as less militant than the ALHMWU.

Under Australia's centralized system of conciliation and arbitration, the Industrial Relations Commissions hears arguments by employers and unions about any changes to awards in the fast-food industry. Arguably individual employees have not participated directly in this process. Unions complain about the lack of access to workplaces. What are the preferences of fast-food MNCs with regard to unions? As one union official from the SDA stated: 'by and large they see us as being not conducive to flexible working practices'. This is particularly so in franchises, which are difficult to unionize because they are run by small business owner/operators who generally see unions as enemies and something to avoid.

In some cases, though, fast-food employers do have a working relationship with unions. The relationship tends to vary from state to state. Generally, employers will seek to negotiate where there is a state award that employers consider as too costly, such as with those that provide pay levels or allowances for weekend work. Unions tend to accommodate this approach as most union policies aim to achieve multi-state standard agreements, which are usually easier to enforce and maintain.

Australian law does not provide for the establishment of European-style statutory 'works councils', nor does the law provide for union recognition ballots as in North America and the UK. Whilst unions may have recognition as parties to awards and at industrial relations commissions hearings, such recognition is generally not translated into many union members.

What does this say about MNC fast-food bargaining strategies and union relations? With a low-cost award wage, a casualized workforce and absence of union pressure, there are few motives for employers to negotiate widespread workplace change either with employees or unions. Workplace changes can then be made unilaterally. According to Royle (1999a, 1999b, 2000), in his examination of McDonald's employment practices in Europe, McDonald's continues to avoid union involvement wherever it can and particularly in terms of statutory forms of employee representation, only where the legislation provides few loopholes has McDonald's finally accepted the role of unions and usually only in terms of centralized collective bargaining. This is also reflected to some extent in Australia. In the absence of union voice mechanisms, employees rely on unilateral managerial prerogatives or internal company grievance mechanisms. Under McDonald's 'people system', provisions are made for employees to raise concerns via an internally designed dispute/grievance system through the Personnel Action Letter (PAL). Employees can use the PAL system to express concerns or grievances. Employees are required to sign these PAL memoranda and they are brought to the attention of either the store manager or corporate office. We infer from interviews with employees, however, that few workers use the system because of their fear of repercussions, their lack of awareness or because they see it as a pointless exercise.

Our survey of university students enabled us to gain another perspective on insight into employees' experiences with unions in fast-food. While unionization levels seem to be very low (less than 9 per cent), a substantially larger proportion of ex-employees expressed a preference to be a member of a union when working in fast-food (24 per cent). This gap between employees' wish to join a union and actual unionization rates undoubtedly reflects a number of factors. These include: a relatively high turnover of casual employees; small workplace size; employer hostility towards unions and the employees themselves. Furthermore, union officials are not regular visitors to fast-food workplaces. Even if unions were active in the workplace, given the high turnover of staff in fast-food and the fragmentation of shifts, it is unlikely that employees would have much experience with unionism, or employer hostility towards it.

Conclusion

This chapter has traced the rise in importance of fast-food MNCs in Australia. With few barriers to entry and relatively low wages, fast-food MNCs are significant employers of young people. Like their counterparts elsewhere, Australian fast-food MNCs follow global strategies based on cost minimization strategy. At the core of these strategies is a 'system' of production, which relies upon young, cheap labour. They have been able to adapt to Australia's centralized system of industrial relations by relying upon an award regime that encompasses inexpensive casualized young labour and minimum award conditions regulating wages and conditions. Whilst fast-food MNCs argue that they adhere to minimum wages laws and awards, their approach is minimalist. Their labour utilization strategy is based on employment of junior and casual workers. Fast-food MNCs are reluctant to deal with unions. Their approach is opportunistic, using union negotiations only when unavoidable and as a substitute for effective and independent employee workplace representation.

This study tends to confirm other research that identifies the close connection between minimum wages and low-skilled labour, as part of a broader cost minimization strategy. But the large size, power, and a willingness of fast-food MNCs to defend their reputation through the courts has tended to shield their operations and employment practices from broader critical analysis. The most interesting conclusions of this research concern employee attitudes. Our interview data from former fast-food MNC employees are paradoxical. Whilst they accept that it is low paid and arduous, they generally found the experience socially rewarding. Fast-food employment clearly has an emotive side associated with the social relations at work, convenient hours and accessible income. Nevertheless, it can hardly be said to offer satisfactory, long-term and rewarding employment.

Acknowledgments

We appreciate the company representatives, franchisees, employees and union officials who gave their time in our interviews, and we also appreciate the assistance of employees and former employees of fast-food companies who completed our questionnaire. Several colleagues have also been very helpful, especially Anthony Gould, and also Ken Lovell and Mary Moloney.

Notes

1 *Hungry Jack's* v. *Burger King*, NSWSC, Case No. 1029, 5 November 1999, Sydney.
2 The cost of living in Australia is generally much lower than that in the UK.

10 Standard recipes?

Labour relations in the New Zealand fast-food industry

Peter Haynes and Glenda Fryer

Introduction

The radical reform of New Zealand's employment laws over the past two decades provides a unique opportunity to study the industrial relations policies and practices of the major international fast-food operators in a changing environment. The responses of the major chains to a shift from a highly regulated, to a minimalist, legislative regime for collective bargaining and wage setting throws their preferred approaches to managing labour into sharp relief. In particular, it is possible to test claims that the major fast-food operators are egregiously exploitative of their workforces and opposed to union organization. At the same time the New Zealand experience sheds light on the complex processes by which labour management practices are transmitted across borders, within the varied organizational context of locally managed, franchise and subsidiary operations.

This review of labour relations in the New Zealand fast-food industry therefore focuses on the following questions. How did the local representatives of the international chains adapt to the greater emphasis on employee protection that existed before 1991? How did these companies alter their bargaining arrangements and the terms and conditions of employment of their employees to take advantage of the liberalization of employment law in 1991? Have there been any local initiatives in HRM? And to what extent have the labour relations policies and practices of the local franchise operators been controlled by the policies and practices of the international company? It outlines and compares the varying approaches to labour relations adopted by the major international operators in New Zealand. It excludes the multitude of locally owned and operated takeaway outlets and small chains. First, though, the development of the fast-food industry in New Zealand is described, and the particular legal context is outlined.

For this review the authors interviewed the human resource managers or managers responsible for human resource management in each of the four major fast-food operators studied, as well as five union officials and a representative of the employers' organization. Some subjects were interviewed more than once. Interviews were semi-structured and were one to two hours in duration. Most were taped and transcribed, but in a few cases the authors took verbatim notes and later cross-checked typed transcripts. Employment contracts, management papers and union archives and other documents supplemented the interview data.

The fast-food industry in New Zealand

Fast-food was established in New Zealand in the 1970s.[1] Kentucky Fried Chicken (KFC) opened its first outlet, in Auckland, in 1971. Pizza Hut followed with its first restaurant in Auckland in late 1974 and McDonald's in 1976 with its first restaurant, in Wellington. All three quickly expanded throughout the country, and were joined in the late 1970s by local operators Homestead Golden Fried Chicken and Georgie Pie (both of which have since ceased business). The first Wendy's restaurant opened in 1986, and the first Burger King outlet in 1994, both in Auckland.

New Zealand's most notable indigenous attempt to compete with the international fast-food giants began with the opening of the first Georgie Pie restaurant in Auckland in 1977. The staple offering was the Australasian culinary icon, the individual serving-sized meat pie. The chain consciously imitated the McDonald's formula, using children's playgrounds to target families, a Ronald McDonald counterpart called Georgie Pie, and so on. A period of rapid expansion began after the company introduced an aggressive pricing formula and competed head-to-head with the major fast-food operators from 1991. Buoyed by the increase in sales following its new pricing strategy, in 1994 the company adopted ambitious expansion plans within New Zealand and Australia. Despite rapid growth Georgie Pie was dogged by poor profitability, and the parent company decided in 1996 to divest itself of the chain. The last outlets closed in 1997.

It has been suggested that economic conditions limited the growth of the industry in the early stages of expansion (*Hospitality*, August 1987: 30). In 1987, more than 10 years after the first three international chains established themselves in New Zealand, there were 121 fast-food outlets in New Zealand, including those operated by the two local imitators (see Table 10.1). By mid-1996, the number of outlets had more than doubled to 289, despite low levels of economic growth between 1987 and 1993. Some rationalization followed the closure of many Georgie Pie outlets and the sale of the remaining seventeen to McDonald's in 1997. By the end of 1999, however, after a period of rapid growth, the five major chains operated 348 outlets in total. Most of the growth in the second half of the 1990s was accounted for by the rapid expansion of the Burger King chain and continuing expansion by the market leader, McDonald's.

Although home-delivery pizza and other fast-food chains compete with the international chains, they are small and occupy a marginal place in the fast-food sector. The largest of these, 'designer burger' chain Wisconsin Burger,

Table 10.1 Number of major brand fast-food outlets in New Zealand, 1987–1999

Brand	1987	1996	1999
McDonald's	25	100	146
KFC	49	87	92
Burger King		19	56
Pizza Hut	31	43	41
Wendy's	1	8	13
Homestead	10		
Georgie Pie	5	32	
Total	121	289	348

Sources: Bliss (1987); McManus (1996), interview data.

has eight outlets (in early 2000) but does not employ standarized operating procedures, and was therefore excluded from the study.

Three decades after its introduction, fast-food has secured a large share of the market for prepared food in New Zealand. The market leader, McDonald's, has achieved its second highest market saturation outside the United States with one outlet for every 25,000 New Zealanders. Although New Zealanders spend an increasing proportion of their food expenditure on fast-food and eating out (see Table 10.2), however, such spending remains somewhat lower, at around 25 per cent, than in Australia (about 33 per cent) and the United States (nearly 50 per cent).

Further, traditional forms of takeaway food continue to provide significant competition for the internationally branded fast-food operators and their local franchisees. The pattern of eating habits revealed by recent surveys indicates that fish and chips, Chinese takeaway and hamburger bar outlets account for a significant proportion of takeaway or quick service food consumed in New Zealand (see Table 10.3).

The labour relations context in New Zealand

New Zealand began the twentieth century with a highly regulated labour market but ended it with one that was very lightly regulated. Shared circumstances in the late nineteenth century saw New Zealand and Australia adopt

Table 10.2 Percentage of weekly household food expenditure spent on takeaway foods

1988/9	1990/1	1992/3	1994/5	1996/7	1997/8
8.1	8.1	10.0	11.4	11.6	11.7

Source: Statistics New Zealand, Household Economic Survey (HEIA.SZAJBZZ2).

Table 10.3 Percentage of respondents aged 10 years and over who had eaten take-away or quick service food in the previous month

	1986 (NZ)	1993 (NZ)	1995 (NZ)	1995 (Auckland)
Fish and chips	53	56	57	48
McDonald's	14	30	39	47
KFC	20	28	34	35
Chinese takeaways	16	23	25	31
Georgie Pie	2	9	21	30
Hamburger bars	12	8	5	5
Burger King	N/A	N/A	5	14
Pizza Hut	6	6	8	9
Wendy's	N/A	N/A	4	5

Source: McManus (1996).

an 'Antipodean solution' to the 'labour problem' (Boxall, 1990), centred on state-sponsored compulsory dispute resolution in which independent trade unions played a pivotal role (Mitchell, 1989). For much of the twentieth century, unionized private sector workers' basic terms and conditions of employment were promulgated in multi-employer 'awards'. The awards were centrally negotiated and usually occupationally based. From 1973, single employer 'agreements' could also be registered under the prevailing legislation, but take-up was limited. Indeed, Harbridge and McCaw (1992: 175) report that only a 'very small number' of private sector employers were parties to agreements following the introduction of a provision in the Labour Relations Act 1987 that required unions to choose between awards and agreements in negotiations with employers. As they were registered in the Arbitration Court and its successors, awards and agreements were treated as extensions of statute and were legally enforceable. A range of statutes such as the Minimum Wage Act 1983, Wages Protection Act 1983, Holidays Act 1981 and Parental Leave and Protection of Employment Act 1987 and their precursors provided further protection for all workers in respect of a limited number of employment conditions.

A high degree of compulsory union membership was another feature of the legal framework prior to the Employment Contracts Act 1991. Although the legal underpinnings varied, with the exception of only two very brief periods in the 1930s and early 1980s, union membership was in effect 'compulsory' for most workers. The Labour Relations Act 1987, which was superseded by the Employment Contracts Act, required any adult worker covered by an award or agreement with a union membership clause to join the union, in effect avoiding 'free riders'. Union membership clauses could also be secured by agreement or through a ballot of workers. The outcome was that in March 1991, a few months before the Employment

Contracts Act came into effect, union membership was 603,118 or 51 per cent of New Zealand wage and salary earners (including managers).[2]

The award system was already being eroded during the 1970s and 1980s prior to the enactment of the 1991 Employments Contract Act, both through legislative change and an increase in 'above award' enterprise bargaining. In the 1980s the 'award system' was further weakened in the wake of the radical reform of product and financial markets, increased labour market flexibility and globalization (Honeybone, 1997). A more permissive approach to enterprise bargaining had already been introduced in 1973 and compulsory arbitration abolished in 1984. Unions, however, did retain their rights of exclusive jurisdiction, blanket award coverage and (in essence) compulsory membership until 1991. It was the Act of 1991 which swept away the last vestiges of the old system and replaced it with a decentralized, contract-based system founded on the individualization of the employment contract. Individual employers and employees were free under the Act to determine their own representation arrangements and to negotiate the type and coverage of employment contracts under a minimalist bargaining, regulatory regime.

The impact of the Employment Contracts Act was dramatic. It was introduced in the midst of a sharp rise in unemployment, at the same time as changes in social welfare benefit entitlements which profoundly disadvantaged many workers in the secondary labour market, characterized by low wage, low skill, casualized and/or part time employment. By 1998, union density was less than 40 per cent of its 1989 level, having declined precipitously (by almost 20 per cent) in 1991–1992 (Crawford *et al.*, 1999). The decline in union density was most marked in the secondary labour market in the early years of the Employment Contracts Act (Boxall and Haynes, 1992). Numbers engaged in collective bargaining fell in tandem, concomitantly with a shift to enterprise bargaining. The swiftest change in both the structure and outcomes of bargaining took place in the first two or three years after 1991. Collective bargaining is estimated to have fallen by 40–50 per cent between 1989/90 and 1993/94 (Honeybone, 1997). By 1999 between 420,000 and 450,000 employees were estimated to be covered by collective employment contracts (Harbridge and Crawford, 2000), compared to some 721,000 in 1989/90 (Honeybone, 1997). Of these, fewer than 9 per cent were covered by multi-employer contracts (Harbridge and Crawford, 2000). There is much evidence that along with the contraction of collective bargaining there was a shift to a 'non-negotiation' model of contract formation by many New Zealand employers under the Employment Contracts Act. Workers and their representatives have little if any influence over either the structure or the outcome of contract formation in this model. This was found to be the case not only in the 'individualized' sector (McAndrew and Ballard, 1995), but also in parts of the service sector where the shell of collectivist relations remained (Haynes and Fryer, 1998; McLaughlin and Rasmussen, 1998). It should be noted, however, that the absence of negotiations does not necessarily imply worker dissatisfaction with the bargaining process and outcomes (Rasmussen *et al.*, 2000)

There has been little research into the processes and outcomes of wage bargaining in the secondary labour market in New Zealand since 1991. It is clear, however, from surveys of trends in the collective contracting sector that the elimination of barriers to temporal and numerical flexibility was swiftest and most complete in the secondary labour market. By 1995, for example, premium or penalty rates were reported to 'have all but disappeared' in the restaurants and hotels sector, and to be 'comparatively rare' in the retail sector and the public and community services sector (Hammond and Harbridge, 1995: 370). Additionally by 2000, almost all young workers (under 20) in the retail food sector were in receipt of 'youth rates'; but youth rates were only present for less than one-third of all workers as a whole covered by collective contracts (Harbridge and Crawford, 2000). A recent survey of retail sector workers gives further insight into the plight of secondary labour market workers under the Employment Contracts Act. These workers were found to have little influence over the choice of contract structure or outcomes, little control over their hours of work, and to have suffered a net loss of wages in real terms after the loss of premium wage payments and allowances (McLaughlin, 2000; see also Ryan, 1997).[3]

Concern about the impact of the 1991 Employment Contracts Act on secondary labour market workers was a key factor in the introduction of the Employment Relations Act by the centre-left coalition government elected in November 1999. The new Act came into effect on 2 October 2000. It does not represent a return to the highly centralized labour law regime prevailing before the Employment Contracts Act, because it retains voluntary union membership and eschews compulsory arbitration. Most importantly for the present study, it seeks to the redress the imbalance created by the ' inherent inequality of bargaining power in the employment relationship', by promoting collective bargaining (Wilson, 2000: 3). The principal means by which it attempts to effect this are by requiring fair treatment in employment matters and by providing unions and union members with improved access and other rights. In particular, unions have the right to enter workplaces to recruit; enjoy the sole right to represent workers in negotiating collective agreements, and may initiate negotiations for new collective agreements (including multi-employer agreements) to which the employer party or parties must respond in 'good faith'. Union membership confers the right to coverage by any applicable collective agreement that may exist. However, while these new rights provide unions with the opportunity to recruit and retain members, their ability to do so may be constrained in practice. There is no requirement to bargain towards a collective agreement and this failure to bargain in 'good faith' is likely to have unfortunate consequences for trade unions in the labour market. It may encourage employers to negotiate standard individual agreements with non-union worker representatives (Boxall, 2001).

HRM and labour relations in the fast-food sector

Without exception, the international fast-food operators surveyed maintain a high degree of control over the New Zealand operations by means of tightly defined operating systems and close monitoring of key financial and operational indicators. Operating manuals and procedures not only specify the technology, tasks and targets of the production and service processes; levels of training, spans of management control, and management development are also detailed and monitored. Furthermore, there is little significant variation between companies, either in terms of the processes employed or in the indicators used to monitor performance. The degree of control and means employed by the international headquarters to maintain control over HRM and labour relations is more complex, however. What follows is an analysis of each of the main organizations included in the study.

McDonald's

On the surface McDonald's New Zealand operation appears to enjoy some autonomy in HRM and labour relations policies and practices. Managers interviewed maintain that there is little direct international oversight of HRM and labour relations in the New Zealand operation beyond ensuring that local practices do not fall below certain set minimum standards. However, if a degree of local autonomy can be tolerated it can only be within centrally determined and well understood guidelines as the defence of the brand allows no alternative. As one McDonald's manager put it:

> Our [HRM] philosophy is very much locally managed. . . . As long as we are within good people practices what we do on [the HRM] side is very much over to the [local operation]. There are certain fundamentals in terms of how you treat people, etc., etc., but they are very generic.

In assessing this quotation it is interesting to note the use of the terms 'certain fundamentals' and 'generic'. An internal corporate 'international consultant' for the HRM function visits New Zealand once a year, and management interviewees maintain that the consultant's role is facilitative rather than prescriptive. However, such visits are also used as an opportunity to discuss 'strategic' HRM issues. Local managers may be permitted to drive the agenda in terms of some local concerns but this does not obviate the corporation's opportunity to confirm the implementation of centrally determined controls.

HRM innovations and ideas diffuse through the extensive interaction and information exchange that takes place between national operations across the globe. All of the HRM practitioners in the New Zealand McDonald's subsidiary have attended the training courses and conferences on HRM provided by the Asia-Pacific division and are enthusiastic about the opportunities these provide to discuss common problems and developments. Further, an 'international ideas exchange' is published quarterly. HRM practitioners contribute innovative policies and practices developed at national level for the consideration of other national McDonald's operations.

Despite the central controls McDonald's in New Zealand decides important human resource management and labour relations matters within a complex process which needs to some extent to reflect the structure of the local operations: about 80 per cent of McDonald's outlets are franchised. Overall, good practice is fostered through a 'best of the best' award for franchisees known as the 'Employer of Choice' award. This is one of three coveted 'premium awards' within the franchisee group. The criteria for award and their application are solely the responsibility of McDonald's New Zealand. An 'Employer of Choice' taskforce, comprising representatives of the franchisees and of the New Zealand subsidiary McDonald's Systems of New Zealand Ltd, generally makes recommendations to franchisees, a majority of whom must agree before a proposed policy is adopted, although inevitably McDonald's tends to have a major influence on the outcomes. Furthermore the practice of HRM and labour relations in the franchised outlets is a matter of concern to the local McDonald's managers. As one manager explained in relation to a checklist developed to assist franchise operators avoid the pitfalls of the disciplinary process:

> Obviously, with 6,000 people employed nation-wide, if one individual messes up on a disciplinary matter, it's going to have brand implications for all of us. We do not want that plastered all over the newspapers.

KFC and Pizza Hut

A local, publicly listed company, Restaurant Brands New Zealand Ltd ('Restaurant Brands'), owns and operates almost all of New Zealand's KFC and Pizza Hut operations (along with the New Zealand Starbucks Coffee franchise). A further eight KFC outlets are operated by six New Zealand-owned franchisees, to whom Restaurant Brands provides management and support services.[4] Restaurant Brands was formed in order to acquire PepsiCo International's holdings in KFC (New Zealand) Ltd and Pizza Restaurants (New Zealand) Ltd. It was listed on the New Zealand Stock Exchange in May 1997. PepsiCo had completed its acquisition of the New Zealand KFC and Pizza Hut operations from the principal franchisees in 1989 and 1995 respectively. The local company reports to the Sydney-based division of Tricon Global Restaurants Inc. ('Tricon'), the international KFC and Pizza Hut franchisor.[5]

Prior to their re-incorporation in 1997, the local KFC and Pizza Hut operations were largely managed out of Sydney. Major HRM and labour relations strategies were determined by the Sydney office and executed in New Zealand within strict boundaries. For example, in 1991 the new collective contract covering KFC staff could not be settled until an Australian-based manager became involved as the KFC advocate. Senior managers maintain that the reorganization of these operations in 1997 allowed for a higher degree of autonomy in management. However, the franchise agreement contains some minimum requirements within the HRM and labour relations field. Managers maintain especially that this does not in practice restrict the local development of HRM and labour relations processes in the area of training.

In late 1999, the local Tricon senior management embarked on an overhaul of reward and recognition, recruitment, leadership development, labour relations strategies, and equal opportunities policies. The senior HRM role was upgraded, made part of the senior executive team, and given a 'blank sheet of paper' on which to formulate policy. Labour law changes following the election of the new Labour-led government in late 1999 were seen as likely to play, as a manager stated, 'a major part in shaping the new labour relations strategy'.

Burger King

As with its major fast-food competitors, New Zealand's Burger King operation appears to enjoy some degree of autonomy in HRM and labour relations. Although many aspects of day-to-day operations in New Zealand's Burger King outlets must conform closely to the operations manual provided by the US licensor, additional local procedures are set out separately. These include most HRM and labour relations policies and practices (a limited amount of material about managing performance problems and health and safety being included in the international corporate manual). The additional policies and procedures are entirely determined by the company responsible for managing the New Zealand operations.[6] One HRM practitioner at the company described the extent of global corporate influence over the HRM function as follows:

> Actually, I don't have any contact whatsoever with the HR people in the [US] Corporation. They don't direct us in terms of HR policies and procedures. It's left to the local franchisee as such.[7]

Wendy's

The smallest of the international fast-food chains operating in New Zealand, Wendy's New Zealand franchise is operated by a privately owned company, Wendco NZ. The local company reports to the Asia-Pacific office of the international franchiser, Wendy's International Inc. It does not employ any dedicated HRM/labour relations practitioners, these functions being the responsibility of the senior operations manager. As a result the operating company is dependent on the policies and procedures provided in the manuals supplied by its US-based franchisor for many aspects of its HRM and labour relations policies. Most of the training material used in New Zealand is US-sourced, for example. Quarterly videos from the US are used to inform and motivate crew-level staff. And, importantly, recent changes to the reward system away from a skills-based system towards non-monetary recognition for good performance are modelled on developments in the international chain's practices. However, Wendy's New Zealand operation has been required to develop its own HRM and labour relations policies and procedures, including selection interview procedures, to fit the local legislative and social context.

Local autonomy: apparent or real?

In assessing the extent of local autonomy of senior management appearance has to be tested against practice. For example, although it can be argued that the degree of direct control is low the actual level of 'unobtrusive' control is high. Unobtrusive control refers to 'the way in which the [international headquarters] shapes and constrains decisions made at plant level through controlling the premises underlying decision-making' (Edwards, 1998: 699). It allows the international company to retain control in the absence of formal policies and guidelines on employment practice, the assignment of expatriate staff and other mechanisms of direct control. Clearly, some unobtrusive control mechanisms may shape the HRM and labour relations policies of the New Zealand fast-food operations. In the case of McDonald's, for example, there are regular meetings of HR managers across the Asia-Pacific region, an international consultant visits regularly to advise on employment-related matters, and HR staff may experience international training. Those HRM policies and practices of the global operation adopted in New Zealand appear to have been diffused internationally by means of interaction with other countries' professionals and training at the corporate headquarters, for the most part.

Although instances were found in which the local operation has deviated from the guidelines of the international headquarters and some have negotiated collective employment contracts, agreeing to some extra legal rights for the union, this does not necessarily mean that control has been devolved. All the evidence suggests, that wherever fast-food companies operate around the globe, commercial success remains predicated on tight control from the centre of both operations *and* employment policies (Royle, 2000). To the extent that local operators are autonomous, this must be largely explained by the level of experience and status of local operators. The more experienced franchise operators are more likely to be monitored less frequently precisely because the corporation knows that it is in the interests of such operators to adhere closely to commonly accepted employment practices. Central control need not be overt to be effective. In the final analysis the McDonald's Corporation is a 'global system'.

Fast-food labour relations before the Employment Contracts Act

Prior to the Employment Contracts Act, the New Zealand Tearooms and Restaurant Employees' Award set fast-food industry workers' terms and conditions of employment. In the late 1980s, the Service Workers Federation of Aotearoa (SWF) negotiated the Award on behalf of its affiliate unions, the regional hotel and restaurant workers' unions.[8] It covered workers in a number of sectors within the food service industry, including industrial catering, unlicensed restaurants, tearooms and coffee bars, as well as the takeaway and fast-food sectors. Grouping workers from differing work situations inevitably entailed a diminution of relevance. This was particularly so in the case of fast-food workers, as the Award was based on a traditional kitchen structure. As the former SWF Secretary recalls:

> people in McDonald's would pick up [the Award] and would not see any reference to swing shifts; they would see no reference to the phrases commonly used. And for people who were flipping hamburgers they were [classified as] cooks. They were cooks engaged to reconstitute pre-cooked or pre-prepared foods. This was just a nonsense to them. It seemed that [the Award] was irrelevant in terms of sick leave. It was written in terms of full-time staff who worked regular shifts.
>
> (Dannin, 1997: 67)

Nevertheless a proposal to split the Award in the late 1980s was resisted by a majority of SWF affiliates on the grounds that the more vulnerable workers in the smaller workplaces would be disadvantaged (interview with former SWF Secretary).[9] Although a number of enterprise-based agreements were made with factory cafeteria employers following a campaign in the mid-1980s, it was deemed too difficult to mount a similar campaign in the fast-food industry (ibid.). The final NZ Tearooms and Restaurants Employees' Award (Document 366) was registered on 7 November 1990 and set to expire on 5 April 1991, one month before the Employment Contracts Act was to take effect.

A significant development in fast-food labour relations during this period was the campaign against lower rates for younger workers. In 1987 the employers proposed youth rates in the process of negotiating a new Tearooms and Restaurants Employees' Award. The SWF mounted a campaign around opposition to this claim, targeting McDonald's in particular. Workers at three McDonald's restaurants in Auckland went on strike and as a result McDonald's management were compelled to abandon lower rates of pay for young workers.

With the defeat of the Labour government in November 1990 and the immediate introduction of the Employment Contracts Bill, the initiative passed decisively to employers. In early 1991, the employers' association proposed returning to lower rates of pay for young workers in the Tearooms and

Restaurants Employees' Award, removing premium rates for weekend work and eliminating certain union rights (including access rights, union subscriptions, and paid 'stopwork' meetings), in return for a 2 per cent wage increase. As a consequence moving towards separate company-level agreements became a matter of long-term survival for the union. The SWF therefore filed for negotiations under the existing Labour Relations Act 1987 for separate Awards and agreements, including KFC, Pizza Hut and contract caterers, in the event that negotiations for the new Award failed.

Fast-food labour relations since 1991

A broad survey of wage-setting outcomes suggests that fast-food labour relations under the Employment Contracts Act (ECA) were not exceptional in terms of the retail and hospitality industries generally. As noted above, premium rates for work on weekends and statutory holidays were eliminated quickly for many retail and hospitality workers after the introduction of the ECA. Such payments were eliminated for new workers across the fast-food sector between 1992 and 1993 and for existing workers by 1995. Similarly, the adoption of youth rates followed the general pattern for less skilled service sector work. After Georgie Pie adopted lower pay rates for young workers in 1993, the other operators had also introduced youth rates by 1995, with the exception of McDonald's referred to earlier.

Georgie Pie

Indigenous fast-food operator, Georgie Pie's major impact on labour relations in the local fast-food industry arose as a result of its ownership by one of New Zealand's largest supermarket groups, Progressive Enterprises. Whereas youth rates were uncommon in the hospitality industry prior to 1991, they prevailed in the supermarket sector. The Georgie Pie division of Progressive Enterprises therefore moved quickly to adopt youth rates following the advent of the ECA, along with the rest of the group. In doing so it initiated a race to introduce youth rates throughout the fast-food sector. The SWF union picketed the first Georgie Pie restaurant opened in Wellington in 1994 in protest at the company's use of youth rates (*Service Worker*, 1994). In 1996, 80 per cent of the Georgie Pie workforce was under 20 years of age, earning youth rates as low as $5 for 15–18 year olds (compared to the starting rate of $8.41 at McDonald's, who as we noted earlier were compelled to remove youth rates because of industrial action and probably concerns about their public image). Despite the cost advantage enjoyed as a result, the company was unable to turn around poor financial performance and, as noted above, the parent company had closed down or sold the properties by 1997.

McDonald's

On 14 May 1991, the day before the ECA came into effect, the first of the enterprise-based collective employment contracts in the fast-food industry was registered.[10] Initially, the McDonald's System collective contract and, to a lesser extent the subsequent relationship of McDonald's with the principal industry union, appeared to demonstrate a degree of openness to collective labour relations that is not usually associated with McDonald's in Anglo-Saxon countries (Royle, 2000). In late 1990 the SWF approached McDonald's management and outlined the problems that it saw with the award, stressing the lack of relevance for McDonald's staff and offering to use McDonald's terminology in a new contract specifically for the operator. McDonald's was the first of the fast-food operators with which the union proposed contract negotiations. According to an SWF official McDonald's management were 'intrigued' to find out that the employee/employer relationships at the local level were problematic. They agreed to address these problems with the franchisees and in order to obtain a majority agreement from the franchisees, the General Manager of the company and the principal union negotiator toured the country presenting the arguments for the new contract. When put to the vote only one franchisee opposed the proposal and a new contract was quickly drawn up, with the SWF representative contributing much of the new wording (ibid.). The contract provided for union fee deductions, two paid union meetings per year and workplace access to any employee who wished to meet with a union representative.

However, the union's central role in collective bargaining proved to be short-lived. At a meeting with the union in January 1992, McDonald's representatives outlined a new contract that specifically excluded the union as a party. In classic union-exclusion terms they reiterated McDonald's 'traditional' philosophy, emphasizing their belief 'in a direct relationship between employer and employee much as the Employment Contracts Act intends'. Furthermore they also pointed out their concern to recognize the views of the approximately 70 per cent of employees who were not union members at that time (McDonald's Employment Contracts: Rationale for Proposed Changes, undated document presented 7 January 1992). Nevertheless, McDonald's representatives maintained somewhat paradoxically that:

> We have a neutral view on unionism . . . [we also] . . . desire to maintain [the positive and mutually beneficial relationship with the union] without prejudicing our desire for direct employer–employee relationships and without compromising the matter of individual choice.

They also undertook to 'be helpful to the union', in agreeing to access to the crew room, facilitating meetings between new employees and union organizers, but 'without compromising individual rights, distribution of union material that is considered to be balanced, and liaising with the union on matters of mutual interest'.

The proposed contract also provided for union fee deductions from wages but only at the request of employees, and for two paid meetings per year. Citing deteriorating economic conditions and increased competition McDonald's proposed eliminating premium rates for overtime, weekend working and working on statutory holidays for new staff. The union therefore had an 'attenuated' role in the new contracting process, which might be more appropriately described as 'consultation' rather than 'negotiation'. In line with the concept of 'local ownership', store managers made 'captive audience' presentations to staff in each outlet; over 400 meetings in all. Although the union met with the McDonald's representatives before the new contract was introduced in March 1992, it was unable to gain significant changes to either the substantive terms or the procedure. The outcome was that each store maintained its own, though identical, contract with poorer terms and conditions for employees.

In 1995 McDonald's took a further step away from the traditional model of collective contracting. A new document entitled *McDonald's Employment Policies* replaced the previous collective employment contracts at each store. As previously, the union was 'consulted' before the new employment conditions were promulgated, but little substantive change was agreed as a result. The new handbook retained the concept of standarized conditions for all McDonald's staff, but in legal terms they were employed on individual employment contracts (in the form of a 'personal letter') incorporating the 'Employment Policies'. The Employment Policies were only to be changed 'by agreement between McDonald's and a majority of staff, nationally, and after consultation with the union' (McDonald's Employment Policies, 1995). They remained in force without amendment until a new contract was introduced in March 2000. By contrast with any meaningful form of collective employment contract, McDonald's Employment Policies (1995) did not include pay rates. But it did include, on the other hand, McDonald's 'philosophy', 'The Customer Ten Commandments'. Although the individual employee's right to choose 'any other person to represent you on matters relating to your employment' was noted, and an entitlement for 'staff' to hold paid meetings provided, the document emphasized the promotion of cooperation and harmony.

In 1999 McDonald's initiated a review of the Employment Policies. At the outset of the review no changes to the form of the policies were envisaged, and the role of the union was not clear.[11] In keeping with an undertaking given to the union in 1995 to consult before changing the Employment Policies, the 'Employer of Choice' Taskforce charged with overseeing the review met with union representatives and incorporated the union's position in its report back to staff. The major conduit for employee influence was a process whereby feedback, from 'break out' groups of staff in all workplaces, along with discussions with union representatives, formed the basis for a report back to staff and an invitation for further feedback from staff along with small focus groups in outlets. The 'Taskforce' also met again with union representatives. By this point the general election campaign was underway and a major debate over the Employment Contracts Act focused attention on the merits of collective bargaining. Not surprisingly, then, some crew and the union raised the need for a collective employment contract. As a result, McDonald's agreed to the concept of a three-year 'collective employment agreement' to which the SWF and its Canterbury counterpart would be parties. Of the 52 per cent of crew members who voted in a secret ballot, over 95 per cent voted for the new contract. Contract formation aside, however, the role of the union at McDonald's is limited in practice to handling a small number of personal grievances, as elsewhere in the low-skilled service sector. Union officials do have access to workplaces to meet with members and non-members, and the company deducts union fees for staff, but there are no delegates' facilities extended by the company (perhaps as a result of a lack of active delegates) or paid union meetings.[12]

Limited evidence of the response of McDonald's employees to their work experience is provided by a small McDonald's supported survey of crew members in Auckland McDonald's outlets (Reid and Melrose, 1999). Not surprisingly some employees were found to view McDonald's as providing opportunities for management training and progression, personal learning opportunities, and enjoyable work experiences, while a smaller number of respondents reported negative feelings about pay, hours of work and work intensity.

Other fast-food chains[13]

The other fast-food operators' approaches to employment contract formation and relations with unions vary to differing degrees from McDonald's'. In one case the operator continues to structure its contractual relations with its workforce on a collective basis, and to negotiate with the union. In this case, the negotiation of the first collective employment contract under the Employment Contracts Act proved more openly adversarial than had McDonald's. An initial approach from the union, along lines similar to that to McDonald's, saw the union refused entry to workplaces to distribute material, and a proposal by the company to distribute its own collective employment contract directly to its staff. Employees were invited to consider negotiating directly with the company, or to appoint a bargaining agent other than the union, as alternatives to authorizing the union to negotiate. It took concerted action, both industrial and legal, by the union before the company joined the union in negotiating a new collective employment contract. The union's campaign reveals how tenuous was its ability to sustain direct industrial action, even early in life of the ECA. At only one store, in the southern town of Invercargill, did a picket of workers force the manager to close the store. At the same time the union mounted a community-based campaign. It used radio advertising telling members not to sign the collective employment contract and pressed community leaders and Labour Members of Parliament to make public statements urging negotiations with the union. This was a novel departure from established practice in New Zealand, inspired by the success of the union's US counterpart, the Service Employees International Union. It also prepared to take the company to the Employment Court over its actions in persuading employees to sign its collective employment contract and, where they were union members, to consider leaving the union.[14] Direct action was buttressed by community campaigning and recourse to a legal solution. The new contract did not include the union as a party but retained union rights to two paid meetings with members per year, union fee deductions, and access to all staff.

Further contracts were negotiated with the union on five occasions between 1991 and 1999. However, it would be inaccurate to characterize the negotiations as evenly balanced. The union succeeded in attenuating some of the employer's proposals, but was unable to prevent some significant deterioration in employment conditions. In 1995 a union official argued the case for the company to continue to negotiate with the union; however, a manager informed him that the company was aware that it did not need to negotiate with the unions, but that it considered the union to be its 'conscience'!

Paradoxically this company allowed union organizers access to potential members in the workplace and to deduct union fees. In 1995, for example, the union mounted a successful membership drive that led to a doubling of membership. Managers were reported by union officials to have been 'relaxed' about allowing the union access to staff: some allowing union organizers to meet with staff *en masse*, or entry into lunch rooms, others allowing union officials to meet with crew individually in the restaurant area. Union literature and a membership form were distributed through the payroll and additional concessions included: provision for the distribution of information about union services by the employer; lists of staff names by the employer at the union's request; and for union access 'not to be unreasonably withheld'; to discuss contractual matters; and allowing discussion of union membership with any other employee who agrees to such a meeting. These provisions were contained in all of the collective employment contracts negotiated by this operator during the period of the ECA. The advent of the ECA in October 2000 did not therefore significantly alter the formal relationship between the union and this company, and there were no discussions about future relations between the union and the company prior to or immediately following the new Act taking force.

In the cases of the remaining New Zealand fast-food operators, the union plays no role in wage setting and contact is limited to a small number of individual grievances. Through the 1990s, collective contracting with the union was superseded by either a collective contract with no union involvement, or (in two cases) individual contracts, the standard terms of which management set with minimal or no consultation with employees. Prior to the introduction of the Employment Relations Bill in February 2000, one of the latter companies maintained that its overall approach to individual staff joining the union was 'neutral'. While it did not deduct union fees or have a formal agreement on access or other union rights, access to staff had been provided 'from time-to-time in different areas'. By August 2000, as the advent of the Employment Relations Act neared, this company initiated a meeting with the union to discuss future relations including the formation of a new collective agreement. The other company that had individual contracting in place in 1999 made no attempt to contact the union.

Across the fast-food sector dealings with the union were reported by 1999 as 'very infrequent', 'virtually non-existent' or 'none at all'. Outside of the pay-fixing consultations, where these occurred, the small number of dealings at head office level related to individual employees. There was some indication that relations with the union would be placed on a new footing in the case of one comapny as a result of the Employment Relations Act 2000. However, there were no indications of sweeping changes in union–management relations within the fast-food industry in the short term. Rather, the union was preparing to target workers for recruitment in other areas of the service sector where it considered its limited resources would be better placed, given the lower levels of organization within the fast-food industry and the higher levels of grievances against their employers held by other service sector workers.

Somewhat paradoxically, considering the dramatic erosion of union membership in the service sector since 1991, which was complemented by a management wish to exclude union influence, most management interviewees still expressed some acceptance of a limited role for unions. Indeed in another study that included hotels, one manager stated:

> I don't have a problem with the union. I don't care whether we have a union or not. If I had a problem with a dismissal and that person's a union member, I've sought advice. Because if you involve the union at the right time, then the union will be helpful, because they want to see their work . . . they want to succeed as well. It's a matter of trust.
>
> (Ryan, 1997: 315)

Conclusions

New Zealand fast-food operators used the freedoms conferred by the Employment Contracts Act 1991 to eliminate or reduce many of their employees' terms and conditions. In particular, they pared away premium wage rates for overtime, weekend and statutory holiday work and (with the 'coerced' exception of McDonald's mentioned earlier) introduced lower pay rates for under-20-year-olds. In some cases, base pay rates for new employees were reduced. A depressed economy and historically high rates of unemployment assisted the process in the early years of the ECA. In this context, the union was unable to prevent the reductions in terms and conditions, as elsewhere in the low-skilled service sector, because of the weakness of its organization at workplace level and the sharp decline in membership density in the fast-food industry to around 5–10 per cent by the late 1990s. Where it was accorded a voice in the determination of wages and conditions it was at best only able to delay or attenuate the process. It must be emphasized, however, that these developments reflect the general pattern of change in the retail and hospitality sectors, in which fast-food operators compete for labour. Base wage movements in the fast-food industry kept pace with increases over the labour market as a whole over the period of the Employment Contracts Act; indeed, in some cases wage rates moved ahead of the service sector in the early 1990s. By comparison with, for example, supermarket workers, many fast-food workers were relatively well paid albeit still at relatively low levels of pay.

A wide range of responses to the freedoms offered by the Employment Contracts Act is evident in the areas of contract formation and recognition of collective rights. While some New Zealand fast-food operators negotiated with the union in the process of contract formation, others structured the employment relationship entirely on an individual, though standardized, basis. Fast-food employers have also varied greatly in their approach to union rights. All allow unions access to members and potential members, although these are statutory requirements. Most but not all deduct union fees for staff, and in one case there is still a contractual entitlement for paid union meetings. The variation in approach to contract formation and union rights appears to reflect a number of factors, including initial levels of unionization, the residual capacity of the union to impose a sanction, New Zealand managers' individual preferences, and possibly even personal relationships. It should be remembered, however, that even where it is afforded a role in contract formation, the union exercises little influence over the outcomes. Rather, labour relations issues as a whole became increasingly marginalized over the period of the Employment Contracts Act after the changes to key terms and conditions introduced in the early 1990s.

It is difficult to predict with precision the patterns of labour relations which will arise in the New Zealand fast-food industry under the Employment Relations Act. Weakened by years of membership loss, the union has prioritized other areas for active membership recruitment, where its organizational strength and levels of worker grievance are greater. On the other hand, early developments indicate that, rather than contesting the union's right to participate in wage determination, fast-food operators in New Zealand are, in compliance with statutory requirements, according the union a formal though limited role. Indeed labour relations in the New Zealand fast-food industry reveal themselves to be more complex and finely nuanced than might be supposed. In the context of continuing deregulation fast-food companies will increasingly do what they want to do with minimal resistance. The logic of tight control of commercial operations implies a tight control of labour relations in the interests of employers and the bottom line.

Notes

1 For the purposes of this chapter 'fast-food' is defined as the provision of a limited, standard menu with quick service, achieved through the rigorous application of scientific management principles. It is the latter feature, in particular, which distinguishes the process from traditional 'take away' or 'carry out' food (for a further discussion see the Editors' introduction).

2 The union membership figure is taken from unpublished data provided by the NZ Department of Labour and reported by Crawford, Harbridge and Walsh (1999). The labour market figure used to calculate union density is taken from the official New Zealand Household Labour Force Survey and includes employers, self-employed or unpaid workers in family businesses, thereby understating union density by around one-fifth. Also, the Household Labour Force Survey data aggregate full-time and part-time workers, but as union membership is calculated on a full-time equivalent basis, total union density is further understated.

3 Note that all of the fast-food operators monitor retail industry wages and conditions closely, as the industry is seen as drawing from the same pool of labour (interview notes).

4 The franchise arrangements are historical, pre-dating the takeover of the principal KFC franchisee in 1989. Restaurant Brands has no plans to increase the number of franchisees.

5 Tricon was formed when PepsiCo divested its Worldwide Restaurant Group into a new public company in October 1997.

6 The New Zealand franchisee for Burger King, TPF Restaurants, owns all Burger King outlets in New Zealand. The four businessmen who set up the operation in 1994 own 50 per cent of the company and Shell New Zealand owns half. But it is Tasman Pacific Foods Ltd, a separate company wholly owned by the four founders of the New Zealand operation, which manages the operation and is therefore responsible for deciding HRM and labour relations policies and practices.

7 It must be remembered that the franchisee (TPF) is a company and that this does not tell us the extent to which individual restaurants have autonomy in the conduct of the employment relationship. Furthermore TPF is also responsible for maintaining the brand [Eds].

8 In May 1991, six of the seven affiliated regional unions merged into the Service Workers Union of Aotearoa (SWU). The Canterbury Hotel, Hospital, Restaurant, Club and Related Trades Union of Workers remained separate. Reflecting the practice, the SWF is referred to as 'the union' where it acted on behalf of its affiliates.

9 The Labour Relations Act 1987 enabled unions to maintain award coverage or negotiate enterprise agreements with employers ('cite out'). However, three-quarters of all registered unions failed to 'cite out' any employers (Harbridge and McCaw, 1992).

10 McDonald's System of New Zealand Limited and Licensees Employees' Composite Award (Document 2668). As the franchisee employers were separate companies, the document took the form of an award. From 15 May 1991, all existing awards and (single employer) agreements were deemed by the

Employment Contracts Act 1991 to be collective employment contracts made under the new Act. The Award is referred to as a contract in the text to avoid confusion.

11 By 1999 only about 5 per cent of McDonald's workforce were members of the SWU, although this is high compared with the UK, US, Canada and Singapore cited in this chapter and lower than in some continental European countries (Royle, 2000).

12 The Employment Contracts Act required employers only to provide access to the authorized union for the purposes of contract negotiations.

13 Undertakings of confidentiality prevent the identification of fast-food operators in this section, with the exception of McDonald's. The cooperation in general of all of the respondents is acknowledged.

14 This is somewhat reminiscent of 'yellow dog' contracts prevalent in the US before they were outlawed in 1932 (Eds).

11 Summary and conclusions

MNCs, regulatory systems and employment rights

Tony Royle and Brian Towers

Introduction

This final chapter offers a summary of the findings and arguments of previous chapters. It also attempts to locate the book within the wider empirical
and theoretical debates around the concepts of globalization and the role of
MNCs. There is no doubt that the fast-food industry is growing in significance not only in terms of sales but also in terms of employment. It could
be argued that fast-food is also promoting a particular perspective on
employment which is encouraging employment 'flexibility' in its worst
sense: insecure, low skilled, poorly paid work. In other words the opposite
of a more positive form of 'flexibility' where employees can develop skills,
earn a good living and have a large degree of control over balancing the
work and non-work aspects of their lives. In addition it is a form of work
that provides little or no opportunity for employee voice and often takes
place in a non-union environment. This situation is undoubtedly driven by
the nature of the business itself, i.e. with labour costs forming a large proportion of the overall cost of the business, with the minimization of such costs
becoming the paramount objective of management. In addition such chain
operations are dominated by systems that in classic scientific management
terms have no room for employees other than as simple and interchangeable
units of production. The notion that employees should have democratic
rights that would allow them to shape the 'system' is generally a non-starter
in this context without trade union and/or state intervention.

Furthermore, these systems are culturally embedded in the industry
particularly in the large Anglo-Saxon multinational 'burger' chains. Careful
selection and training of management help to maintain a strong corporate
culture of which McDonald's activities in Russia are a prime example. Its
'leave Russia at the door' policy and its 'summer camps' for workers show
the extent to which companies of this kind can persuade their managers to
adopt and promote corporate values regardless of societal norms. This is
not to say that large-scale MNCs do not allow *some* autonomy for their
operations under different regulatory regimes in different societies. But this
is strictly limited given the over-riding imperative of maintaining efficient,

globally profitable systems: excessive autonomy would undermine the organizational logic of MNCs in the fast-food industry. Franchising drives much of the expansion in this industry but although some authors have alluded to seemingly autonomous employment practices in franchises, what is clear is that these are largely a matter of form, not substance. Overall, such well-established and powerful systems create considerable problems for independent and effective employee representation even in the countries of mainland Europe where legislation supporting employee rights is comprehensive and more strictly applied than elsewhere. The following summary of the findings revolves around two main themes: first, that of the characteristics of the fast-food workforce and the pay and conditions in the industry; and second, the issue of employee representation.

The fast-food workforce

In part, fast-food companies are able to pursue these employment practices because they are able to target weak and marginalized segments of the labour market, employing workers likely to be acquiescent to managerial prerogative. In Chapter 2, Leidner, reporting on the US, suggests that most fast-food employees are likely to be young, female and part-time, and in many other countries workers are also likely to be young with little previous experience of work and often no knowledge or experience of trade unions. Many simply move on to other jobs after a short time and, because of the transitory nature of this employment experience, they may have little interest in joining unions or in taking even limited collective action to improve their pay and working conditions. Indeed, Leidner points out that in the US, where individualism and meritocracy are deeply embedded in the culture, fast-food workers receive little support from the wider public or even other workers. Fast-food employment is also seen as an 'appropriate' first work experience for teenagers. Hence, there is little sympathy for older fast-food workers who stay with the company because they are seen to have 'failed' and therefore deserve what they get. Of course this perspective overlooks the fact that labour is not homogeneous; individuals in the labour market are not equal, they vary widely in their characteristics and opportunity of access to employment. It is also a mistake to think that fast-food restaurants are entirely staffed by young workers and that labour turnover is always high. As we saw in Chapter 5, in countries like Germany, labour turnover is much lower than in countries such as the US, Canada, the UK, Australia and New Zealand. This is because a large proportion of fast-food workforces are made up of ethnic minorities (such as those of Turkish descent) and economic migrants (mostly from Eastern Europe) who cannot find work elsewhere and are also more likely to be older workers, some of whom are highly qualified.[1] Additionally, Royle (2000) points out that in Austria the situation is similar to that in Germany and regions such as the south of Italy where unemployment amongst fast-food older workers is high, the workers are older and stay longer in the industry.

Furthermore, in ethical terms, why should workers regardless of age, ethnic background, qualifications and experience be required to endure poor working conditions and low pay simply because there is no other work available to them? And why should young workers, who often lack previous experience, be discriminated against in terms of rights, pay and conditions of work when previous experience is irrelevant for this kind of work? There is no inexorable law of labour market behaviour that precludes intervention by trade unions, and especially the state, to promote and protect good pay and conditions in employment. Nor are employers themselves necessarily exempt from introducing and maintaining good employment practices. Indeed there are many instances of employers outside the fast-food sector in large MNCs doing so without damaging, and even contributing to, their commercial success. Even within the sector, as Royle (2000: 160) suggests, there are examples where conditions are somewhat better than elsewhere. Due to the intervention of trade unions and state legislation the disposable income of McDonald's employees in Norway in 1999 was 90 per cent of the average for all workers with Denmark and Sweden not far behind with more than 70 and 65 per cent respectively. Yet McDonald's remains a profitable enterprise in Scandinavia. By contrast, the worst example, perhaps not surprisingly, where trade union intervention is non-existent and legislation minimal, was the US with a figure of 40 per cent.

Pereira's chapter on Singapore also illustrates the extent to which fast-food companies are able to target acquiescent sectors of the labour market. When adequate numbers of young workers could no longer be hired in Singapore, McDonald's was able to make use of 'McAunties' and 'McUncles' (i.e. older workers) who were only too pleased to find work in air-conditioned surroundings. In this way the company, with no additional cost to itself, improved its public image as it provided employment for a particularly vulnerable segment of the labour market (older workers) experiencing high levels of unemployment. In a similar way in Chapter 6 Benders and colleagues point out that the promotion of female and ethnic minority employment at McDonald's coincided exactly with the Dutch government's employment policies. In Russia McDonald's specifically targeted young workers from amongst the vast numbers of people applying for jobs with the company. These workers were much more likely to take on the values of the corporation than older workers who may still harbour the vestiges of collectivism and worker solidarity. In all these cases workers are likely to be acquiescent: either workers need the job and are therefore unlikely to put their jobs at risk by questioning managerial prerogative; or they have no previous experience and know nothing else; or simply have no interest in criticizing management because they will move on to something else before long. In the case of disabled workers McDonald's is a proactive employer with its 'McJobs' programme. However, the US government subsidizes the corporation for each disabled employee at an average rate of $800 (Royle, 2000). These workers also form part of the acquiescent workforce in some restaurants, as those who, in many other cases, cannot find work elsewhere. Such opportunism in hiring practices may well not be unwelcome to those employed, but it should not be confused with altruism.

Employee representation in fast-food

One important lesson to be drawn from this study is that whatever the systems of employee representation in countries – and these vary widely from the least regulated of North America, Britain and Singapore to the highly regulated systems of continental Europe – large MNCs have in many cases been able to tame, neutralize or subvert these systems, particularly at workplace level. Some countries rely more on trade unions and collective bargaining to advance and defend employee rights whilst others rely on a combination of both legal regulation – including statutory works councils and collective bargaining. There is also the supranational form of regulation in the EU, notably the European Works Council and the forthcoming EU directive on information and consultation for works councils at national level. Other forms of intervention such as the EU working time directive and directives on health and safety also have implications for employee representation. Nor is the balance between collective bargaining and state intervention stable. As trade union membership and collective bargaining retreat most countries have sought to regulate the labour market directly through the law, including the US.

Yet in the US and the UK, fast-food corporations still have the ability to promote their interests virtually untrammelled by trade unions and legal regulation. In the UK, despite the Employment Relations Act of 1999, according to the Prime Minister the UK still remains 'the most lightly regulated labour market of any leading economy in the world'. Nor is there any evidence that the new statutory recognition procedure will have any impact on the UK fast-food industry, given the bargaining unit determination constraints, continued employer opposition and the absence of an effective union presence. As Chapter 4 indicates there are, as yet, no recognition agreements in the sector and only a small number of union members in one or two firms. In the US there is a similar situation. Although according to Leidner (Chapter 2) there have been a few sporadic and determined attempts to unionize individual fast-food restaurants but 'no broader movement to unionize McDonald's or the rest of the fast-food industry has yet materialized. This outcome is not unconnected with American labour law, which, despite its aim of encouraging collective bargaining, under the central statute enacted as far back as 1935, has, if anything, done the opposite (Gould, 1994; Human Rights Watch, 2000).

In Canada, the nature of the work and the characteristics of the workforce have been strong impediments to union organization. Despite some successes – such as KFC in British Columbia, where, though its workers had an existing agreement inherited from the previous owner of the restaurants – the industry remains almost entirely non-union. The labour laws in all Canadian provinces are not universally union-friendly, despite the generally more favourable legal contexts in Canada relative to the US and the much higher incidence of union membership and collective bargaining. Nor do Canadian employers behave significantly more sympathetically towards unions, who, Reiter (Chapter 3) suggests, are faced with the 'usual combination' of legal, quasi-legal and sometimes illegal practices. Perhaps the collective lesson to be drawn from the entire North American experience is the ability of employers, as elsewhere, to avoid the strictures of even reasonably favourable labour law even where the law defining the bargaining unit and the availability of card counts is more favourable to unions.[2] In countries like Singapore (Pereira, Chapter 8) there is no state provision for mandatory unionization or employee interest representation. Given strong employer preferences, it is hardly surprising that the fast-food industry in Singapore is completely union free.

In Russia, McDonald's is the only major fast-food MNC and it has not so far been significantly challenged by its employees or the Russian trade unions. As Sheksnia and colleagues point out:

> McDonald's has been criticized for steadfastly refusing to deal with trade unions seeking to represent its employees and has also refused the implementation of a collective agreement that would undoubtedly improve conditions and wage levels.
>
> (Sheksnia *et al.*, Chapter 7 this volume: 134)

Significantly, they also note on the same page that 'the less than fully developed state of Russia's legislation and legal practices may have helped the corporation to implement its strategies in this regard'. More recently McDonald's, after the intervention of the Russian parliament, has recognized a small union of seventeen workers in its Moscow 'McComplex' processing plant. However, this agreement only provides union representatives with an office space and a small administrative budget and two hours per week to work on union activities. There is as yet no sign of an agreement on terms and conditions of work despite the recognition of the union (York, 2001). This is typical of the kind of employer delaying tactic found in the US and Canada and not only in the fast-food industry. Employers know that the longer they wait to start meaningful negotiations towards a contract, the more likely it is that the union's influence will diminish and leave it vulnerable to a de-certification challenge. It is also significant to note that the very limited trade union success in Russia followed the intervention of a state institution, and that even this small victory is likely to be short lived. In this newly emerging 'democratic' society, the Russian government is planning to introduce restrictions on the rights and benefits of workers in the interests of attracting inward investment. York (2001) reports that the Kremlin is planning to draw up a new labour code which will remove many of the Soviet-era trade union guarantees that still exist and, in a way which will undoubtedly delight many employers, will slash maternity leave, lower the minimum working age and allow a 'voluntary' 12-hour workday.

Ostensibly the more highly regulated systems in Australia and New Zealand should provide less favourable contexts for MNCs in the fast-food industry. However, as Allen and colleagues (Chapter 9) illustrate, Australian unions have felt obliged to make significant concessions. In order to gain recognition the unions have had to agree to lower rates of pay and no premium rates for weekend work. There are also instances of the state siding with MNC fast-food operators as, for example, in Queensland where special award conditions have been granted to fast-food companies on the grounds that the industry employed a low skilled, predominantly student workforce. In 1983 following an award, MNCs such as McDonald's, Hungry Jack's and KFC returned to their familiar, aggressive non-union practices, which included the termination of all check-off agreements. In New Zealand, following government deregulatory intervention introduced in the 1991 Employment Contracts Act, bargaining power shifted decisively towards employers, seen in the early elimination of weekend and statutory holiday employment followed by the adoption of lower rates of pay for young workers. However, and significantly, after concerns about its image brought on by industrial action carried out by some of its employees, McDonald's dropped the lower rates of pay for young workers. This anti-union climate, not of course confined to fast-food, eventually attracted the attention of the new government, which, in 2000, introduced the more protective Employment Relations Act. Whilst it is too early yet to assess the impact of the new legislation, it is probable that the anti-union culture established in the 1990s will take some time to erode, if at all. Employers in the industry remain powerfully entrenched faced with the very limited organizational strength of employees and their representatives.

Germany, because of its highly juridified industrial relations system, the formal legitimation of the trade union role and the extensive system of works councils, may be seen as one of the more favourable contexts for the development of effective employee representation in the fast-food industry. Yet, as Royle (2000: chapter 5) indicates, the German unions continue to have difficulty in raising basic pay levels, ensuring adequate adherence to collective agreements and establishing union supported works councils, particularly amongst Anglo-Saxon corporations. Indeed, despite companies such as Burger King, McDonald's and Tricon (Pizza Hut, KFC) easily meeting the statutory thresholds for numbers of workers, they have no supervisory boards and very few, or no, works councils. Low pay remains a feature of a labour market that has high levels of unemployment amongst unskilled workers and absorbs large numbers of economic migrants (mostly from Eastern Europe) desperate to find work in the West. Royle illustrates how companies such as McDonald's have successfully managed to avoid collective agreements for 18 years, and continue to resist works councils. Indeed McDonald's appears to have developed a whole range of 'avoidance strategies' (Royle, 1998, 2000). These include, for example, changing ownership of restaurants; buying out workers en masse; capturing works councils by appointing company-friendly employees and managers; and various other effective stratagems. There is much evidence to conclude that though most German national fast-food companies tend to adopt more cooperative relations with unions and works councils, there are some who take an anti-union stance. However, it also evident that even some of the more union-friendly companies are also becoming less willing to accept unions and statutory works councils as they adopt increasingly systematized working methods, removing more experienced and more expensive skilled workers as the sector as a whole consolidates into a smaller number of larger scale operations. What remains surprising is the extent to which Anglo-Saxon fast-food MNCs, in particular, are able to avoid key elements of seemingly strict regulation and impose their own employment systems and corporate cultures.

In the Netherlands, until the *Accoord of Wassenaar* in 1982, relations between McDonald's and the Dutch unions were highly conflictual. However, the outbreak of peace following Wassenaar was conditional. The Accoord which was partly designed to promote the employment of ethnic minorities and women, did in fact, perfectly match McDonald's employment profile. Furthermore, the incomes policy aspects of the *Accoord* favoured the Corporation's aim of controlling its labour costs. Since that time relations with unions at sectoral level have been reasonably cooperative. However, throughout the 1990s McDonald's continued to resist works councils in its restaurants, so that by 1998 only three or four works councils existed in over 160 restaurants. More recently the Corporation, presumably mindful of its public image, has agreed to the establishment of a company-level works council although the council represents only 10 per cent of its total workforce employed in company-owned restaurants, and it is too early as yet to see how effective it will be in practice. What is clear is that in a country characterized by consensual industrial relations any inward investor has to appear to be cooperative. However, as Benders (Chapter 6 in this volume: 116) and colleagues argue, 'this policy change must not be mistaken for a humanitarian concern for democracy'.

EU level regulation promoting employee consultation and information rights through legislation such as the European Works Council (EWC) Directive has been much vaunted but in practice has been largely ineffective in the fast-food sector, especially when one consider such cases as the EWCs at McDonald's (Royle, 1999b, 2000) and PepsiCo/Tricon. To begin with, the EWC directive does not cover franchise operations and therefore excludes the majority of employees in fast-food MNCs in Europe.[3] Second, the voluntary arrangements provided for in the directive have allowed determined employers such as PepsiCo/Tricon and McDonald's to infiltrate and control the process of establishing the councils to suit their own interests and agendas. Both corporations have specifically excluded, unless unavoidable, the involvement of national unions and international union organizations. As further insurance, employee representatives are often, where possible, hand picked to ensure adherence to corporate values and strategies (Crowley, 1996; Hazan, 1996; North, 1996; Royle, 1999b, 2000).

Some wider considerations: globalization and the MNC

This volume appears at a time of fierce political and academic debate, reflecting widespread dissatisfaction with the claimed inevitability and beneficence of a globalizing economy, increasingly dominated by MNCs. At the same time there is a continuing debate as to the meaning and extent of globalization to which both industrial relations academics and others of varying disciplines have contributed. Some of these debates have involved a revival and re-working of the convergence and divergence theses. Recent work in the industrial relations field has included that of Locke (1992, 1995); Frenkel (1993); Katz (1997); Katz and Darbishire (2000).

The question we consider here is to what extent do the findings on the global fast-food industry, detailed in these pages contribute empirically and theoretically to the debate on the nature of global industrial relations transformation, including the role of the MNCs within that transformation? That there is some form of global transformation is not seriously contested; however, partly drawing on the authors cited above, we argue that this transformation is largely driven by a 'convergence' across seven main dimensions:[4]

1 An increasing domination of the enterprise, mainly in the form of the MNC, and, driven by the relocation of sites to cheaper production areas, contracting out and (in this study) franchising. This form of convergence can also be associated with a shift towards the management of global commodity chains.
2 The relative decline in the significance and regulatory power of national systems.
3 The often non-existent, weak or ineffective nature of supranational regulation. Examples are: the relative failure of public and corporate codes of conduct; NAFTA's virtual exclusion of social policy clauses; and the 'menu' driven nature of EU regulation, which often leaves many loopholes that MNCs can exploit.
4 The growth of HRM employment practices and associated forms of work organization and flexibility. These may not necessarily advance employment rights and in fact may lead to the opposite.
5 A tendency towards low wage employment.
6 A global, though uneven, decline in trade union membership.

7   A continuing divergence of practices within national systems associated with particular sectoral requirements and modes of production, as Locke (1992, 1995) suggests.

The evidence of the studies in this volume is unequivocal on the domination of large MNCs in the global fast-food industry. Though McDonald's is by far the most prominent, other corporations are significant competitors either across regions such as Europe or globally. Traditional domestic players have had to become larger and/or multinationals themselves in order to compete, leading to increasing concentration in all countries reported here. That the favoured form of organization is the franchise does not limit this finding. Indeed, franchises offer substantial advantages to MNCs in the provision of start-up capital and the driving down of labour costs in a labour intensive industry, but without losing control of a standardized, Fordist labour process. Indeed the increasing use of information technology allows MNCs to maintain an even tighter grip on franchise activities. As we argue in the introduction, franchises are de facto subsidiaries of MNCs in the fast-food industry but without many of the attendant costs and problems. As we suggest above, the use of franchises can also be seen as being part of the larger trend towards the management of global commodity chains.

Franchisees can also be important in the context of the relationship between the industry's MNCs and the regulatory systems of the countries within which they do business. It can be deployed in the letter of the law, though not the spirit, to evade regulations linked to exemptions for small businesses. This remains the case under EU-wide consultative institutions and in countries such as the UK which retain employment cut-offs under a number of regulations including trade union access to statutory recognition procedures. However, the law *can* be changed to remove the franchise exemption as in the case of the Canadian province of British Columbia, noted earlier.

Beyond the still obvious opportunities offered to MNCs by the franchise, the wider evidence on the regulation of national systems is somewhat less equivocal. MNCs in fast-food – particularly in countries such as the US, Canada, the UK, Russia and Singapore – have little difficulty in subverting and avoiding national regulations which conflict with their interests and policies. Indeed regulation in some of these is so weak that no conflicts arise. In the countries of mainland Europe particularly in Scandinavian countries (Royle, 2000, 2002) they are much more constrained by the presence of strong social democratic traditions and stringent regulation and higher levels of union membership. However, even in these countries, where MNCs have in most cases finally had to take part in sectoral bargaining arrangements of one form or another, effective employee representation at the workplace is often weak or non-existent, with MNCs effectively undermining statutory mechanisms. Furthermore despite collective bargaining arrangements either being enforced by law, or through the pressure of successful union action and media pressure (as in Germany, for example), pay in fast-food in mainland Europe is still low in many countries. The only real exception to this being in Norway and Denmark (see Royle, 2000). To a lesser extent fast-food MNCs in Australia and New Zealand have also been constrained by national regulation and practice. However, in practice such constraints have been far from onerous; MNCs have benefited from changes in government policy supporting more business friendly approaches, with the outcome that, once again, effective employee representation at the workplace is poor or non-existent and pay and conditions have suffered. Overall, although the limitations of national regulatory regimes can be restrictive it remains clear that, in general, the evidence from fast-food is that determined, well-resourced MNCs can largely exempt themselves from key elements of such restrictions.

It would be difficult in general to characterize fast-food MNCs as following the HRM paradigm, even the 'hard' variant. Unlike the automotive industry which has, by a mixture of choice and compulsion, to some extent moved away from Fordist systems and controls whilst seeking to implement 'high performance' working practices such as job rotation, teamwork and quality enhancing techniques – all within a framework of employee involvement and consultation and commonly an active trade union presence – fast-food remains 'backward'. Although fast-food MNCs have at times introduced teamwork and employee involvement practices, independent employee representation is absent. The imperative behind such practices is the maintenance of a highly disciplined employment relationship and standardized systems of control and service that preclude any serious national or local autonomy. In this context, and by this logic, effective employee representation has no place. It is also relatively easy to avoid, given the frequently transient and acquiescent nature of the fast-food labour force. The outcomes, as already indicated, are endemic low pay, no effective voice for the workforce and, wherever possible, the avoidance of collective bargaining. The chapter on Germany, for example, shows how McDonald's resisted collective agreements for many years and was only forced to the bargaining table by increasing media pressure.

However, there is some limited evidence of variation *within* countries in the fast-food sector as Locke (1992, 1995) suggests is the case in other industries. Whilst American and British-owned MNCs tend to adopt similar practices, especially with regard to resisting employee representation, non-Anglo-Saxon companies show some differences, even though these tend to be national players and not MNCs. However, the explanation for the difference in approaches to such issues as employee representation is not just 'country of origin effect'; it also reflects the history of ownership of the company concerned and the attitudes of individual managers.

In general, the absence of trade unions in the workplace and low levels of trade union membership are largely explained by the nature of the fast-food labour force, the Fordist nature of fast-food production systems, and the sustained hostility of the corporations and their franchisees (albeit sometimes masked by the rhetoric of cooperation in some countries). Evidence from the US, across all industries, also shows that potential union membership is strongly influenced by hostile managerial attitudes (Freeman and Rogers, 1999). Similarly Teague (2001), commenting on the work of Katz and Darbishire (2000), suggests that across various industries and countries systems of labour market governance have been destabilized and are underperforming in one way or another. Trade union revival, in such contexts, is certainly not guaranteed by even vigorous, well-led and well-funded organization strategies, as again the US reveals. The evidence, including this study, increasingly suggests that a necessary, though not sufficient, condition for the revival of union representation is strong public policy intervention to control employer resistance whilst encouraging the development of more positive corporate strategies.

Fast-food: limited prospects for employment rights?

The future for employment conditions in the fast-food industry does not look very positive. Overall the triangular relationship between employers, trade unions and other representative and consultative bodies and the state is both unequal and shifting. The experience of the international fast-food industry suggests that trade unions on their own are always handicapped in the power relationship between themselves and large corporations, particularly MNCs, commanding highly superior resources. In this unequal relationship the role of the state is crucial. The stance that it adopts towards either of the parties will tend to determine the outcome. In the fast-food industry, in particular, the characteristics of the labour force and low union strength make state intervention essential both directly, in the form of legislation protecting and advancing individual employee rights and, indirectly, through the positive encouragement of collective bargaining and other forms of employee representation. Even in the case of strong and well-established state intervention the outcomes are far from always favourable to the interests of employees, given the much greater power available to employers, even in unionized workplaces. Nor are the organizational targets easily recognized: fast-food MNCs, as in other industries, can be seen merely as the apex of a vast superstructure of supply and control as MNCs increasingly become 'brand managers' of global commodity chains rather than 'manufacturers', whilst retaining and extending control over power and resources. Hence the task of regulation is both more difficult and more complex. As Ramsay (2000) pointed out in his insightful analysis, if trade unions want to become more effective in combating MNCs, they may need to develop strategies to find and act on weaknesses within these global commodity chains. They must also seek to forge effective partnerships wherever possible with national governments and international institutions. And the state in all of its manifestations cannot be left out of the equation.

Finally, although in this study we have been centrally concerned with the employment rights of workers within the MNC and in one industry, such rights should also be viewed in their wider social and political dimensions. Freedom of association and the implied rights to form trade unions, bargain collectively and strike are now well grounded as fundamental or human rights in international law and the laws of regional associations such as the European Union. Human rights as inalienable democratic rights are too important to be left to the amoral imperatives of private, profit-maximizing corporations.

Notes

1 Royle's (2000) study for example cites the cases of a university professor from Sri Lanka, a teacher from Krakow and a hotel manager from the Philippines working as hourly paid employees in Paderborn in Germany.
2 In the US ballots under the auspices of the NLRB are mandatory, although unions can seek recognition by the employer accepting a card count as evidence of employees' wish to be represented. This voluntary approach remains rare but was commonplace in the early years after the 1935 Wagner Act. In almost all Canadian provinces and for federal employees card counts can be accepted as an alternative to a ballot. This procedure inhibits the employer's use of negative tactics during the recognition election. It is broadly equivalent to the automatic recognition procedure under the UK Employment Relations Act of 1999, which was itself partly influenced by the Canadian example (Towers, 1999b; Dubinsky, 2000).
3 This is due to the fact that the directive has been interpreted as being about ownership rather than control and is one of the issues raised by the ETUC in the review of the directive undertaken by the social partners. Interestingly in the Canadian province of British Columbia the labour board has ruled that franchise and non-franchise KFC outlets have a common employer, thus making it possible for the trade union to negotiate a collective agreement for all KFC's employees in British Columbia.
4 It should be noted here that our interpretation of 'convergence' is partly based on the Weberian 'globalization' analysis of writers like Robertson (1990) who argue that globalization is driven by a common mass culture and the old functionalist thesis of Kerr *et al.* (1960) in which each society is likely to converge towards a single set of basic principles, on the basis of choices rationally made by its members in relation to individual and collective advancement. In this sense 'convergence' crosses over into the broader concept of 'globalization'. However, space does not allow us to develop these discussions here, but we do recognize that any serious discussion of 'globalization' needs to take into account not only economic and political but also cultural processes.

References

Abbott, B. (1993) 'Small firms and trade unions in services in the 1990s', *Industrial Relations Journal*, 24, 4: 308–17.

ABS (1999a) *Australian Social Trends 1999*, Cat. No. 4102.0, Canberra: Australian Bureau of Statistics.

ABS (1999b) *Take Away and Fast Food Retailing Outlets in Australia, July, 1999*, unpublished data, Canberra: Australian Bureau of Statistics.

ABS (1999c) 'Trade union statistics, August, Australia', Cat. No. 6323.0, Canberra: Australian Bureau of Statistics.

Ackers, P., Smith, C. and Smith, P. (1996) 'Against all odds? Trade unions in the new workplace', in Ackers, P., Smith, C. and Smith, P. (eds) *The New Workplace and Trade Unionism*, London: Routledge.

ACLU. (2000) 'Workplace rights – wrongful discharge', American Civil Liberties Union Freedom Network: http://www.aclu.org/issues/worker/legkit6.html (9 May 2000).

ACTU (1987) *Future Strategies for the Trade Union Movement*, Melbourne: Australian Council of Trade Unions.

Adams, G.W. (1993) *Canadian Labour Law*, 2nd edn, Ontario: Aurora.

Adams, R.J. (1999) 'Why statutory union recognition is bad labour policy: the North American experience', *Industrial Relations Journal*, 30, 2: 96–100.

Ardagh, J. (1987) *Germany and the Germans: An Anatomy of Society Today*, London: Hamish Hamilton.

Ballot, M. (1995) 'Labor relations in Russia and Eastern Europe', *Labor Law Journal*, March: 169–74.

Bamber, G.J. and Davis, E.M. (2000) 'Changing approaches to employment relations in Australia', in Bamber, G.J., Park, F., Ross, P., Lee, C. and Broadbent, K. (eds) *Employment Relations in the Asia Pacific: Changing Approaches*, Sydney: Allen & Unwin, pp. 23–45.

Bamber, G.J. and Lansbury, R.D. (eds) (1998) *International and Comparative Employment Relations: A Study of Industrialised Market Economies*, 3rd edn, Sydney: Allen & Unwin.

Barber, T. (1999) 'Germany's blame game', *The Financial Times*, 24 February: 27.

Barlow, M. and Robertson, H. J. (1994) *Class Warfare*, Toronto: Key Porter Books.

Barron, P. and Maxwell, G. (1998) 'Employee job perceptions: a comparison of Scottish and Australian fast food units', *Australian Journal of Hospitality Management*, 5, 1: 33–9.

Barshay, J. (1993) 'Pepsi takes a seat on Moscow Fast-food express', *New York Times*, 11 June.

Beaumont, P.B. (1995) *The Future of Employment Relations*, London: Sage.

Beaver, W. (1999) 'Fast-food invades the schools', *Business & Society Review* 104, 2: 191–7.

Bedrijfschap Horeca en Catering (2000) *Statistisch Zakboekje 1999; Horeca*, Zoetermeer: Bedrijfschap Horeca en Catering.

Bellah, R.N., Madsen, R., Sullivan, W.M., Swidler, A. and Tipton, S.M. (1985) *Habits of the Heart: Individualism and Commitment in American Life*, Berkeley, CA: University of California Press.

Bello, C. (1987) *Observaties van een zwartwerker; Over de arbeidsomstandigheden in Amsterdamse pizzeria's*, Amsterdam: Van Gennep.

Bernstein, A. (1998) 'Striking while the griddle is hot', *Business Week*, 4 May: 6.

Black, L. (1988) 'Bolshoi Mak: why the soviets are eating out of George Cohon's hand', *Globe and Mail Report on Business Magazine*, August: 30–6.

Blank, D. (1999) 'Short-staffed Disney, McDonald's siphon offshore labor pool', *Nation's Restaurant News*, 12 July, 33, 26: 1.

Blasi, J. and Panina, D. (1994) 'The emerging industrial relations system in Russia's privatized enterprises', *Labor Law Journal*, August: 523.

Bliss, K. (1987) 'Big and brash – and bringing in the bucks', *Hospitality*, 23, 8: 29–41.

Blom, E., van der Velden, T. and Cremers, J. (1985) *Zien, oordelen, handelen: de voorgeschiedenis en ontwikkeling van de KWJ-beweging van werkende jongeren*, Utrecht: Jongerenbeweging FNV.

BLS (1998) '1998 national occupational employment and wage estimates: service occupations', Bureau of Labor Statistics, United States Department of Labor: Washington, D.C. http://stats.bls.gov/oesnl/oes%5Fserv.htm#b65000 (15 March).

BLS (1999a) 'Employer costs for employee compensation – March 1999'. News release USDL: Bureau of Labor Statistics, United States Department of Labor: Washington, D.C., http://stats.bls.gov/news.release/ecec.toc.htm, 99–173 (24 June).

BLS (1999b) 'BLS releases new 1998–2008 employment projections'. Press release, Bureau of Labor Statistics, United States Department of Labor: Washington, D.C., http://stats.bls.gov/news.release/ecopro.nr0.htm (30 November).

BLS (2000a) 'Union members in 1999'. Press release, 19 January, Bureau of Labor Statistics, United States Department of Labor: Washington, D.C.: http://stats.bls.gov/news.release/union2.nr0.htm (1 June).

BLS (2000b) 'Career guide to industries: eating and drinking places 2000–2001', 19 April 2000. Bureau of Labor Statistics, United States Department of Labor: Washington, D.C. http://stats.bls.gov/oco/cg/pdf/cgs023.pdf (3 July).

BLS (2000c) 'Labor force statistics from the current population survey (unemployment rate, civilian labor force, aged 16 and over)', 2 June, Bureau of Labor Statistics, United States Department of Labor: Washington, D.C.: http://146.142.4.24/cgi-bin/surveymost (27 June).

Blundy, A. (1999) 'Russian workers accuse McDonald's of blocking union', *Independent*, 23 June: 14.

Blyton, P. and Turnbull, D. (1998) *The Dynamics of Employee Relations*, 2nd edn, Basingstoke: Macmillan.

BNA (1991) *Bureau of National Affairs (USA): Bulletin to Management*, 7 March: 66–71.

Bond, P. (1998) 'Help really wanted: as a tight labor market becomes tighter, retailers and restaurateurs are having a difficult time finding and keeping good employees', *Atlanta Journal and Constitution*,11 October: 1R.

Boyer, G.R. (ed.) (2001) 'Introduction, Review Symposium', *Industrial and Labour Relations Review*, April, 54, 3: 681–716.

Borisov, V., Clarke, S. and Fairbrother, P. (1994) 'Does trade unionism have a future in Russia?', *Industrial Relations Journal*, March: 19–23.

Boston Globe (2000) 'McDonald's to open 9 restaurants in Russia', February: F2.

Boxall, P. (1990) 'Towards the Wagner framework: change in New Zealand industrial relations', *Journal of Industrial Relations*, 32: 523–43.

Boxall, P. (2001) 'Evaluating continuity and change in the Employment Relations Act 2001', *New Zealand Journal of Industrial Relations*, 26 (forthcoming).

Boxall, P. and Haynes, P. (1992) 'Unions and non-union bargaining agents under the Employment Contracts Act 1991: an assessment after 12 months', *New Zealand Journal of Industrial Relations*, 17: 223–32.

Bozec, L. (2001) 'Profits rise 30% for PizzaExpress group', *Caterer and Hotelkeeper*, 8 February: 12.

Braam, S. (1994) *De blinde vlek van Nederland; Reportages over de onderkant van de arbeidsmarkt*, Amsterdam: FNV/van Gennep.

Brown, W., Marginson, P. and Walsh, J. (1995) 'Management: pay determination and collective bargaining', in Edwards, P.K. (ed.) *Industrial Relations: Theory and Practice in Britain*, Oxford: Blackwell.

Burger King Australia (1998) Press Release, Sydney, 11 June.

Campbell, N.D.C. (1999) 'The next working class speaks out', *Our Times*, 15 March: 23–30.

Canadian Hotel and Restaurant (1955) 'Getting on the take-out bandwagon', 15 September: 23.

Canadian Restaurant and Foodservice Association (1999a) 'Foodservice facts 1999', *Foodservice and Hospitality Magazine*, November: 35–47.

Canadian Restaurant and Foodservice Association (1999b) 'Research catalogue 1999', http// www: crfa.ca//m-research.htm.

Canadian Women's March Committee (2000) 'It's time for change: demands to the federal government to end poverty and violence against women', unpublished pamphlet, September: 1–30.

Centraal Bureau voor de Statistiek (2000) 'Oudere werknemers vaker lid vakbond', *Webmagazine*, 6 October (http://www.cbs.nl/nl/nieuws/artikelen/0628k.htm).

Centraal Bureau voor de Statistiek (2001), 'Ledentallen van vakverenigingen aangesloten bij vakcentrales', *Statline*, 21 February.

Chain Store Age Executive with Shopping Center Age (1999) 'Challenges abound in training', December, 75, 12: 3C.

Chan, P.J. and Justis, R.T. (1990) 'Franchise management in East Asia', *Academy of Management Executive*, May: 75–85.

Charlton, A. (1999) 'Natalya Gracheva is giving McDonald's heartburn', *Associated Press*, 23 June.

Chau, P.S. and Justis, R.T. (1990) 'Franchise management in East Asia', *Academy of Management Executive*, May 75–85.

Chew, S.B. and Chew, R. (1995) *Employment-driven Industrial Relations Regimes: The Singapore experience*. Aldershot: Avebury.

Chew, S.B. and Chew, R. (1996) 'Introduction', in Chew, S.B. and Chew, R. (eds) *Industrial Relations in Singapore Industry*, Singapore: Addison-Wesley, 2–29.

Chiu, S.W.K., Ho K.C. and Lui T.L. (1997) *City-states in the Global Economy: Industrial Restructuring in Hong Kong and Singapore*, Boulder, CO: Westview.

Clark, A. (2001) 'Mine's a McLatte', *Guardian*, 1 February: 3.

Clarke, S. (ed.) (1995) *Management and Industry in Russia: Formal and Informal Relations in the Period of Transition*, Aldershot: Edward Elgar.

Cleveland Plain Dealer (1996) 'Restaurant employment agreement criticized', 24 February: 1–B.

Cohon, G. with Macfarlane, D. (1999) *To Russia with Fries*, Toronto: McClelland & Stewart.

Coker, M. (1999) 'Russia: clawing its way back to life', *Business Week*, 13 December: 70–4.

Coller, X. (1996) 'Managing flexibility in the food industry: a cross-national comparative case study in European multinational companies', *European Journal of Industrial Relations*, 2: 153–72.

Colton, M. (1998) 'Big Mac attack: did somebody say strike? The kids who took on McDonald's – and won', *Washington Post*, 26 April: F1.

Cook, C. (1999) 'Trends in commercial and non commercial foodservice: the 1999 Hospitality Market Report', *Foodservice and Hospitality Magazine*, November: 30–4.

Cooke, W.N. (1997) 'The influence of industrial relations factors in U.S. foreign direct investment abroad', *Industrial and Labor Relations Review*, 51, 1: 3–17.

Craig, W.J.A. (1986) *The System of Industrial Relations in Canada*, Toronto: Prentice Hall.

Crawford, A., Harbridge, R. and Walsh, P. (1999) 'Unions and union membership in New Zealand: annual review for 1998', *New Zealand Journal of Industrial Relations*, 24: 383–95.

Crowley, D. (1996) 'Row at Pepsi over K-Club incident', *Irish Sunday Tribune*, 9 June: 5.

Cully, M. (2000) 'Unions at a loss: members and earnings', *Australian Bulletin of Labour*, 26, 1: 11–17.

Cully, M., Woodland, S., O'Reilly, A. and Dix, G. (1999) *Britain at Work: As Depicted by the 1998 Workplace Employee Relations Survey*, London: Routledge.

Dannin, E.J. (1997) *Working Free: The Origins and Impact of New Zealand's Employment Contracts Act*, Auckland: Auckland University Press.

Deijen, H. (1995) 'Audiovisueel "hessup" bij McDonalds geintroduceerd', *Het Financieele Dagblad*, 18 November.

Delsen, L. and Jacobs, A. (1999) 'The case of the Netherlands', *Labour*, 13, 1: 123–82.

De Vos, T. (1981) *U.S. Multinationals and Worker Participation in Management*, London: Aldwych.

Deyo, F. (1981) *Dependent Development and Labour Subordination: An Asian Case Study*, New York: Praeger.

Dowling, P.J., Schuler, R.S. and Welch, D.E. (1994) *International Dimensions of Human Resource Management*, London: Wadsworth.

Drapp, B. (1998) 'Strikers sought respect, dignity from McDonald's, *Cleveland Plain Dealer*, 13 May: 1E.

Dubinsky, L. (2000) *Resisting Union-busting Techniques: Lessons from Quebec*, London: Institute of Employment Rights.

Duve, F. (1987) *Unternehmermethoden gegen Betriebsratswahlen (Reportagen aus Grauzonen der Arbeitswelt)*, Hamburg: Rowohlt Taschenbuchverlag.

Eberwein, W. and Tholen, J. (1990) *Managermentalität: Industrielle Unternehmungsleitung als Beruf und Politik*, Frankfurt: FAZ.

Economic Newsletters (1999, 2000) Cambridge, MA: Davis Center for Russian Studies: February 1999, December 1999, January 2000.

Edgecliffe-Johnson, A. (1999) 'Comment and analysis: burger with fries and videos to go: the fast-food war for American stomachs is moving into the internet age', *The Financial Times* USA Edition, 7 April: 7.

Edwards, P.K., Hall, M., Hyman, R., Marginson, P., Sisson, K., Waddington, J. and Winchester, D. (1998) 'Great Britain: from partial collectivism to neo-liberalism to where?', in Ferner, A. and Hyman, R. (eds) *Changing Industrial Relations in Europe*, Oxford: Blackwell.

Edwards, T. (1998) 'Multinationals, labour management and the process of reverse diffusion: a case study', *International Journal of Human Resource Management*, 9: 696–709.

EIRR (1997) 'McDonalds serves up improved social relations', *European Industrial Relations Review*, 279 (April): 19–21.

EIRR (2001a) 'Moderation characterises bargaining in 2000', *European Industrial Relations Review*, 328 (May): 21–5.

EIRR (2001b) 'Government outlines new co-determination rules', *European Industrial Relations Review*, 325 (February): 24–7.

Ellis, V. and Ellingwood. L. (1998) 'Welfare to work: are there enough jobs?', *Los Angeles Times*, 8 February: A1.

Euromonitor (1998) 'Market research Europe: European markets, fast-food', August: 1–32.

Euromonitor (2000) 'Market research GB: market report: leisure, fast-food restaurants', December: 83–105.

Fantasia, R. (1995) 'Fast-food in France', *Theory and Society* 24, 2: 201–43.

Featherstone, L. (1999) 'The Burger International revisited', *Left Business Observer*, 91, 31 August: 4f.

Feiter, A. (1996) 'Onze filosofie is dat we kleurenblind zijn', *SER-Bulletin*, 36, 1: 22–3.

Felstead, A. (1993) *The Corporate Paradox: Power and Control in the Business Franchise*, London: Routledge.

Ferner, A. and Edwards, P. (1995) 'Power and the diffusion of organisational change within multinationals', *European Journal of Industrial Relations*, July, 1, 2: 1–35.

Ferner, A. and Hyman, R. (1998) 'Introduction: towards European industrial relations?', in Ferner, A. and Hyman, R. (eds) *Changing Industrial Relations in Europe*, Oxford: Blackwell.

Financial Post (1934) 'Red labor leaders call fake strikes to upset industry', 5 May: 3.

Financieel Dagblad (1990) 'Hamburgerconcern wil meewerken aan sociale vernieuwing', 21 July.

Flecker, J. and Schulten, T. (1999) 'The end of institutional stability: what future for the "German model"?', *Economic and Industrial Democracy*, 20: 81–115.

Foodservice (2000) 'Marken machen Märkte', April: 18–50.

Foodservice and Hospitality Magazine (2000) '30th annual top 100 listings', July, 33, 5: 35–58.

Freeman, R. and Rogers, J. (1999) *What Workers Want*, Ithaca, NY: ILR Press.

Frenkel, S. (1990) 'Australian trade unionism and the new social structure of accumulation'. Paper presented to the Asian Regional Conference, International Industrial Relations Association, Manila.

Frenkel, S. (1993) 'Theoretical frameworks and empirical contexts of trade unionism', in Frenkel, S. (ed.) *A Comparative Study of Trade Unionism in Nine Countries*, Ithaca, NY: ILR Press.

Friedman, S., Hurd, R., Oswald, R.A. and Seeber, R.L. (eds) (1994) *Restoring the Promise of American Labour Law*, Ithaca, NY: ILR Press.

Gale, W.R. (1997) 'Wal-Mart unionized despite overwhelming "no" vote', *Employment Bulletin*, 7: 3–4.

Geoghegan, T. (1999) 'Tampering with the time clock', *New York Times*, 24 January, Section 4: 15.

Ginsberg, S. (1999) 'Wanted: hamburger helpers; as economy booms, fast-food workers are in short supply', *Washington Post*, 14 January: M03.

Glazer, N.Y. (1993) *Women's Paid and Unpaid Labor: The Work Transfer in Health Care and Retailing*, Philadelphia: Temple University Press.

Gould, W.B. (1994) *Agenda for Reform: The Future of Employment Relations and the Law*, Cambridge, MA: MIT Press.

Gouldner, A.W. (1964) *Patterns of Industrial Bureaucracy*, New York: Free Press.

Grancelli, B. (1988) *Soviet Management and Labor Relations*, London: Allen & Unwin: 107.

Hammond, S. and Harbridge, R. (1995) 'Women and enterprise bargaining: the New Zealand experience of labour market deregulation', *Journal of Industrial Relations*, 37: 359–76.

Hamstra, M. (1998a) 'McD places order for new kitchens at operator confab', *Nation's Restaurant News*, 30 March, 32, 13: 1.

Hamstra, M. (1998b) '"Made-for-you" maneuvers signal competitive shift in QSR category', *Nation's Restaurant News*, 13 April, 32, 54.

Harbridge, R. and Crawford, A. (2000) 'The Employment Contracts Act and collective bargaining patterns: a review of the 1999/2000 year', in Harbridge, R., Crawford, A. and Kiely, P. (eds) *Employment Contracts: Bargaining Trends and Employment Law Update 1999/2000*, Wellington: Victoria University of Wellington.

Harbridge, R. and McCaw, S. (1992) 'Award, agreement or nothing? A review of the impact of S132(a) of the Labour Relations Act 1987 on collective bargaining', *New Zealand Journal of Industrial Relations*, 17: 175–83.

Haynes, P. and Fryer, G. (1998) 'Contracting or bargaining? Enterprise bargaining in the New Zealand major hotel industry', International Industrial Relations Association Conference, Bologna, October.

Hazan, P. (1996) 'Pepsi met un syndicat en ébullition', *Liberation*, 10 June: 21.

Herzberg, F. (1966) *Work and the Nature of Man*, New York: Staples Press.

Hertz, N. (1997) *Russian Business Relationships in the Wake of Reform*, London: Macmillan Press.

Hirst, P. and Thompson, G. (1996) *Globalisation in Question: The International Economy and the Possibilities of Governance*, Cambridge: Polity Press.

Hochshild, A.R. (1983) *The Managed Heart: Commercialization of Human Feeling*, Berkley, CA: University of California Press.

Holden, N., Cooper, C. and Carr, J. (1998) *Dealing with the New Russia*, Chichester: John Wiley.

Holliday, R. (1995) *Investigating Small Firms: Nice Work?*, London: Routledge.

Honeybone, A. (1997) 'Introducing labour flexibility: the example of New Zealand', *International Labour Review*, 136, 4: 493–507.

Honig, N.E. and Dowling, D.C. (1994) 'How to handle employment issues in European deals', *Preventive Law Reporter*, Spring, 13, 1: 3–9.

Huff, W.G. (1994) *The Economic Growth of Singapore*, Cambridge: Cambridge University Press.

Huijgen, F. and Benders, J. (1998) 'Het vallende kwartje; Directe participatie in Nederland en Europa', *Tijdschrift voor Arbeidsvraagstukken*, 14, 2: 113–27.

Human Rights Watch (2000) *Unfair Advantage: Workers' Freedom of Association in the United States Under International Human Rights Standards*, London: Human Rights Watch.

IDS (2001) 'The national minimum wage in pubs and restaurants', *Incomes Data Services*, March: 1–8.

ILO (1997) 'ILO highlights global challenge to trade unions'. Press release 4 November 1997, ILO/97/28. International Labour Organization, Geneva: http://www.ilo.org/public/english/bureau/inf/pr/1997/28.htm (1 June 2000).

Ingram, J. (1994) 'Fast-food pioneer braves Russia's market', *New York Times*, 17 July.

d'Iribarne, P. (1989) *La logique de l'honneur: Gestion des entreprises et traditions nationales*, Paris: Editions du Seuil.

Jacobi, O., Keller, B. and Müller-Jentsch, W. (1998) 'Germany: facing new challenges', in Ferner, A. and Hyman, R. (eds) *Changing Industrial Relations in Europe*, Oxford: Blackwell.

Jardine, A. (1999) 'McDonald's still facing a McLibel backlash', *Marketing*, 16 September: 15.

Jekanowski, M.D. (1999) 'Causes and consequences of fast food sales growth', *Foodreview* 22, 1: 11–16.

Katz, H.C. (1997) 'Introduction and comparative overview', in Katz, H.C. (ed.) *Telecommunications: Restructuring Work and Employment Relations Worldwide*, Ithaca, NY: ILR Press.

Katz, H.C. and Darbishire, O. (2000) *Converging Divergences: Worldwide Changes in Employment Systems*, Ithaca, NY: ILR Press.

Kelly, P.F. (2000) 'Union organizing in the new economy: can new efforts reverse labor's long goodbye?', *Labor Watch*, March, Capital Research Center, http://www.capitalresearch.org/LaborWatch/lw-0300.htm (6 June 2000).

Kerr, C., Dunlop, J.T., Harbinson, F. and Myers, C.A. (1960) *Industrialism and Industrial Man*, Harmondsworth: Penguin.

Key Note (2000) *Fast-Food and Home Delivery Outlets*, London: Key Note Ltd.

Khoo, C.K. (1983) *Census of Population 1980 Singapore: Administrative Report*, Singapore: Singapore Department of Statistics.

Klein, N. (2001) *No Logo*, London: HarperCollins.

Kleiner, I. (1998) 'Ontario overhauls union certification process', *Lawyers Weekly*, 21, 9, October: 7f.

Kotthoff, H. (1994) *Betriebsräte und Bürgerstatus, Wandel und Kontinuität betrieblicher Mitbestimmung*, München-Mehring: Rainer Hampp Verlag.

Kreuger, A.B. (1991) 'Ownership, agency, and wages: an examination of franchising in the fast food industry', *Quarterly Journal of Business and Economics*, 106, 1: 75–102.

Krikke, H. (1994) 'Nee hoor, we hebben geen speciaal beleid', *OR Informatie* 21 (29 March): 30–3.

Lane, C. (1989) *Management and Labour in Europe*, Aldershot: Edward Elgar.

Lane, C. (1991) 'Industrial reorganisation in Europe: patterns of convergence and divergence in Germany, France and Britain', *Work, Employment and Society*, 5, 4: 515–39.

Lane, C. (1994) 'Industrial order and the transformation of industrial relations: Britain, Germany and France compared', in Hyman, R. and Ferner, A. (eds) *New Frontiers in European Industrial Relations*, Oxford: Blackwell.

Langenhuisen, R. (1995) 'McDonald's kauft sich von Betriebsräten frei', *Kälner Express*, 7 December: 36.

Lardner. J. (1999) 'OK, here are your options: employee stock plans are spreading fast – and not just at high-tech firms', *US News and World Report*, 1 March.

Lawrence, P. (1996) *Management in the USA*, London: Sage.

Laxer, K. (1999) 'Youth roll-call', *Our Times*, 18, 1, 15 March: 34–9.

Lecher, W. and Naumann, R. (1994) 'The current state of trade unions in the EU member states', in Lecher, W. (ed.) *Trade Unions in the European Union*, London: Lawrence and Wishart.

Leggett, C. (1993a) 'Corporatist trade unionism in Singapore', in Frenkel, S. (ed.) *Organized Labor in the Asia-Pacific Region: A Comparative Study of Trade Unionism in Nine Countries*, Ithaca, NY: ILR Press, 223–49.

Leggett, C. (1993b) 'Singapore', in Deery, S. and Mitchell, R. (eds) *Labour Law And Industrial Relations in Asia : Eight Country Studies*, Melbourne: Longman, 96–136.

Leidner, R. (1993c) *Fast Food, Fast Talk: Service Work and the Routinization of Everyday Life*, Berkeley, CA: University of California Press.

Leming, J. (1998) 'Workers benefit from tight market', *Journal of Commerce*, 15 June: 5A.

Levitt, T. (1972) 'Production line approach to service', *Harvard Business Review*, 50, 5: 41–52.

Liddle, A. (1997) 'Jury finds Taco Bell guilty in wages suit', *Nation's Restaurant News*, April, 21, 31: 1.

Liddle, A. (2000) 'McDonald's drive-thrus to test wireless debit technology', *Nation's Restaurant News*, 7 February, 34, 6: 4.

Lienert, A. (1998) 'Employees benefit in tight job market: firms offer more pay, perks amid record employment', *Detroit News*, 24 August: A1.

Lipset, S.M. (1991) 'American exceptionalism reaffirmed', in Shafer, B.E. (ed.) *Is America Different? A New Look at American Exceptionalism*, Oxford: Clarendon Press.

Locke, R. (1992) 'The demise of the national union in Italy: lessons for comparative industrial relations theory', *Industrial and labour Relations Review*, 45, 2: 229–49.

Locke, R. (1995) 'The transformation of industrial relations? A cross-national review', in Wever, K.S. and Turner, L. (eds) *The Comparative Political Economy of Industrial Relations*, Wisconsin: Industrial Relations Research Association.

Love, J.F. (1995) *McDonald's Behind the Arches*, London: Bantam Press.

Lowrie, H. (1995) '£1 for a 5 hour shift at Burger King: clock-on, clock-off scandal', *Today*, 19 September: 1–2.

Lucas, R. (1996) 'Industrial relations in hotels and catering: neglect and paradox?', *British Journal of Industrial Relations*, 34, 2: 267–86.

Luhrs, N. (2000) 'Books (was In Defense of Mrs. Elton)', Piffle discussion list. Online posting 24 May 2000.

Lyons, K. (1999) 'Fast food franchising and the future', *Franchising Magazine*, 12, 5: 2–7.

MacDonald, D. (1997) 'Sectoral certification: a case study of British Columbia', *Canadian Labour and Employment Law Journal*, 5: 243–86.

Mangan, J. and Johnston, J. (1999) 'Minimum wages, training wages and youth employment', *International Journal of Social Economics*, 26, 1/2/3: 415–29.

Mansfield, B. (2000) 'Challenges facing unions in Australia', in Bamber, G.J., Park, F., Ross, P., Lee, C. and Broadbent, K. (eds) *Employment Relations in the Asia-Pacific*, Sydney: Allen and Unwin.

Maharaj, D. (1998) 'Restaurant, retail jobs go begging', *Los Angeles Times*, 5 October: A1.

Marchington, M. (1995) 'Involvement and participation', in Storey, J. (ed.) *Human Resource Management: A Critical Text*, London: Routledge.

Market Share Reporter (1998) Annual edition: 324.

Marquardt, R. (1998) *Enter at Your Own Risk: Canadian Youth and the Labour Market*, Toronto: Between the Lines Press.

McAndrew, I. and Ballard, M. (1995) 'Negotiation and dictation in employment contract formation in New Zealand', *New Zealand Journal of Industrial Relations*, 20: 119–41.

McCarthy, D.J. and Puffer, S.M. (1997) 'Strategic investment flexibility for MNE success in Russia', *Journal of World Business*, 32, 4: 293–319.

McCarthy, W. (1992) 'The rise and fall of collective laissez faire', in McCarthy, W. (ed.) *Legal Intervention in Industrial Relations: Gains and Loses*, Oxford: Blackwell.

McDonald's (1995) *McDonald's Employment Policies*, McDonald's New Zealand, company handbook.

McDonald's Education Service (1997) *Student Information Pack*, East Finchley, UK: McDonald's Education Service.

McDonald's (1998) *Submission to Junior Rates Inquiry*, Australian Industrial Relations Commission, Case No. C. No 33985 of 1998, 22 December, Print no. Mis 917/98 S Print Q9610 at p. 57.

McDonald's (1999) 'Canadian McFacts', public relations package.

McDonald's Web site (2000) 'Welcome to Russia: Celebrating its 10th anniversary', http://www.mcdonalds.com/surftheworld/europe/russia/russia.html

McGovern, P. (1998) *HRM, Technical Workers and the Multinational Corporation*, London: Routledge.

McKay, B. (1993) 'Inflation bites Russians, who still bite into Big Mac', *Advertising Age*, 64, 15 March: I–3, I–23.

McLaughlin, C. (2000) '"Mutually beneficial agreements" in the retail sector? the Employment Contracts Act and low-paid workers', *New Zealand Journal of Industrial Relations*, 25: 1–17.

McLaughlin, C. and Rasmussen, E. (1998) '"Freedom of choice" and "flexibility" in the retail sector', *International Journal of Manpower*, 19: 281–95.

McManus, G. (1996) 'Rapid roll-out', *Marketing*, 15, 4: 10–19.

Meyers, M. (1998) 'Temp agency feeds the food industry', *Minneapolis Star Tribune*, 5 April: 1A.

Milne, S. (1998) 'Analysis, union recognition: Will Tony Blair pay his dues?', *Guardian*, 17 March: 15.

Morgan, O. (1999) 'Interference on the line', *Observer*, 28 November: 4.

Mitchell, R. (1989) 'State systems of conciliation and arbitration: the legal origins of the Australasian model', in MacIntyre, S. and Mitchell, R. (eds) *Foundations of Arbitration*, Melbourne: Oxford University Press.

Mol, B. (1996) 'McDonaldisering van Operaties en het Personeelsmanagement: Een Case-Study naar Culturele en Institutionele Invloeden bij Overdracht naar de Nederlandse Maatschappij', unpublished Master's thesis, Nijmegen Business School.

Mulder, J. (1997) 'Het prille leven van een fast food-OR; Medezeggenschap bij McDonald's', *Praktijkblad voor Medezeggenschap*, 19, 11: 15–17.

Mulhern, C. (1998) 'Chain reaction: do you have what it takes to run a string of stores overseas . . . in Siberia?', *Entrepreneur*, April: 42.

Müller-Jentsch, W. (1995) 'Germany: from collective voice to co-management', in Rogers, J. and Streeck, W. (eds) *Works Councils: Consultation, Representation, and Co-operation in Industrial Relations*, London: University of Chicago Press.

Munro, J. (1992) 'Hopping in hamburger heaven: youth underemployment in the service sector', *Youth Studies Australia*, 11, 3: 25–33.

Murphy, H.L. (1996) 'Help wanted', *Franchise Times*, August, 2: 1.

Nagelkerke, A. and de Nijs, W. (1998) 'Labour relations research: changing perspectives', in Evers, G., van Hees, B. and Schippers, J. (eds) *Work, Organisation and Labour in Dutch Society: A State of the Art of the Research*, Dordrecht/Boston/London: Kluwer Academic Publishers, 63–104.

Narodnoe, K. (1987) 'SSSR za 70 let (USSR National Economy, 70 Years)', *Finansy i Statistika*: 1–20.

Nathan, S. (1999) 'Take this job, please: shortage of summer workers has employers scrambling', *USA Today*, 28 May: 1B.

National Restaurant Association (2000a) 'Issue briefs', 23 June, http://www.restaurant.org/govt/issues.html, 1 July 2000.

National Restaurant Association (2000b) 'Save American free enterprise!', http://www.restaurant.org/govt/safe/index.html, 1 July 2000.

Nation's Restaurant News (1997a) 'Krystal to settle wage litigation for $13 million', 3 February: 2.

Nation's Restaurant News (1997b) 'Female cashiers prevail in suit vs. Hardee's', 15 September, 31, 37: 2.

Nation's Restaurant News (1997c) 'Union opposes the addition of Big Mac to NYC's hospital menus', 10 November, 31, 45: 21.

Nation's Restaurant News (1998) 'Akron QSRs to ask for union cards', 6 July, 32, 27: 4.

Nation's Restaurant News (1999) 'BK to hire welfare recipients', 8 March, 33, 10: 3.

Naughton, K. (1998) 'From the frying pan to the factory', *Business Week*, 1 June: 106.

Newman, K.S. (1999) *No Shame in My Game: The Working Poor in the Inner City*, New York: Alfred A. Knopf and Russell Sage Foundation.

Nobis, E. (2000) 'Veertig nationaliteiten bij McDonald's', *Het Financieele Dagblad*, December: 28.

Norman, J. (1999) 'Taco Bell overtime case now class-action suit', *Orange County Register* (California), 2 September: C-2.

North, S.J. (1996) 'PepsiCo bullies its staff council', *Sunday Business*, 9 June: 8.

OECD Employment Outlook (1996) *Women's Work: A Report*, Geneva: Organization of Economic Cooperation and Development.

Ostrow, J. (1992) 'Fast-food prices jump in Russia', *Advertising Age*, 63, 6 January.

Papiernik, R.L. (1999) 'Diversity at work: welfare recipients', *Nation's Restaurant News*, May, 33, 21: 238–9.

Palmer, J. (1988) *Europe without America? The Crisis in Atlantic Relations*, Oxford: Oxford University Press.

Pauly, H. (1998) 'Restaurants are hungry for labor: employers try new incentives to lure workers', *Chicago Sun-Times*, 21 December: 50.

Pereira, A.A. (2000a) 'McAunties and McUncles: older crew members in Singapore's fast food industry', *Research in the Sociology of Work*, 9: 129–45.

Pereira, A.A. (2000b) 'State collaboration with transnational corporations: the case of Singapore's industrial programmes 1965–1999', *Competition and Change*, 4, 4: 1–29.

Perry, M., Kong L. and Yeoh, B. (1997) *Singapore: A Developmental City State*, Chichester: John Wiley.

Petrick, J.A. and Rinefort, F.C. (1999) 'Occupational health and safety in Russia and the Commonwealth of Independent States', *Business and Society Review*, 104, 4: 417–38.

Pfeffer, J. (1994) *Competitive Advantage through People*, Boston, MA: Harvard Busines School Press.

Pilger, J. (1999) *Hidden Agendas*, London: Vintage.

Pot, F. (2000) *Employment Relations and National Culture: Continuity and Change in the Age of Globalisation*, Cheltenham: Edward Elgar.

Prewitt, M. (1999a) 'Purdue study: low benefits boost turnover, increase net labor cost', *Nation's Restaurant News*, 6 December, 33, 49: 1.

Prewitt, M. (1999b) 'Operators say "living wage" trend not a solution to industry's labor crisis', *Nation's Restaurant News*, 13 December, 33, 50: 1f.

Price, C.C. (1996) 'The U.S. foodservice industry looks abroad', *Foodreview* 19, 2: 13–17.

Price, C.C. (1998) 'Sales of meals and snacks away from home continue to increase', *Foodreview* 21, 3: 28–30.

Puffer, S.M., McCarthy, D.J. and Zhuplev, A.V. (1998) 'Doing business in Russia: lessons from early entrants', *Thunderbird International Business Review*, 40, 5: 461–84.

Puffer, S.M., McCarthy, D.J. and Naumov, A.I. (2000) *The Russian Capitalist Experiment: From State-owned Organizations to Entrepreneurships*, Cheltenham, UK: Edward Elgar.

Purdue University (1999) 'Benefits for fast-food workers improve bottom line'. Press release, Purdue News, October, West Lafayette, IN.: http://www.purdue.edu/UNS/html4ever/990827.Lalopa.turnover.html (June 30 2000).

Quiney, M. (1994) *An Introduction to GMB Organisation in Hotel and Catering*, London: General Municipal and Boiler Makers Union.

Rainnie, A. (1989) *Industrial Relations in Small Firms: Small Isn't Beautiful*, London: Routledge.

Ramsay, H. (1997) 'Fool's gold? European works councils and workplace democracy', *Industrial Relations Journal*, 28, 4: 314–22.

Ramsay, H. (2000) 'Chain reactions: responding to new modes of organizing production', 2000 AFL-CIO/UCLEA Conference, Milwaukee, WI, April.

Rasmussen, E., McLaughlin, C. and Boxall, P. (2000) 'A survey of employee experiences and attitudes in the New Zealand workplace', *New Zealand Journal of Industrial Relations*, 25: 49–67.

Rasnic, C.D. (1995) 'Balancing respective rights in the employment contract: contrasting the U.S. 'Employment-at-Will' rule with the worker statutory protections against dismissal in European Community countries', *Journal of International Law and Practice* 4, 3: 441–504.

Reeders, R. (1988) 'The fast food industry', in E. Willis (ed.) *Technology and the Labour Process*, Sydney: Allen & Unwin, 142–54.

Reid, M. and Melrose, M. (1999) *Career Development for McDonald's Family Restaurant Staff: Phase One Research Report*, Auckland: Auckland University of Technology.

Reiter, E. (1996) *Making Fast-Food*, 2nd edn, Montreal: McGill Queens University Press.

Ritchie, P. (1990) 'McDonald's: a winner through logistics', *International Journal of Physical Distributions and Logistics Management*, 20, 3: 21–4.

Ritzer, G. (1996) *The McDonaldization of Society*, 2nd edn, London: Sage.

Robb, D.J. (1998a) 'NLRB gets union cards from Macedonia McDonald's workers', *Cleveland Plain Dealer*, 2 June: 1B.

Robb, D.J. (1998b) 'McDonald's workers win NLRB support', *Cleveland Plain Dealer*, 28 August.

Robb, D.J. (1999) 'McDonald's, strikers settle beef', *Cleveland Plain Dealer*, 10 February: 1B.

Robertson, R. (1990) 'Mapping the global condition: globalization as the central concept', in Featherstone, M. (ed.) *Global Culture: Nationalism, Globalization and Modernity*, London: Sage.

Rodriguez, C. (2000) 'Service with a shrug: firms struggle to find, keep good employees', *Boston Globe*, 16 January: A1.

Romano, M. (1993) 'With victory at O'Hare, union looks to future', *Restaurant Business*, 10 February, 92, 3: 16.

Rothstein, M.A., Craver, C.B., Schroeder, E.P., Shoben, E.W. and VanderVelde, L.S. (1994) *Employment Law*, St Paul, MN.: West Publishing Company.

Royle, T. (1998) 'Avoidance strategies and the German system of co-determination', *International Journal of Human Resource Management*, 9, 6: 1026–47.

Royle, T. (1999a) 'The reluctant bargainers? McDonald's, unions and pay determination in Germany and the UK', *Industrial Relations Journal*, 30, 2: 135–50.

Royle, T. (1999b) 'Where's the beef? McDonald's and its European works council', *European Journal of Industrial Relations*, 5, 3: 327–47.

Royle, T. (2000) *Working for McDonald's in Europe: The Unequal Struggle?*, London: Routledge.

Royle, T. (2001) 'Employers' associations and union exclusion strategies: multinational corporations in the German fast-food industry', *International Human Resource Management Conference*, World Trade Centre, Barcelona, 19–22 June.

Royle, T. (2002) 'Union exclusion strategies in the European food service industry', *Industrial Relations Research Association Conference*, Atlanta, USA, January, (forthcoming).

Rubinfien, E. (1993) 'PepsiCo's Taco Bell pulls into Moscow aboard the metro', *Wall Street Journal*, 11 June.

Rudolph, W. and Wasserman, W. (1995) 'Kleinvieh macht auch Mist', *Die Mitbestimmung*, 2: 33–6.

Russian Business Monitor (2000) 'McDonald's to open 15–20 restaurants in Russia annually', 30 October: 4.

Ryan, R. (1997) 'Market rules: industrial relations in hotels and restaurants', in AIRAANZ (ed.) *Proceedings of the 1997 Conference of the Association of Industrial Relations Academics of Australia and New Zealand*, Brisbane: 311–19.

Sacks, K.J. (2000) 'Restaurants', *Standard & Poor's Industry Surveys*, 168, 8: Section 1.

Sadowski, D., Backes-Gellner, U. and Frick, B. (1995) 'Workers councils: barriers or boosts for the competitiveness of German firms?', *British Journal of Industrial Relations*, September, 33, 3: 493–513.

Salmon, J.L. (1998) 'McDonald's, employees reach pact; strike ends; Va. protest leader is still unsatisfied', *Washington Post*, 23 October: C3.

Sanginesi, W. (1999) 'Organizing restaurant workers: some observations', Toronto: York University, unpublished paper

Sauga, M., Student, D. and Weidenfeld, U. (1996) 'Längst auf dem Weg', *Wirtschaftswoche*, 9 May, 20: 16–18.

Schein, E.H. (1984) 'Coming to a new awareness of organisational culture', *Sloan Management Review*, Winter: 3–16.

Schlosser, E. (1998) 'Fast-food nation: the true cost of America's diet', *Rolling Stone*, September: 3.

Schlosser, E. (2001) *Fast-Food Nation*, Boston, MA: Allen Lane.

Schnabel, C. (1998) 'The reform of collective bargaining in Germany: corporatist stability vs. firm flexibility', in Hoffman, R., Jacobi, O., Keller, B. and Weiss, M. (eds) *The German Model of Industrial Relations between Adaptation and Erosion*, Düsseldorf: Hans-Böckler Stiftung.

Service Worker (1994) 'Picket over youth rate embarrasses Georgie Pie', March: 5.

Shafer, B.E. (ed.) (1991) *Is America Different? A New Look at American Exceptionalism*, Oxford: Clarendon Press.

Shapiro, J. and Murray, B. (1997) 'Fast food and welfare reform: success of the effort may hinge on "dead-end" burger-flipping jobs', *U.S. News & World Report*, 18 August.

Sherghneva, E. and Feldhoff, J. (2000) *The Culture of Labour in the Transformation Process: Empirical Studies in Russian Industrial Enterprises*, New York: Peter Lang.

Singapore Straits Times (1995) 'How the elderly can get the most out of extended worklife', 19 November: A 12.

Singapore Straits Times (1996a), 'McDonald's older staff are model workers', 7 February: A 13.

Singapore Straits Times (1996b), 'Back to work scheme: 350 jobs filled in 30 days', 14 November: A 1.

Singapore Straits Times (1999) 'Mac Boss is hungry for more.' 4 July: Q 1.

Slomp, H. (1995) 'National variations in worker participation', in Harzing, A.-W. and van Ruysseveldt, J.J. (eds) *International Human Resource Management*, London: Sage, 292–317.

Smart, T. Stoughton, S. and Behr, P. (1999) 'Working their way up: economy's expansion has lifted those on the bottom rung, but will gains last?', *Washington Post*, 12 September: H01.

Sparrow, P., Schuler, R. and Jackson, S. (1994) 'Convergence or divergence: human resource practices and policies for competitive advantage world-wide', *International Journal of Human Resource Management*, 5, 2: 268–99.

Specter, M. (1995) 'Borscht and blini to go: from Russian capitalists, an answer to McDonald's', *New York Times*, 9 August: D1, D3.

Der Spiegel (1981) 'Land des Lächelns', 22: 72–5.

Der Spiegel (1997) 'Zehn Prozent Abschlag', 45: 138–39.

Statistics Canada (1998) 'Labour force historical review', 1: 1–120.

Statistics New Zealand (2001) *Infos* (Information Network for Official Statistics), Wellington: Statistics New Zealand.

Steinberg, R.J. and Figart, D.M. (eds) (1999) *Emotional Labor in the Service Economy*. Special issue of *The Annals of the American Academy of Political and Social Sciences* 561 (January).

Stern (1999) 'Abgebraten bis die Kasse stimmt', 4 November, 45: 115–28.

Streeck, W. (1997) 'German capitalism: does it exist? Can it survive?', *New Political Economy*, 4: 251–83.

Summers, C.W. (1995) 'Worker dislocation: who bears the burden? A comparative study of social values in five countries', *Notre Dame Law Review* 70, 5: 1033–73.

Summers, C.W. (2000) Letter to the author, 26 June.

Swann, D. (1988) *The Economics of the Common Market*, Harmondsworth: Penguin.

Tan, C.H. (1995) *Labour Management Relations in Singapore*, New York: Prentice Hall.

Tannock, S. (2001) *Youth at Work: The Unionized Fast-food and Grocery Workplace*, Philadelphia: Temple University Press.

Teague, P. (2001) 'Review symposium: converging divergences and European employment relations', *Industrial and Labour Relations Review*, April, 54, 3: 688–94.

Terry, M., (1994) 'Workplace unionism: redefining structures and objectives', in Hyman, R. and Ferner, A., (eds) *New Frontiers in European Industrial Relations*, Oxford: Blackwell.

Tilly, C. (1996) *Half a Job: Bad and Good Part-time Jobs in a Changing Labor Market*, Philadelphia: Temple University Press.

Timo, N. (1996) 'Globalisation? Industrialisation? Democratisation? McDonaldisation? A case study of fast food', in Dundas, K. and Woldring, K. (eds) *Towards Real Reforms in Employment Relations: Can the Adversarial Culture Be Replaced?* Proceedings of the Fourth Annual Conference of the International Employment Relations Association, Southern Cross University, 10–13 July, 477–505.

Tocqueville, A. de. (1969) *Democracy in America*, trans. G. Lawrence, ed. J.P. Mayer, Garden City, NY: Anchor Books.

Towers, B. (1997) *The Representation Gap: Change and Reform in the British and American Workplace*, Oxford: Oxford University Press.

Towers, B. (1999a) '. . . the most lightly regulated labour market . . . The UK's third statutory recognition procedure', *Industrial Relations Journal*, 30, 2: 82–95.

Towers, B. (1999b) *Developing Recognition and Representation in the UK: How Useful Is the US Model?* London: Institute for Employment Rights.

Trevilyan, P. and Lyons, K. (2000) 'The name that Jack built', *Franchising Magazine*, 13, 1: 2–8.

Turner, L. (1998) *Fighting for Partnership: Labor and Politics in Unified Germany*, Ithaca, NY: Cornell University Press.

Uchitelle, L. (1998) 'Signing bonus now a fixture farther down the job ladder', *New York Times*, 10 June: A1.

U.S. Industry and Trade Outlook 1999 (1999) New York: McGraw-Hill Companies and U.S. Department of Commerce/International Trade Administration.

Van Casteren, J. (1997) 'Big Mac is watching you', *De Groene Amsterdammer*, 121 (7 May): 16.

Van der Burgh, Y. and Kriek, F. (1992) *Naleving van de wet op de ondernemingsraden; Stand van zaken medio 1992*, Den Haag: Ministerie van Sociale Zaken en Werkgelegenheid/VUGA.

Van Giezen, R.W. (1994) 'Occupational wages in the fast-food restaurant industry', *Monthly Labor Review*, 117, 8: 24–30.

Van Lier, J. (2000) 'The best of both worlds', in Benders, J., Noorderhaven, N., Keizer, A., Kumon, H. and Stam, J. (eds) *Mirroring Consensus: Decision-making in Japanese–Dutch Business*, Utrecht: LEMMA, 105–13.

Vidal, J. (1997) *McLibel: Burger Culture on Trial*, London: Macmillan.

Vikhanski, O.S. (1992) 'Doing it all for you at Moscow McDonald's: an interview with Glen Steeves, restaurant manager, Moscow McDonald's', in Puffer, S.M. (ed.) *The Russian Management Revolution*, Armonk, NY: M.E. Sharpe: 274–81.

Vikhanski, O.S. and Puffer, S.M. (1993) 'Management education and employee training at Moscow McDonald's', *European Management Journal*, 11, 1: 102–6.

Visser, J. and Hemerijck, A. (1997) *'A Dutch Miracle'; Job Growth, Welfare Reform and Corporatism in the Netherlands*, Amsterdam: Amsterdam University Press.

Wadhams, N. (2000) 'Court rules against McDonald's in case of punished union worker', *Associated Press State & Local Wire*, 16 October.

Walraff, G. (1985) *Ganz Unten*, London: Methuen.

Watson, J.L. (ed.) (1997) *Golden Arches East: McDonald's in East Asia*, Stanford, CA: Stanford University Press.

Watson, J.L. (1998) 'Introduction: transnationalism, localism and fast foods in East Asia,' in Watson, J.L. (ed.) *Golden Arches East: McDonald's in East Asia*, Cambridge: Cambridge University Press, 1–38.

White, J. (1993) *Sisters and Solidarity: Women and Unions in Canada*, Toronto: Thomson Educational Publishing.

Willmott, H. (1993) 'Strength is ignorance; slavery is freedom: managing culture in modern organisations', *Journal of Management Studies*, 30, 4: 515–52.

Wilson, M. (2000), 'Signalling a seachange', *Employment Today*, Issue 55: 3–4.

Windmuller, J.P., de Galan, C. and van Zweeden, A.F. (1990) *Arbeidsverhoudingen in Nederland*, Utrecht: Het Spectrum.

Wooden, M. (1996) 'The youth labour market: characteristics and trends', *Australian Bulletin of Labour*, 22, 2: 137–60.

Wu, D.Y.H. (1997) 'McDonald's in Taipei: hamburgers, betel nuts, and national identity', in Watson, J.L. (ed.) *Golden Arches East: McDonald's in East Asia*, Stanford, CA: Stanford University Press.

Yalnizyan, A. (1998) *The Growing Gap*, Toronto: Centre for Social Justice.

Yan, Y. (1997) 'McDonald's in Beijing: the localization of Americana', in Watson, J.L. (ed.) *Golden Arches East: McDonald's in East Asia*, Stanford, CA: Stanford University Press.

York, G. (2001) 'Workers of McDonald's unite in Moscow union', *Toronto Globe and Mail*, 12 June: 3.

Zeiger, S. (1994) 'Shelley Zeiger on the promise and pitfalls of doing business in Russia', *Central Business*, June 22, 7, 13: 25.

Zuber, A. (1999a) 'EEOC suits put harassment on operators' front burner', *Nation's Restaurant News*, 1 February, 33, 5: 1.

Zuber, A. (1999b) 'McDonald's tests new automated ordering machines', *Nation's Restaurant News*, 23 August, 33, 34: 6.

Zuber, A. (1999c) 'McDonald's says Made for You, overseas expansion to hike profits', *Nation's Restaurant News*, 15 November, 33, 46: 4.

Zuiderveld, U. (1995) *Snelle hap; De geschiedenis van de Nederlandse cafetaria- en fastfoodsector*, Doetinchem: Misset.

Index